My Ghost
Has a Name

My Ghost
Has a Name

memoir of a murder

Rosalyn Rossignol

THE UNIVERSITY OF SOUTH CAROLINA PRESS

Published by the University of South Carolina Press
Columbia, South Carolina 29208

www.sc.edu/uscpress

Manufactured in the United States of America

26 25 24 23 22 21 20 19 18 17
10 9 8 7 6 5 4 3 2 1

Library of Congress Cataloging-in-Publication Data
can be found at http://catalog.loc.gov/.

ISBN: 978-1-61117-826-5 (paperback)
ISBN: 978-1-61117-827-2 (ebook)

This book was printed on recycled paper with
30 percent postconsumer waste content.

For Nell

As, therefore, the storm that prevents a sailor from putting into port is more dangerous than that which does not allow him to sail, so those storms of the soul are more serious which do not allow a man to compose or to calm his disturbed reason; but pilotless and without ballast, in confusion and aimless wandering, rushing headlong in oblique and reeling courses, he suffers a terrible shipwreck, as it were, and ruins his life. Consequently for this reason also it is worse to be sick in soul than in body; for men afflicted in body only suffer, but those afflicted in soul both suffer and do ill.

Plutarch, *Animine an corporis affectiones sint peiores*

And let me speak to th'yet unknowing world
How these things came about.

Horatio, *Hamlet,* act 5, scene 2

Contents

Prologue

The Phone Call

It's one of those days when I am haunted. My ghost has a name but no local habitation, which explains how I could move from Iowa to Maryland and still see her—hazel eyes, long blond hair parted in the middle, brilliant smile—mostly in my dreams, but sometimes out of my eye's corner, filling my peripheral vision, a dark shadow against the sun. Until I blink and turn my head and she is gone. And I stop to wonder where she is, from what dimension her spirit occasionally obtrudes into this material one. I do not wonder if she is at peace. I *know* she cannot be at peace.

The last time I saw Nell she was pregnant with Sarah, who would be the oldest of her three children. Even though Nell was still two months from her due date on that January afternoon, her belly was colossal, much too big, I felt, for her slight frame. Still she was full of energy and optimism, happy with her husband, Joe Nickel, and her job as an x-ray technologist in Hilton Head, South Carolina. When she left, my mother said, "That was sure nice of Nell to stop by. I'm so glad you were home."

The next time I heard my mother say Nell's name I was one thousand miles away from our childhood home in Augusta, Georgia. I was sitting on the secondhand sofa in the sunroom of our wood-frame house in Dubuque, Iowa. I had just come home from work at Loras College, two blocks away, where I taught English writing and literature. My son, Rich, answered the phone. I took the phone from him, making a face because I didn't really feel like talking to Mama. I said hello.

"Did you hear about Nell?" she asked, not bothering with her usual greeting and small talk.

"What do you mean did I hear about Nell? What are you talking about?"

"Nell Crowley," she went on, as if I knew more than one. "The one you used to go around with in high school. The one who was your maid of honor when you married Bill. She was murdered, they say it's by her daughter, with a baseball bat."

I held the phone, my gut filling with horror. I was unable to speak, or even breathe for a moment. The sensation was so physical, I felt as if I'd been punched in the stomach, hard. Mama's voice came back over the line. "Are you there? Did you hear what I said?" I managed to choke out a yes, furious that she could simply call me and make such a statement in such a calm voice. Swallowing my rage, I responded, "I have to go now," and hung up.

Then the dreams started—right away, that very night. At first they were all violent: A zombie-Nell ambushing me from beneath a shadowy stairwell, trying to cut my throat, her own face livid and swollen with the blows that killed her. Or Nell alive again, whole and beautiful, inviting me into her room to listen to a new band on her stereo, then stabbing me in the chest. Was this survivor's guilt, I wondered? Or some bizarre, atavistic fear of the dead? Was I being haunted by her ghost?

I called her mother, Julia, to express my sympathy for her loss. I asked about Nell's father, Jack. Julia said that he had died, mercifully, of a heart attack the previous February. She missed him terribly but was so thankful he didn't have to live through this horror, which was, and would be always, unbearable. Julia felt that the entire incident had come about as a result of Sarah getting mixed up with the wrong crowd, and the wrong drug—crack cocaine.

Even though I didn't know Sarah, I told Julia I had a hard time believing Nell's sixteen-year-old daughter had killed her. Julia said there were two other teens involved, both male, but that there was just too much evidence suggesting Sarah's participation to believe otherwise. Plus, Julia said, Sarah had written about hating her mother in her journal and told some of her friends she would like to kill her.

Although it took more than a year for Sarah to go to trial, I kept up with her case and read accounts of the proceedings in Beaufort County, South Carolina, newspapers. Claiming that she had had no part in her mother's murder, Sarah pleaded innocent. Sarah's journal, however, was more damning than Julia's initial characterization of it had suggested. In one entry, composed almost exactly one year before the murder, Sarah had written, speaking of her brother and half sister, "I love her and Willie to death and I would never let anyone hurt them but I know I'll end up hurting them both when I kill mom. She deserves to rot in the fiery pits of hell. I'll take her there myself." *My God,* I thought, *she really did do it.* Yet Sarah continued to assert her innocence, so vehemently and so convincingly that I was torn.

A memory: Mama stands at the door to my room, Kool Filter King in one hand, highball glass in the other. Nell and I sit on the white shag carpet that covers my bedroom floor, the butt end of a joint smoldering in an ashtray I had made in ninth-grade art class. We silently watch its smoke curl upward in a thin spiral. Mama says, "Nell, you better make sure you have something to wear to church tomorrow if you're spending the night." Nell and I exchange looks; she says, "Well, Mrs. Hunnicutt, we thought Rosalyn might spend the night at my house, if that's OK." Mama likes Nell, thinks she's a good influence because she gets good grades. Still she wants to say no, has always preferred saying no; I have no idea why and never will. But sometimes she says yes. "Well, all right, but next weekend I want you to go to church with us." Mama bobs and weaves her way back to the kitchen, where she is playing cards with her sister and two of my uncles. We finish the joint, and I pack a paper bag with a change of clothes. If I could, I would never come back.

Following Nell's death my son once asked me, "Why was she your best friend?" There were the usual reasons. I thought she was beautiful; I loved the way she moved her hands. I loved the fact that, although she was smarter than me in algebra and geometry, I could always best her in English. But mostly I loved her because she was my refuge. I grew up in a home with a widowed mother who had never wanted to have a child, but whose terminally ill husband had somehow talked her into the idea that I would be better than nothing. Nine months later he died, leaving her with a baby girl whom she saw primarily as a burden. As a child I escaped my sense of alienation in books and a rich fantasy life. But there were some things I couldn't escape, one being the sense that I was forever in the way, an unwelcome distraction in my mother's busy social calendar. As I entered my teens, my sense of alienation grew into a profound loneliness. That loneliness ended, however, when I changed schools and started attending John M. Tutt Jr. High

Nell was one of the first people who sat with me at lunch, who asked me to come over after school, and to spend the night on weekends. At her house, where everyone slept late on Sunday morning, and then had a big pancake breakfast cooked by her dad, I always felt welcomed, and valued for myself. When we had sleepovers, something that happened most weekends, and many, many summer nights, we would take turns tickling each other's backs, and I loved the way she touched me, soothing me into sleep when my turn came second. Before long I was spending more of my afternoons and weekends at Nell's than I did at home.

Unlike most other girls we knew (this was the Deep South, in the 1970s), Nell and I had career plans, weren't content to just get married and have babies. Her parents were well-educated professionals, her father career military, her mother a professor at the Medical College of Georgia. They encouraged us to go to college, and for a long time we planned to attend the same one, to major in the same subject, biology, and to pursue the same career, medical technology.

Another memory: Nell's wire-rimmed glasses slide down her nose as she bends over the clear flow of a natural spring, her long, narrow fingers lifting anacharis fronds from the water. We are at Heggie's Rock, an area just west of Augusta where a huge granite outcropping stretches for miles, like the surface of the moon dotted by occasional oases of pine trees or scrubby bushes. We are supposed to be looking for lichens, but the stream and the cool shade under the trees have drawn us, along with blue damselflies that hover and dip their tails into the water. Nell finds another plant, one I don't recognize. She plucks a small handful and, to my horror, pops it into her mouth. "It's watercress," she explains, but I watch her carefully for the next half hour, wondering if she's poisoned herself. Most of the plant life at Heggie's Rock is lichens. Because we have been studying these in physical science class, we gather enough of them to fill a large platter, artfully arranged. We label each sample and present the platter to Mrs. Hadden, our teacher, who keeps it for years, until the last lichen has crumbled into pale green dust.

While Nell stuck to the plans we had made in high school, taking courses that would prepare her for admission to the medical college, I let myself be seduced into a less practical major by the lure of beautiful language, the language of writers like Virginia Woolf and Sylvia Plath, that moved me far more than the images of amoebas and hydras that I searched for through the lens of my student microscope. I met other people who shared and expanded my interest in the arts, while Nell fell in with those who were planning careers in the sciences. We attended different study groups, obsessed over the quirks of different professors, and, without making any conscious decision to do so, began going our separate ways.

So why is it so important to me now to understand what happened when Nell was murdered? Here, at the beginning, I cannot say. I know it has something to do with feelings I had toward my own mother when I was Sarah's age, though it's hard to imagine what Nell's relationship with her daughter could have had in common with my experience. I know it has something to do with how strongly I once felt about Nell, and about the guilt I now feel for having let our friendship so casually end. As absurd as it sounds, I have the sense that I could have done something to prevent her death. Finding out exactly how it came about will help me lay that absurdity to rest. And this is why, in the fall of 2004, just days before the anniversary of her murder, I left the peace and tranquility of my home to begin my descent into hell. That it was a hell inhabited by others, a place I would only visit from time to time, made the journey seem bearable, at least at the beginning.

Death in the Afternoon

Murder is a crime ordinarily consigned to darkness: the shadowed alleyway, the murky gloom of midnight in someone's bedroom, the dimness of the forest. Just after 5:00 P.M. on October 20, 1999, on an afternoon that had been warm and sunny, but was now threatening rain, Deputy Kelly Cotner received a call from Beaufort County Dispatch to respond to the location 31 Bellinger Bluff Road in the area known locally as Lemon Island, but more often referred to as Okatie, in the coastal town of Bluffton, South Carolina. Cotner was at first told there was a gunshot victim on the premises; then, in route to the scene, he received clarification. The as yet "unknown victim" had been stabbed and beaten with a baseball bat.

Bellinger Bluff is one of several short side roads branching directly off the main road to Beaufort, along a stretch of highway that leads through

Photograph of the Davis home, where the murder occurred,
on Bellinger Bluff Road. Photograph by the author.

endless acres of green-and-brown salt marsh, over bridges that span the branching arms of the intracoastal waterway. The houses built on these short cul-de-sacs exhibit both the affluence and the craving for privacy of their owners. They have swimming pools, docks, and detached garages and are thoughtfully landscaped. Of the several houses on this particular road, number 31 is the most striking—a large Cape Cod with white siding and tall, many-paned windows overlooking a wide front porch and broad grassy lawn.

When Cotner arrived he found in the house, not a body, but two very lively children, one a petite blond girl who appeared around five years of age, the other a thirteen-year-old boy who identified himself as Willie Nickel. Willie told the officer that he thought his mother, Nell Davis, who had been home with the children, had left to take his older sister Sarah to a friend's house. Finding nothing in the house to arouse suspicion or confirm the information from dispatch, Cotner began a tour of the grounds. He was joined by Mike Davis, the clean-cut, dark-haired owner and proprietor of Main Street Pharmacy in nearby Ridgeland. Mike was the father of Haley, the youngest child; stepfather to Willie and Sarah; and husband to Nell, whose car was indeed missing. But if she was gone, taking her daughter to a friend's house, who could be the victim?

By now the towering cumulus clouds that had been building all afternoon in the sunlit sky had begun to darken, bringing an early dusk. As Officer Cotner walked the grounds in the fading light, the voice of the dispatcher crackled over his radio once again. More information trickled in. This time Cotner was advised that the victim's body would be located behind a garage-like shed. Sure enough, just around the back corner of this detached structure, beneath the dark shade of ancient trees hung with Spanish moss, the strong beam from Cotner's flashlight illuminated a pool of blood congealing on thick blades of Bermuda grass. But still no body. He felt the first heavy drops of rain. Then the final call came. He was told that the body had been stuffed into a green compost bin on the far side of the garage. He turned another corner. The beam of light cut through the thickening dusk, spotlighting the green plastic bin with its gabled lid. Cotner moved closer, lifted the lid, and there she was.

Five years later I stand with Lieutenant James Bukoffsky in the hallway just outside his office. Bukoffsky was one of two lead detectives originally assigned to the case. He had joined Cotner shortly after the discovery of the body and taken pictures with a digital camera to document the scene. Fearful of the ordeal awaiting me, I am comforted by the presence of this solidly built man with the face of a friendly bulldog. I like his bristly salt-and-pepper mustache and the way that he smells—warm and spicy, like an old tobacco barn. He smiles sadly as he opens the door to the office, his large hand holding a gallon-sized ziplock bag with several white envelopes inside. "Are you sure you want to do this?" he asks, taking a seat behind his desk, motioning me into a chair beside him. I nod my head, wondering if the reality can come anywhere near the nightmare images thronging my imagination. He sighs heavily, removing one envelope from the bag and placing it on the desk. "I'm going to set this up for you in some kind of order. If you want to stop, just say so."

The first photos show the shed and driveway, some of the trees festooned with yellow-and-black crime-scene tape. The light is murky, because of the coming storm. Another picture shows the back yard, another the large bloodstain behind the garage, the rabbit pen nearby. "You ready?" he prompts. I nod, whisper, "Yes," in case the nod wasn't affirmative enough. The next photo is of the Rubbermaid compost box, its green plastic gleaming in the rain that must have begun by now.

I see what Deputy Cotner saw: the green bin, first with its lid intact. In the second photo, taken from the same frontal position, the lid has been removed. A bare foot protrudes above one side of the enclosure, like the foot of a doll tossed carelessly into a toy box. One foot, from the ankle to the toe. My mind flashes to a scene of Nell sitting in a beanbag chair watching TV, one foot propped on her knee in exactly the same position. The next photo, of her body inside the box, shows a petite woman wearing a white t-shirt soaked with crimson blood, the gashes made by the knife so large I can see her pale, bruised flesh through the tears in the cloth. Yet what strikes me most is her posture: head tucked into her right shoulder, her legs crossed, her arms extending naturally, almost peacefully, by her side. Her layered hair is curly, damp with sweat, blood, and rain, but the position of her head hides the devastating damage done to her right temple. Her wire-rimmed glasses, which must have fallen or been knocked off when she was struck, lie in her lap. Pale-blue EKG patches still cling to her chest, arm, and leg. Irrationally I think, "She looks like she's still alive."

Then, when I see the next photo, I realize that the only dead people I've seen have been embalmed and beautified by the art of an expert mortician. This photo is from the autopsy. Nell's head lies on the cold steel table, her mouth open, her skin ashen white, cobwebby, and drawn. Like Dracula struck by the rising sun, she has aged forty years in an instant.

It is at this moment, while viewing my friend's dead body, that I decide I must tell this story. When I get back to my room, I begin sifting through the photocopies I made of files at the sheriff's office and the Beaufort County Courthouse. The files contain incident reports, statements taken at the scene, and transcripts of formal interviews conducted at the Beaufort County Detention Center. One odd thing I discover during this process is that the alleged perpetrators were issued "tickets." When I ask, "Do you mean tickets like the ones for traffic violations?" Debbie Szpanka, the public information officer for the sheriff's office, confirms my suspicion. "Yes," she says. "It's what the officers do when they don't have a warrant." *Geez,* I think. *A ticket for murder.*

■ ■ ■

The drive from Augusta, Georgia, where Nell and I grew up, to Bluffton, South Carolina, takes you through a kind of no-man's-land. Leaving Georgia almost immediately, you enter Beech Island, where the two-lane blacktop stretches its length between open fields and wooded areas, occasionally interrupted by small, medium, and sometimes large houses that sit on "land" rather than "lots," most of them planted in the middle of at least two acres with long driveways, some paved, mostly gravel, leading to the road. There are churches, here in the middle of nowhere, with names like Mt. Olive Baptist and Jerusalem Holiness—more churches, it seems, than houses. I imagine the preachers competing for congregation members.

The land is heavily forested, the trees predominantly pine. I see a few political signs for the November 2004 election, most of them for South Carolina Republicans, though there are two signs proclaiming, "Re-elect Laura Bush." Occasionally a trailer park occupies several acres of land, the trailers packed in closely among spindly pines, black-and-red "No Trespassing" signs on doors and in windows. A convenience store by the name of Kool Corner rests at the bottom of a steep hill as if to catch all the cars as they come down, before they gather momentum to climb the next hill. A portable marquee in front of a church reads "Don't be afraid of ghosts; believe in the Holy Ghost."

By the time I approach Allendale, South Carolina, the halfway mark, the houses begin to bunch together signifying something like suburbia, though I am downtown and then through it before I can blink twice. The hills and curves in the road disappear and the tarmac stretches straight and flat, an arrow pointing, for me, in one direction.

The scenery begins to feel oppressive, even hostile. Although it is late October, technically fall, most of the leaves are still green. The ones that have turned are an ugly, withered yellowish brown. On an isolated stretch of road I rout a flock of crows; they rise into the swirling wind like tattered black ashes. I wonder, not for the first time, if I have lost my mind, subjecting myself to the horror that I know awaits me at the end of my journey.

The oppressiveness of backcountry roads dissipates when I merge onto I-95, the most-traveled interstate on the East Coast, for the final leg of my journey. Surrounded by eighteen-wheelers traveling at lethal speeds, I could be anywhere, at least until I see the exit markers bearing the names of the towns I will be visiting over the course of the next several years—Coosawhatchie, Ridgeland, and finally Highway 278 to Bluffton and Hilton Head, which is where I get off.

Bluffton is where I will be staying, with a friend of a friend who also happens to work for a local paper, the *Island Packet*. Although I would have stayed anywhere within reasonable driving distance of the places I needed to visit, I couldn't have picked a more central location, with Hilton Head to the east, Beaufort to the north, Ridgeland to the west, and Savannah, Georgia—all places I need to go, with people I need to see—forty-five minutes to the south.

What a difference that short stretch of I-95 has made. It is as if I have entered an entirely different culture. There are housing developments, new condos, and apartment complexes everywhere, although they, like the shopping centers (even Walmart) are concealed from the road behind a screen of trees. Small unlit signs, their size and appearance regulated by city ordinance, discretely announce the presence of hidden shopping oases. This means that if you are traveling after dark and not entirely familiar with the area, you might spend an extra half hour (as I did one night) searching for the correct turnoff. Access roads, screened by a healthy growth of water oak, bay laurel, palmetto, and various smaller trees and shrubs, provide the means to approach apartments, banks, supermarkets, and Wendy's hamburgers. From the perspective of Highway 278, which is the town's thoroughfare, the most visible evidence of the area's high-density population is the amount of traffic. During rush hour, cars are as jam-packed and slow moving as a Washington, D.C., suburb.

The total effect is surreal, as if I have finally encountered a place where the South's penchant for façade has overwhelmed any other consideration. I am sure many people admire this arrangement, see it as evidence of superior city planning, and certainly it is easier on the eyes than a mass of tacky signage lining the highway. But there's a menacing side to it as well—a sense of something in hiding—waiting, brooding there among the twisted branches of the bay laurel, the swinging beards of the Spanish moss.

The night of my arrival, Vic Bradshaw, who's putting me up in his spare bedroom, insists that we go out driving, despite my feeling that the last thing I want to do is get back into a car. He wants to show me around a bit, help me get the lay of the land so that, hurrying to my appointments the next morning in rush-hour traffic, I'll have an easier time of it. We head toward Beaufort, since the Beaufort County Sheriff's Office is the first stop on my agenda. After we've gone about five miles I say I'm tired, and he says that's OK, he's got a map at his apartment. On the drive back I ask if he knows where Bellinger Bluff Road is. That's the road Nell's house is on— was on—and I am anxious to see where she died. He says no, mentions the map again, and we leave it at that. We've pretty much run out of the kind of small talk two unintoxicated strangers engage in upon their first meeting. Only a moment has passed when a road sign looms out of the darkness on the right-hand side of the highway. Its green-and-white reflective surface glows eerily in my headlights like something out of a David Lynch movie. "Bellinger Bluff" it says. I shiver but say nothing, and I do not turn around.

Death in the Afternoon, Scene 2

The 9-1-1 call that brought officers to the Bellinger Bluff crime scene was made from a location about ten miles away, a mobile home on Knowles Island Road in Jasper County. Seventeen-year-old Heather Nelson made the call. In a written statement, Ms. Nelson noted that it was around 5:00 P.M. when Sarah Nickel came running through her yard. Heather and her grandmother Mary, who'd had hip-replacement surgery several days before, were watching *Guiding Light* on television when they heard their German shepherd barking and the sound of a woman screaming. Heather went to the window that overlooked the front yard, just as Nickel ran up the steps and burst through the front door, slamming it behind her. She was crying hysterically and yelling, "Help me! They killed my mom!"

From the window, Heather could see two white males wearing black t-shirts running toward the house after Nickel. Heather grabbed the phone, punched in 9-1-1 with one shaking finger. She could hear her brother James yelling at the men but couldn't make out what he was saying.

Listening to the tape of the 9-1-1 call, I can hear Heather yelling at the dispatcher, saying they have to get some cops out there, trying to tell them that her friend Sarah Nickel just came running up to the Nelsons' trailer, screaming, "They killed my mama." She describes the approach of two young men, who followed Sarah right up to the front door. The next thing I hear is Heather yelling at her grandmother, "Grandma, *please* get out of the door!" Sarah, in the background, is sobbing, "My little brother and sister are all alone."

Speaking to the dispatcher, Heather repeated the information she had gotten from Sarah—how, after coming home from school and work, the

girl and her mother had gone behind her garage to check on their rabbit
when the suspects stepped out and hit Nell in the head with a baseball bat
and then stabbed her. After the assault on her mother, Sarah had said, the
two men forced her to drive them away from the scene in her mother's
green Chevy Tahoe. She added that she knew who the men were and provided names: John Ridgway and Kevin Bergin.

The officers who responded at Knowles Island Road quickly established a perimeter around the woods where the male suspects had fled and
were waiting for the Beaufort County Sheriff's Department K-9 Tracking
Team.

Sergeant Joey Woodward, who came to the scene from Bellinger Bluff,
took Sarah Nickel's statement, which added quite a bit to the information provided by Heather Nelson. Sarah claimed that she had called John
Ridgway, whom she knew from school, the day before, October 19. She had
wanted to talk to him about a court date that John had scheduled for October 21. The court case involved a previous runaway attempt and a stolen
car. Sarah was to testify against Ridgway. She would later say that John told
her to lie in her testimony, to say she was too drunk to remember anything
that had happened in reference to this episode, which had occurred several
months before. During this alleged conversation, Ridgway had also told
Sarah that he and his friend Kevin, whom she didn't know, were coming to
her house tomorrow, and that they were going to kill her family, but, she
insisted, she didn't "take him seriously."

The following day, her mother picked her up from school. Shortly after they arrived at the Bellinger Bluff house, Sarah stated that she noticed
John and Kevin standing behind the shed. They were wearing the same
color clothes, green shirts and brown pants. When she went to speak to
them, Sarah reported, they told her to go and get her mother or she, Sarah,
would be killed instead. Sarah returned to the house and quickly came
back with Nell. Kevin struck the older woman with a baseball bat just after
she rounded the corner of the shed. When Nell fell to the ground, Sarah
said, John grabbed her mother by the throat and started choking her. Sarah
claimed that she was then taken into the garage by John. She heard a series
of thumping noises, and, when Kevin came into the garage, she saw that
his clothes were bloody. In one hand he dangled a large, blood-smeared
knife. Kevin and John changed out of their bloody clothes and John took
Sarah into the house, where she grabbed some of her own clothes and her
mother's purse, which held the keys to her SUV. When they came out of

the house, John and Kevin picked up her mother's body and heaved it into the compost box. Then John, Kevin, and Sarah got into the car and drove away, with Sarah at the wheel.

Sarah drove out Highway 170 and took Snake Road into Jasper County, where, she told Officer Woodward, she had to stop for gas. Ridgway and Bergin told her they wanted her to drive them to Detroit via I-95 North. After getting gas she pulled onto the freeway but then got back off at the exit for Coosawhatchie. When Ridgway asked her what she was doing, she explained that they were taking a short cut. From Highway 462, she turned onto Knowles Island Road, where her father, Joe Nickel, lived. When she saw that his car wasn't outside his house, she continued up the road to the Nelsons'. She knew the family and could see one of them, Heather's brother James, in the yard. Slamming the gearshift into park, Sarah jumped out of the vehicle, leaving it in the middle of the road, and ran to the Nelsons' mobile home. John and Kevin followed her at first but then turned around and fled into the woods.

After speaking with Sarah, Woodward quickly determined the necessity of following up several leads, one of which was the stop for gas by the suspects and the use of the bank card, which would provide proof for part of Sarah's story. As well as statements from any available witnesses, the gas station/convenience store (it turned out to be a Texaco) in Ridgeland might also provide video footage of the suspects.

Upon arrival at the Knowles Island Road crime scene, the K-9 units were provided with information that would help them identify the suspects, who had been observed entering the woods on the opposite side of the road just beyond a fenced horse pasture. These officers set off into the woods, using bloodhounds to track the two men through the rainy darkness. Next, working alongside Lieutenant David Randall and Sergeant Robert Tuten, Woodward began the arduous task of processing the crime scene in what had now turned into a downpour. Blue tarps had been set up to protect the green Chevy Tahoe and its immediate environs, but Woodward was concerned about the difficulty of collecting evidence that had been thrown into the woods by the two boys when they exited the vehicle. He approached the ditch that separated the road from the wooded area, shining his flashlight into an adjacent briar patch. Stuck to the briars as if attached to a Velcro display board were latex gloves, hairnets, pantyhose, and a white sock. Further on, just beyond a wooden fence, officers gathered another pair of latex gloves, a bag of clothes, a pair of tan pants stained copiously with blood, a pair of black Converse athletic shoes, and one Nike Air shoe, as well as a large, black-handled knife with blood on its blade.

Back at Bellinger Bluff Road, the sudden storm had turned, as Lieutenant Bukoffsky described it, into "a real gully washer," a situation complicated by the increasing darkness. Those responsible for processing the crime scene struggled frantically to secure evidence before it washed away into the marsh abutting the Davis home site. Tarps were erected to lessen the rain's impact; photographs were taken to preserve visual evidence of vulnerable clues, such as tire tracks, a piece of gray wire in the driveway, and footprints behind the shed. A search warrant was obtained for the incident location, which allowed officers to give the residence a thorough going-over. Items were seized from Sarah's bedroom, which, in the words of Lieutenant Bukoffsky, looked as if someone had "lobbed a grenade in there," while the rest of the house was neat and orderly. Since Sarah's statement had indicated her acquaintance with one of the boys who attacked her mother, particular attention was given to her room in case her belongings should provide some clues. Sergeant Sam Roser said they didn't know exactly what they were looking for, but when they found a lot of handwritten material, in both notebooks and a file box, they knew they had to take a look at it.

Meanwhile, at approximately 7:45 P.M., Lieutenant Michael Thomas of the South Carolina Department of Natural Resources intercepted a radio call stating there had been a murder in the Lemon Island area (a.k.a. Okatie) of Beaufort County. The suspects, two white males wearing dark t-shirts and jeans, had been sighted in adjacent Jasper County, on Knowles Island Road off Highway 462. Being familiar with the area, which was largely wooded with some homesites and fenced fields, Lieutenant Thomas headed out that way to see if he could provide assistance. Turning off the highway onto Roseland, which would intersect with Knowles Island Road in about a mile and a half, Lieutenant Thomas hoped to reinforce the perimeter established earlier by officers from the sheriff's department. Reaching the intersection more quickly than he expected, and wondering if he might have missed anything in the gathering darkness, Thomas turned around, heading back toward 462.

He hadn't gone far when he saw two dark-clad figures, their white faces and arms making them look like floating fragments of human beings, moving down the roadside toward his vehicle. He stopped his truck and shined his flashlight into their faces. The boys stood still, blinded by the flare of white light. Thomas stepped out of the vehicle, identified himself as a law enforcement official, and instructed the suspects to raise their hands above their heads, and then to lie face down on the pavement. Following guidelines for dealing with potentially violent suspects, he placed his feet carefully on their necks, waiting for back-up. Almost immediately another officer came around from the opposite side of the vehicle to provide cover. It was now 8:40 P.M. Lieutenant Thomas advised the two suspects that they were under arrest and read them Miranda. When Thomas asked them where they were from, they answered, "Hilton Head," and stated that they wanted to turn themselves in. Shortly thereafter officers from the Jasper County Sheriff's Office arrived to take them into custody.

In the backseat of another Department of Natural Resources vehicle sat Sarah Nickel, the sixteen-year-old daughter of Nell Davis, who claimed also to have been a victim of Ridgway and Bergin, the two males she had run away from in order to report her mother's murder. Heather Nelson, who had already provided the police with her written statement regarding Sarah's appearance at her residence, stood on the roadside, trying to get the attention of one of the officers who were striding hurriedly back and forth in the rainy darkness, trying to make sure they had gathered all the evidence both inside and out of the stolen Chevy Tahoe. They were also anxious to get the two males, one of whom was already confessing, back to the detention center where formal interviews could take place.

Finally Heather snagged the attention of Sergeant Woodward. When he approached she said, quietly, that she did not want to get involved but, understanding the seriousness of the case, felt she ought to tell the officer that the earrings and watch Sarah was wearing actually belonged to Sarah's mother and had been removed from the murdered woman's body. Woodward felt a distinct flip-flop in his gut. He approached Nickel and asked her to get out of the truck. It was hard to talk to the girl because she kept asking, "When can I call my Daddy? I want my daddy to come and get me." Woodward almost felt sorry for her. Until he noticed the earrings. They looked like diamonds. "Are those your mother's?" he asked, indicating first the earrings, then the watch. "Yes," Sarah answered, looking somewhat bewildered. As if sensing what was about to happen, she slipped them out of her ears and handed them, with the watch, to Officer Woodward. Woodward then informed her that taking the jewelry after her mom had been murdered was a criminal offense and therefore she was under arrest.

Nickel's reply, as recorded by Woodward, stood in stark, vivid contrast to her previous emotional flatness. "I'll see you in fucking hell!" she raged. "Fuck you!"

Sarah wasn't the only suspect with whom Woodward had contact on Knowles Island Road. When Mike Thomas drove up with Ridgway and Bergin, they were transferred to separate police cruisers. During the transfer Woodward identified himself to Ridgway, noted that this was a murder investigation, and asked if Ridgway remembered having his Miranda rights administered. Ridgway answered yes and further stated that he wanted to cooperate, was in fact so eager to do so that he volunteered to take Woodward to the bloody knife and clothes he and Bergin had thrown from the vehicle when Sarah "bailed." But since the items in question had already been seized, there was no need. Woodward turned to leave, wishing to speak to Bergin before he was taken from the scene, but Ridgway kept talking, hurriedly, excitedly. His large boyish face animated by fear, the words came pouring out before Woodward could get away. "Kevin just lost it on Sarah's mom, and killed her." Woodward acknowledged the statement but indicated that, because of the weather conditions and location, the suspects would have to be transported to the Beaufort County Sheriff's Office for a formal interview. The officer also informed Ridgway that he was under arrest for the murder of Nell Davis. He started to walk away again but heard Ridgway call after him, "It was Sarah's idea. She knew everything!"

Bergin was less forthcoming. Sitting in the rear seat of a Jasper County police cruiser, he was told of the murder charge, and that he would be interviewed in Beaufort, since the murder had occurred in Beaufort County. The slender, dark-haired Bergin, his thinness accentuated by his drenched black clothing, quietly stated, "I understand. I'll see you there."

In spite of the rain, scene-of-crime officers had collected sixteen pieces of evidence near the abandoned vehicle. There were the potentially inconsequential items like an empty Marlboro pack and a plastic cup, but most of the objects' importance was obvious from the start: the pantyhose that had been used to disguise the boys' features, the rubber gloves, the bloody clothes, the shoes, and the black-handled kitchen knife. From inside the Chevy Tahoe, officers recovered more items. These included, most notably, a Hillerich and Bradsby bat found on the floor of the backseat passenger side. Visual assessment at the scene suggested that there was dried blood and hair on the hitting end of the bat, so the bat was swabbed and hair samples taken immediately. Nell's black leather purse lay on the floorboard in the front-seat passenger side. Suitcases and bags in the rear contained clothing belonging to the suspects. An athletic bag, gray in color, was filled with books on the occult, which, in the trial to come, would surface as important evidence of what some would come to see as the most compelling motive for Nell's murder.

3

He Said/She Said

The nightmares have started again. This time I dreamed I was visiting Nell's parents, as I have done several times in my nocturnal sojourns. It's never completely clear to me, either dreaming or awake, why I'm there. Sometimes I'm looking for Nell, who obligingly shows up to spend some time with me, to show me the latest addition to her music collection for instance, but I always feel somewhat uneasy; my dream self knows something isn't right. Lately, I suppose because of my ambivalence about writing this book, my dreams often take me to Nell's parents' house to talk to them about what I am writing. Her father, who died the year before Nell did, is there and always says he appreciates what I am doing, that he wants the truth to come out. Nell's mother is more hesitant, refuses to speak, shaking her head whenever I ask. Last night's dream, however, was more disturbing. Instead of the home Nell grew up in, this time I was going to the one where she was murdered—31 Bellinger Bluff Road. I was shown to her room, told that I would be sleeping in her bed. Instead of a mattress and frame, the "bed" consisted of a green Rubbermaid compost box. I woke up with a pounding heart. My resolve to tell this story faded. I stayed away from it for a few days, wondering how, if I'm having nightmares at this stage of the game, I will fare when I start digging into the dark stuff, the really disturbing material, that surfaced at Sarah's trial.

■ ■ ■

On October 21, 1999, at sixteen minutes after midnight, John Ridgway was formally interviewed by Staff Sergeant Joey Woodward, assisted by

Lieutenant David Randall, at the Beaufort County Sheriff's Office. At just over six feet tall, overweight despite his height, Ridgway still wore the black t-shirt and pants he'd been picked up in, which were now damp with rain and perspiration. He seemed the epitome of remorse. In the videotape of the interview, everything about him sags—the corners of his mouth, his eyebrows, shoulders—as he sits hunched over a table across from the two officers who will be questioning him. His hazel eyes are unusually deep set under thick eyebrows, his eyelashes so large and dark he appears to be wearing mascara. He has short dark-brown hair, and sideburns an inch wide frame his cheeks. His eyes are his best feature in the gambit he is about to make. On the other hand, his overt eagerness to help with the investigation has been replaced by a strange, kinetic blend of enthusiasm and resignation. He blinks, taps his fingers on the table, and clears his throat, anxious for the interview to begin. His desire to exert some control over this situation, to interpret the facts as favorably as possible, must be threatened by a growing awareness that, this time, neither his repudiation of what happened, nor his parents' intervention, will blunt the edge of what is coming.

After going over Ridgway's Miranda rights again, and having him sign a statement that his rights had not been violated, the officers begin with their questions. Ridgway is asked to give "an overall view of what happened." Later, based on that information as well as evidence from the two scenes—the home on Bellinger Bluff Road and the abandoned vehicle site on Knowles Island Road—they will ask him questions to fill in the blanks. This interview, like Kevin Bergin's, is videotaped.

Ridgway right away implicates Sarah.

"Um, well actually the past couple of days we've been talking to Sarah. Um, off and on, um, she had wanted to leave." These are the first words out of his mouth, once the interview has passed beyond the stage of preliminary legalities. Ridgway then admits that he wanted to leave too, but knew that he "had a serious court date" he had to be back for. Presumably he is speaking of the October 21 court date—scheduled for the day after the murder—so of course this bit about being back for court must be nonsense. He goes on to say that since his friend Kevin was in town, he figured he would go ahead and leave with him. Then he describes speaking to Sarah on the phone the evening of October 19:

"I talked to her personally, you know. . . . Basically what happened was today, we decided we were going to go to Sarah's mother's house, at Sarah's request, and Kevin was going to, well at that time it was undecided, going to knock her out with some object."

He goes on to describe going to a music store on Hilton Head to sell some CDs. This was necessary to get cab fare for the trip to Sarah's house in Bluffton, some twenty-five miles away. He also mentions visiting a CVS pharmacy to purchase the latex gloves and hairnets that would be found at the crime scene on Knowles Island Road. These preparatory tasks concluded, he and Bergin returned to Ridgway's parents' house in Hilton Head Plantation, an exclusive gated community, where they packed their bags and were picked up by a driver from Yellow Cab.

Once they reached the residence at Bellinger Bluff, Ridgway continues, they went to wait behind the storage shed for about an hour, until Sarah and her mom came home. This too, he claims, was done at Sarah's suggestion. When Sarah and her mother and siblings arrived home, Sarah came out to speak to Ridgway and Bergin and fed a pet rabbit in a cage on the far side of the shed. According to John, Sarah then announced that she was going to lure her mom outside by saying that something was wrong with the rabbit. When Nell came outside, John says, Kevin "could knock her out with the bat in order for us to get the code to a safe" that was in the house. The idea that someone who has been knocked out with a bat might be unable to communicate the combination to a safe seems not to have occurred to Ridgway at this time.

The suspect continues with his story, stating that he and Bergin wanted to get into the safe where, Sarah had told him, there was "a bunch of money and guns. . . . Kevin wanted the guns. I wanted the money." Then, almost as an afterthought, he adds, "Sarah wanted the money."

Things went pretty much as planned, Ridgway notes. Sarah brought her mom to see the rabbit. As soon as she rounded the corner of the shed, Kevin hit her with the bat in the head, "God knows how many times." Later, asked to elaborate on what happened to Sarah's mom, Ridgway says, his tone incredulous, as if he can't believe what had happened, "Kevin just went, as he put it, he went out of control." When pressed to specify the number of times Nell had been struck with the bat, Ridgway claims he had closed his eyes during the attack, but heard a whacking sound four or five times. Upon opening his eyes he saw the woman still standing for a moment. Then she fell. Asked to describe the scene, he states that Nell had "blood coming out of her nose. One eye was open . . . she was lying on the ground . . . all bloody."

If Ridgway's story is true, Bergin evidently suffered from the same mis-apprehension about an unconscious person's ability to speak the combination to a safe. Ridgway has Kevin demanding, "What's the fucking code to the safe, bitch?" and then saying, "Oh fuck, I think I killed her." To Kevin, Ridgway recalls saying, "I don't believe you were, you really, that you were really going to do it." Ridgway had then turned away and run upstairs with Sarah to pack her stuff.

Of Sarah he says, "She was kind of freaking out, so I gave her a hug and I was freaking out too and I told her I was." After packing they went downstairs, where Sarah's brother Willie and sister Haley were watching TV. Ridgway told the children his name was Jeff.

Waiting for Sarah, Ridgway sat down in the room with Willie and Haley. He'd seen a poster for the band Korn in Willie's room and started talking to the thirteen-year-old about music, "to keep my mind off what just happened." Before leaving the house, Ridgway accompanied Sarah to her mother's room, where she grabbed some diamond earrings, a wristwatch, and her mother's purse off the dresser. Ridgway stashed the purse in his pants.

When he and Sarah came back outside, Ridgway continues, they found Kevin now strangling Nell, "making sure she was dead," saying, "I don't know what to do with this fucking bitch." Nell was, by this time, "going blue. Her tongue was hanging out of her mouth." Ridgway grabbed the bags of clothes. Sarah, he says, "was still afraid and freaking." Ridgway wanted to "get the hell out of here," but Kevin insisted on burying the body. Realizing they hadn't enough time to dig a grave, the two young men decided to dispose of Nell's remains in the compost box. Accordingly Ridgway grabbed her ankles, Bergin took her arms, and they deposited her in the green Rubbermaid bin, where she was later found. Ridgway left to put things in the car. Sarah walked back and forth to the car, saying she couldn't look. Sarah's sister and brother were told that Nell had gone to a neighbor's house, and that Sarah and "Jeff" were going to fetch her so she could drive them to Jeff's house. When Bergin, Ridgway, and Nickel were all in the car, Ridgway recalled asking Bergin, "Is she really dead?" Bergin replied that he had wanted to make sure she was, so he had "stabbed [her] a bunch of times" after the body was in the compost box.

They left the house at Bellinger Bluff Road with Sarah driving, Ridgway beside her, and Kevin in the backseat. With less than half a tank of gas, they decided to stop and fill up at a Texaco in Ridgeland.

When asked whether he had ever attempted to intervene in what was happening to Mrs. Davis, whether he might have tried to help her or anything, Ridgway replied, "I was so terrified of what I had just witnessed. I couldn't move. I was scared. There were times when I would say, when I was laying on the ground [in the woods at Knowles Island Road], praying that my heart would stop or . . . I talked to Kevin. Should we kill ourselves. I talked to him till . . . I didn't know what to do. I still don't know what to do. Basically I went along with the plan 'cause I thought it was a really big thing. But I misjudged . . . and I never thought I'd be. I had no intention."

There are a lot of blanks in these sentences, some more consequential than others. He never thought he'd be _____ ? What? Observing someone kill another person? Abandoned by Sarah? Arrested and charged with murder when he didn't actually swing the bat or wield the knife? And then there's the "I had no intention": intention of _____ ? That the incident would actually lead to murder? That he would get caught?

And when he abandoned the vehicle on Knowles Island Road and ran off into the woods, what was going through John Ridgway's head? "So we're in the woods," he says, in storytelling mode. "Running around. We didn't move till it got dark. We walked around in the bushes. I was trying to explain this to Kevin. I was just trying to tell him to just turn himself in, and he told me that an animal, when he gets shot at, runs or dies. So why would we turn ourselves in? So we kept walking through, walking all over the place, fields, fences, bushes and woods and God knows what else. Finally it started raining off and on. It was horrible. I was freaking out. Two people freaking out. I know we eventually got to the point where, oh about nine o'clock and I was just so sick of it, I told him, told Kevin, do you want to spend the rest of your life like this? Running, running all over the place, in bushes and thorns? And he said no."

■ ■ ■

I stare at the faces of Sarah Nickel, John Ridgway, and Kevin Bergin, comparing press photos taken at the time of the murder to those appearing on the South Carolina Department of Corrections website. In the latter all I can see is their faces. Sarah appears to have lost weight. Her face is gaunt, her cheeks hollowed, but these changes only accentuate the most startling fact of her appearance: she could be her mother's twin. I feel the unsettling sensation that I am staring at a picture of Nell at sixteen. John Ridgway still appears overweight, despite his large frame and his height, and Kevin

Bergin, although his face is puffy, seems as slender as he was on the day of his arraignment. John stares at the camera, his expression bold and defiant. Kevin looks smaller (and at five feet six, he is)—somehow sad and diminished. I know I can't really tell anything about these young people from their photos, so I stop trying. But I must know more about them than their criminal history and their participation in this tragedy, so I write to them in prison. Sarah is the only one who writes back.

■ ■ ■

At approximately 1:30 A.M. on October 21, Staff Sergeant Joey Woodward and Lieutenant David Randall began their taped interview with Kevin Bergin. Sergeant Woodward, or "JoJo," as he is known to nearly everyone in the community, is a muscular man in his forties with thick silver hair and the kind of light-blue eyes that seem to pierce right through whatever, or whomever, gets caught in his gaze. Right now Kevin Bergin is their target. Woodward begins with a series of questions such as, "Do you know what your social security number is?" and "Who're your parents?"—questions designed to indicate, on tape, Bergin's identity, his ability to undergo the procedure, and his legal waiver of Miranda. These formalities taken care of, the officers ask the suspect to go over events leading up to the previous day.

Bergin's demeanor contrasts strongly with that of his friend, John Ridgway. Watching Ridgway, noting the young man's eagerness to talk, the way he met the officers' eyes when he answered questions at the scene, Woodward must have known right away that he was going to provide them with plenty of information, some of it useful and true, some of it self-servingly distorted. Kevin Bergin was a different story from the beginning. When he was apprehended at Knowles Island Road, Kevin had stared at the rain-soaked pavement as he mumbled answers to the officers' questions, using his long dark hair as a screen to hide his features.

Here in the bright lights of the law enforcement center Kevin Bergin is at least more visible, and he does agree to answer questions. But the answers he gives are as elusive as his darting eyes. He will not let himself be pinned by Woodward's gaze. He wears a Beaufort County Sheriff's Office windbreaker draped around his shoulders to keep him from shivering. The fingers of one hand clutch it closed. One thick lock of black hair hangs down over his left eye, but it isn't enough, under the bright lights of the deputy's room, to hide his fear. Nonetheless, at the beginning of the interview, when offered the chance to tell "his side of the story," he proceeds readily enough, though the information he gives is sketchy at best. His voice is low and raspy, clearly a smoker's voice. His goatee and hollow cheeks, his pale skin and ungroomed hair lend him a gaunt, haggard appearance.

Bergin, who has been living with his parents in Connecticut, tells Woodward and Randall that he had come down to the Beaufort area for a visit. He was staying with John Ridgway, an old friend who also formerly lived in Connecticut. Once Kevin arrived at John's house, he says, "everything's cool for a while." Then "this girl, who I never met before called and said she wanted to, like, take her parents' car or something, and head out. And she said something about, like, killing her parents or something, but I wasn't too into that you know, and I won't do it. So, we went over there and everything gets a little hazy for me."

Bergin seems to lose his train of thought at this point, because after explaining that this isn't the first time he's had "a blackout thing," he continues on to say, "I don't know, I went over there and I don't remember killing someone, I tell you that much."

The next thing he recalls, he says, is "coming out of the woods . . . getting told by two guys, cops in a pickup truck, to get down on the ground, put my hands behind my head."

Perhaps puzzled by Bergin's suggestion that he never met Sarah before, Woodward redirects the narrative, asking, "Do you know Sarah?" to which Bergin shrugs and answers, "I don't know her." This seems rather odd if the three young people had, together, planned this murder. The exchange that follows does little to clarify the issue, as Bergin indicates that he "thinks" he knows Sarah now, but he had never met her before the day of the murder.

Woodward has a bit more success when he questions Bergin about Sarah's contact with John Ridgway. Bergin affirms that he had heard John talking by phone with Sarah, and that, although he wasn't sure, he thinks Sarah had cooked up the plan that had been executed on the afternoon of October 20. But when asked if the Sarah he spoke about now was the same "girl that drove out of that place today in the car with you," Bergin's account breaks down again. He claims he can't remember driving out of the place, or even exactly how he and John had gotten there. Nor does he remember bringing a bat or a knife or anything—with the exception of "traveling bags" of clothes—with him to the scene.

The next set of questions aims at establishing a history for Bergin's relationship with Ridgway, which the young man describes as being "like brothers." When Woodward asks what kind of person John is, Bergin responds, "I'd say he's a good guy," noting that when they had first met, "Me and him just clicked, you know. It was a long time ago when we met and we started hanging out and we got hanging out all the time. And then he moved down here. Kept in contact with him and I came down here."

When asked what he thinks and feels about Sarah, Bergin answers, "I feel like she led me into a bad situation and now she's trying to make it look as if I did something that I'm responsible for. This was her situation to begin with." Asked to elaborate, he does so: "As far as I know she had a situation with her parents. She had a situation with court and stuff. I feel as if I got mugged somehow." Seeing this as an opportunity to bring Bergin back to the scene of the murder, Woodward asks if Sarah's parents were at home when he arrived at her house the previous afternoon. Bergin's memory fails him again. "I don't know." Trying to focus in on the moments immediately preceding the attack on Nell Davis, Woodward asks the young man if he remembers seeing Sarah at the house, when she had come out to talk to John behind the shed. He gets no response.

Frustrated by the lack of progress they are making in the interview, Woodward decides to take a different tack, leaning forward in his chair and asking Bergin if he thinks he has done anything wrong.

Bergin answers, "I don't believe that I've done anything wrong. I don't remember doing anything, you know?"

Knowing how critical it is to break through Bergin's resistance, Woodward decides to confront him directly with what police already know, hoping that will spark a desire to cooperate.

Woodward leans forward, says, "You remember standing out behind the garage, Kevin? Cause I can tell you after speaking with everyone else, I can ask you these questions because I believe, I believe you were there. In fact, I know you were there and I'm just trying to get the story straight, that's all. There's got to be a story and it's got to be straight. Everybody has been basically 100%. Basically 100% or trying to be 100%. That's all I'm asking from you. I'm not demanding you tell me anything. I'm simply asking you to do what you think's right. I mean sometimes people do things for the weirdest reasons, sometimes people get involved when they ain't even there, you know what I'm saying? I'm asking you, you remember being behind the garage today?"

Finally, Bergin admits being behind the garage. Initially unwilling to "answer any questions for anybody else," Bergin reluctantly says that Sarah was there behind the garage, with her mom, and admits that "maybe" he had seen Sarah choking her mom. That said, the information starts to flow a little more freely.

Woodward: "Did you see Sarah hit her mom?"

Bergin: "A couple of times."

Woodward: "With what?"

Bergin: "Something, something heavy."

Woodward: "What did you think or what did you see?"

Bergin: "It could have been a two-by-four, it could have been a baseball bat.

And this is where things get strange. Woodward holds up a ball-point pen, saying, "Let me ask you something, what is this?"

"That's, that's a pen."

Bergin waffles again, saying, "It could have been a bat, it could have been a two-by-four."

Woodward reminds him that, as he had stated previously, he was standing five feet away. Bergin doesn't respond. Woodward says, "OK, it's very important for me to know that Sarah was hitting her mom with a bat. I mean it's important for our case cause it's important to tell the truth about it."

The first time I read Woodward's statement, "It's very important for me to know that Sarah was hitting her mom with a bat," I remember all the reruns of *Law and Order* I've seen and think, "Well isn't that just like a cop in a TV drama—he's trying to put words into the mouth of a guy who apparently doesn't have the slightest interest in telling the truth."

Bergin gives an equivocal response to Woodward's question about the bat, saying, "If that was the weapon . . . that would be it. I know it was wooden."

"It was what, wooden?" Woodward asks, trying for clarification.

Bergin gets walleyed, as if he would rather go anywhere, do anything, than answer this question. He stumbles over the words, speaks haltingly. "Like when . . . something . . . basically, like something traumatic happened today, I don't really . . . I remember . . . bits and pieces come back."

At this point in the questioning, the detective can see that he is close to losing Bergin. The pale-faced young man sits silent, hunched over, and when he does speak, his voice rises barely above a whisper. Woodward returns to an earlier thread, backing up to the last statement that contained anything remotely affirmative. "How many times do you think she hit her?" There's no response to that question, so he changes tack and asks Bergin where she was hitting her mom.

"I think she hit her in the head."

Another tiny piece of the puzzle clicks into place. But when Woodward tries to use that to jump-start a narrative of events that followed, Bergin turns evasive again. He isn't sure what Sarah had done next. He thinks she may have "left or something." Then there are questions about the clothing Bergin was wearing, and whether he changed it at any point. This is another key issue, because officers had retrieved a bag of men's bloody clothing from a ditch a few feet away from the abandoned Chevy Tahoe. Bergin admits he had been wearing something else when he arrived at Bellinger Bluff yet denies owning the green shirt and pair of brown pants that Woodward describes. Later he denies having changed at all, protesting, over and over again, "I don't know, I honestly don't know," and denying that he had hit Sarah's mother, or done anything wrong that he can remember. Frustrated and clearly running out of patience, Woodward asks if Bergin would like to know what John Ridgway has told investigators about what had happened. Using what he knows will be his last bit of leverage, the detective then says, after pausing to consult his notes, and to give Bergin time to stew a bit, "He said . . . that you did it, that you went crazy."

Bergin seems genuinely surprised. He meets Woodward's gaze for the first time. His eyes flash from hazy to focused. "He said that I did . . . crazy?"

Reading from his notes, the officer continues, "He [Ridgway] said, 'Why'd you do it?' You [Bergin] said, 'I just went crazy. I lost it.'"

Seeing how much of an impact these words have on Bergin, Woodward tries to soften their effect by adding, "I think it was as traumatic to him as it was you," but then quickly adds, "Yeah, I asked John about the whole situation, too. The whole thing. He basically, he basically told me the same story you told me, about the plan, but he also told me who killed Sarah's mother."

Upon hearing these words, Kevin swallows hard and pushes himself back in his chair, straightening up for the first time since the interrogation began. He squints, blinking rapidly, and his head seems to roll back. The news that his best friend, his blood brother, has let him down strikes him like a physical blow. As if unable to believe what he has just heard, he asks, "He said I hit her?" but then immediately issues a denial, saying, "I don't remember anything," and asks for a cigarette. His request is ignored.

Woodward knows from experience that it is only a matter of minutes before Bergin breaks. And when he does, it is just like you see in the movies, or on reruns of *Law and Order,* except he will not get to have that cigarette.

Now Woodward tries to get more information about Sarah's participation, asking Bergin who had told him what he was supposed to do when he arrived at the Davis house. Bergin answers, "Sarah," supporting Ridgway's statement that the plan had been formulated by Sarah Nickel. When Woodward zeroes in on the moments before Nell's death, asking, "When Sarah came out, what did she tell you?"

Bergin answers, "She told me to kill her mother."

The experience of reading these words as they are printed on the transcript of the interview is markedly different from hearing and seeing Kevin Bergin speak them on the videotape. The words are the same, but the long hesitation in the middle of the sentence, "She told me . . . to kill her mother," speaks volumes. So does Bergin's body language; his eyes dart furiously in every direction. He is a cartoon caricature of someone trying to formulate a lie on short notice. Yet his claim that Sarah said she would signal her mom's approach with a wink provides the kind of dovetailing detail that gives his story credence. Ridgway had also mentioned Sarah using a wink.

"All right. Fuck it. I freaked out all right," Bergin finally says, now sitting up and looking Woodward straight in the eye. He has hit the breaking point and now proceeds to tell a partial version of events that will eventually find its way into the courtroom. He admits hitting Nell with the bat but says he did it because Sarah told him to. And no, he says, revising his former accusation, Sarah did not hit her mother; but she did, he adds, kick Nell after she had fallen. When asked if he cared whether or not Nell was alive when he left the scene, Bergin's response is weirdly defiant, and his eyes flash with anger. "I cared. I know that family lost somebody. If that was my mother and somebody did that to my mother I'd fucking kill them and I hate myself for this."

Sensitive to the anger Bergin feels over the idea of someone attacking his own mother, Woodward sees another chance to bring Sarah into the conversation, asking Bergin what Sarah had been saying when he was hitting her mom.

"The only thing I remember she said was, 'The bitch is going to die.'"

"While you were hitting her mom?"

"No, she said that before. Before she came out."

Asking for clarification of Sarah's exact words, Woodward says, "One more time, what did she say?"

"The bitch is going to die."

These words, unlike his previous, "She told me . . . to kill her mother," are spoken without hesitation, without, apparently, much thought, but with absolute conviction.

The rest of Bergin's story coincides closely with Ridgway's. And like Ridgway's interview, Bergin's ends with a question. Sergeant Sam Roser, speaking for the first time, says, "Can I ask you one thing? Who stabbed Mrs.?"

Kevin doesn't let him finish the sentence. "I don't know," he answers, and Woodward concludes the interview by noting that the time is 0237 (2:37 A.M.) on October 21, 1999, the day Sarah Nickel was to have testified against Kevin's good friend, John Ridgway, in court.

■ ■ ■

While the interviews police conducted with John Ridgway and Kevin Bergin were videotaped, the interview with Sarah Nickel was not. The typed transcripts of the interviews with Bergin and Ridgway are in question-and-answer format. Sarah Nickel's interview, conducted by Sam Roser and James Bukoffsky, takes a different form, relating what the officers asked and how Nickel answered, but nowhere in the written report is there any indication of what her precise words were.

Nickel was interviewed at approximately twenty minutes after midnight, in the deputy's room at the Beaufort County Sheriff's Office. According to the report, she was advised of her Miranda rights and signed a written waiver of those rights, though I was unable to locate a written record of her waiver, despite an extensive search of courthouse files. Nickel denied using narcotics or alcohol on the day of the murder but admitted that she had used both in the past. Sergeant Sam Roser, a stocky man who reminded me of Bruce Willis (without the dimple), asked most of the questions and compiled the written report. Bukoffsky, Roser later informed me, was the quiet "good cop" half of their interview team.

And it was important to have someone play that role, because the pretty, blond-haired, blue-eyed sixteen-year-old, who sat across from them in the spacious, impersonal surroundings of the Beaufort County Sheriff's Office deputy's room, was most obviously inclined to be neither cooperative nor evasive. She was, as far as they could tell, consumed by one emotion: rage. She didn't lash out at them initially and, like Ridgway, looked them in the eye when she answered their questions. But, according to the sergeant, her answers rang with defiance, as if she, rather than her mother, were the victim.

Nickel's version of events began with the story of a runaway attempt that had taken place two weeks ago. She had gone to Ridgway's house. According to Sarah, John had said he also wanted to run away, and he is the one who suggested killing her family. She notes that Ridgway was supposed to go to court on this very day, October 21, for a previous runaway, in addition to charges stemming from a recent knife attack on another teen. Sarah admits here that she wanted to go away with John, and the report again notes that he "told her that he was gonna kill her family on the 20th." Asking if her parents had any guns, Ridgway allegedly informed her that "they were gonna hit her [presumably Nell] and try and get the combination for the safe, that was where her parents kept the guns." From this point forward, Sarah's account of events accords with that of John Ridgway, with few notable exceptions. The biggest one is Sarah's refusal to acknowledge that there was any real plan to kill her mother or stepfather.

When Sergeant Roser asked Nickel directly why the boys had killed her mother, she is reported as saying she "did not know why," but then adds that "when John told her that he was gonna kill her family she did not take him serious." Interestingly this comment parallels one made by Adam Thomas, a friend of Ridgway's who had been in close contact with Ridgway and Nickel in the week prior to Nell's murder. In the short time that they had known each other, Thomas stated, he and Ridgway had attended Narcotics Anonymous together. On one such occasion, according to Thomas, Ridgway had tried to convince him to go into a meeting and "kill and rob everyone in there." At the time Ridgway made the remark, Thomas said, he believed that John was kidding but later "realized that he was not joking." What spurred this realization is not included in the report.

To Roser's question about why she didn't warn her mother, Nickel replies that there were too many windows in the house to lock them all. She does admit, however, to telling her mother that something was wrong with the rabbit, which caused her mother to come out into the yard, but when Roser repeats the question, "Why didn't you warn your mother?" and adds, "Or ask her to call 9-1-1?" Sarah clams up, refusing to answer. Asked why she got into the car with Bergin and Ridgway, she claims that she was scared for her safety, but when asked if they had threatened her in any way, she says no.

Frustrated by the girl's straightforward but scant answers, Roser goes over the details of the killing again, asking who wielded the bat and knife, and receives the same answers she had given previously: Kevin hit her mother with the bat, and although she did not see it, she believes he is the one who stabbed her as well because she saw John give him the knife. Roser asks Sarah for the third time why she didn't warn her mother. She answers that she does not know. Bukoffsky asks the last question, abruptly dropping the "good cop" façade when he says, "Why did you kill your mother and stuff her in the green compost box?" Rather than recording a direct response from Sarah, the report states that she requested an attorney. As Sam Roser remembers the interview, he adds that Sarah also asked for her daddy, Joe Nickel, which is not recorded in the report.

Five years later I sit in the same room, the deputy's room, listening to Lieutenant Bukoffsky relate his memory of this interview. He recalls Sarah's sudden rage when he asked the final question of the interview, "Why did you kill your mother and stuff her in the green compost box?" and tells me something that is conspicuously absent from the report: Sarah sprang out of her chair and got right up in Bukoffsky's face. Remembering the situation, he adds, with a wry smile, "I had to drop her."

"Drop her?" I ask, seeking clarification.

"Sit her down."

"Oh," I say, relieved that he didn't punch her.

Leaning back in his chair and stroking his moustache, Bukoffsky gazes over my shoulder as if trying to recall something else from that distant interview, conducted in the small hours of the morning. His eyes slide back into focus, he looks at me. "I'll tell you something else. When I went to the bond hearing for those three, I told the judge that if he let them out on the street pending trial, it would be over my dead body." His face is stern but then relaxes into a chuckle. "I guess that judge had to sit me down." He pauses, grows thoughtful again. "But it was so awful, one of the worst cases I've ever been on."

When I ask if it was the crime's brutality that made it so awful, he nods but indicates that the brutality was only part of it. "I thought at the time that the case suggested sexual abuse," he says, catching me by surprise. "I used to work in a unit that dealt with sex crimes against children, and this case had all the earmarks." He notes Sarah's promiscuity, as recorded in her diaries, and her hatred of her mother who, though not the abuser, could have provided access to her daughter, enabling the abuse. In Bukoffsky's opinion Sarah, not Kevin Bergin, wielded the knife and "stabbed her mother," because of the rage that would have to attend upon such an attack. "It's what we call 'overkill,'" he says, asking if I am familiar with the term. I am, but I wait to hear how he will define it. "Overkill happens when the attacker has so much rage that they keep on going—hitting, stabbing, whatever—long past what it would take to kill the victim."

I think of the crime scene and autopsy photos, the huge gaping wounds in Nell's chest, her bruised and swollen skull. I can certainly see why he would classify the attack as overkill. This is the first I've heard anyone mention abuse, and I begin to wonder about the handsome stepfather, Mike Davis. Could he have abused his stepdaughter? If he had, why wasn't he killed? But then, according to Ridgway's statement, Sarah *had* wanted to kill Mr. Davis, had "wanted to kill her step-father herself," but was prevented because Ridgway and Bergin wanted to make sure they were off the property before Mr. Davis got home.

Of Ridgway, Bukoffsky delivered the following opinion, smiling and ruefully shaking his head. "I think she manipulated the Ridgway boy. You should have seen him. He was just a big softie."

I wrote "softie" with a big question mark in my notes.

Bukoffsky continued, offering clarification. "Yeah, the way I see it, he was just an average guy just wanting to slide through high school, maybe go to college. Sarah got him in her clutches. She's a pretty little girl, paid him some attention. You know."

Now it was my turn to smile and shake my head. I couldn't wait to meet her.

Just before our interview was over, Bukoffsky asked me if I had seen Sarah and talked to her. I told him I had spoken to her on the phone, and that I was going to visit her at Camille Griffin Graham Correctional Institution in Columbia, South Carolina, before heading back home to Maryland. He looked at me for a long moment, then said, "Have you asked her if she did it?"

I said no, not yet, but then told him that her first letter to me had closed with these words: "I would like to say, for the record, that I in no way wanted my mom to die."

Another long stare. Without breaking his gaze, Bukoffsky said, "I tell you what. I would like to look her in the eye and hear her say she didn't stab her mother."

"Would you know if she was telling the truth?" I asked, extremely interested in the answer, because the question was one that I would be asking Sarah in just a few days.

There was another pause, another long, shrewd look from those light brown eyes. "Yeah, I'd know," he finally said.

Ridgeland Cemetery,
October 20, 2004, 4 P.M.

I returned to Vic's apartment, where I cooked an omelet with lox and cream cheese—comfort food, and boy did I need it. Vic was the night editor for the *Island Packet,* so he wouldn't be home until after midnight. I turned on the TV to distract myself from the horrors of the past few days. Flicking through the channels, something caught my eye—an aerial view of a woodland that fragmented into a sixteen-faceted repetition of the same view—insectovision as my kids used to call it. Thinking I'd stumbled on a nature show of some kind, I settled back on the sofa to eat. The fly descended into the trees, branches whirled past, then there was a close-up of something red and meaty. The insectovision vanished with a buzzing sound, and I found myself looking down at a faceless corpse, while the theme song for *CSI,* one of television's most popular series, played. I grabbed the remote and searched frantically for the one channel I knew I could count on—TV Land—and heaved a sigh of relief when a close-up of Opie Taylor's grinning face emerged on the screen. I'd lost my taste for the omelet, but *The Andy Griffith Show* eventually calmed me enough so that I was able to get up off the sofa and go to the bathroom to brush my teeth in its too-bright light. I decided not to wash my face because I didn't want to close my eyes, even for a moment. When I got into bed, I immediately took half an Ambien, one of the sleeping tablets I occasionally use, and began reading one of Vic's books about the history of rock and roll, a subject I have absolutely no interest in. The book I had brought with me, Truman Capote's *In Cold Blood,* I turned face down and hid under the bed.

The following day—the five-year anniversary of Nell's murder—I had intentionally kept my schedule open, but when I got up in the morning, still groggy from the sleeping pill, I realized there was too much to do for me to do to take the day off. So I drove over to the sheriff's office to finish making copies of the case files. When I had a complete set and went downstairs to pay at the accounting office, the woman who took my check informed me that she had just gotten off the phone with someone asking about the Davis murder. "Really?" I said, hoping for more information.

"Yes. It was a woman who wanted to know what house Davis had lived in on Bellinger Bluff Road. She said she was considering renting a house there, but didn't want to live in Nell's house because she's already had one bad experience with ghosts and doesn't want another."

"So what did you tell her?" I asked, wondering if Nell's husband, Mike Davis, who was getting married again in a few weeks, had decided to move. I knew one thing. If I were his new wife, I wouldn't be living in the house where his last wife was murdered.

"I said we don't give out that kind of information over the phone," she answered, which makes sense, I guess, in terms of protecting people's privacy. Later I would learn that it wasn't Mike's house after all, and that he did take his new wife there to live. I wondered if she ever visited the spot behind the garage where the compost bin used to be.

In the afternoon I stopped by Lemon Island Marina, situated on the bank of the Chechessee River, just before the Okatie Bridge. Its location, less than a quarter mile from Bellinger Bluff Road, made me think that the people who worked there would remember the murder and might be able to give me some insight into how people in the local community had reacted. The marina's main structure was a weathered shed-like building, its sign made of tin roofing painted white with pale blue showing through its surface like blue veins under pale white skin. Inside, casting nets like gigantic cobwebs hung in the large plate-glass windows. The cement floor was spotless. Fish and shrimp piled inside the iced display cases gave off the bracing, fresh smell of the open sea.

Clark Lowther, the marina's proprietor, was a handsome man in his fifties with leathery tanned skin and thick salt-and-pepper hair. He had a sailor's eyes that, when they were not looking at you, slid away to the horizon, scanning it for signs of weather. When I asked him about the murder, he squinted into the distance, saying yes, he recalled it happening, but he didn't know many of the details. "I was probably on the road," he explained.

"I deliver crabs up and down the coast." When I told him my desire to talk to people in the area, he told me, "This area doesn't really have a community. Mike and Nell Davis were from Ridgeland. People really only started moving out here, building houses and stuff, five or six years ago. People are still confused about what to call the place. Is it Lemon Island? Okatie? Bluffton? Everybody seems to call it something different." This was true. It's reflected in the various newspaper accounts as well as police reports.

I told Mr. Lowther that I was getting ready to drive over to Ridgeland to look for the cemetery where Nell is buried. I had bought a miniature rose bush to put on her grave. When I asked if he could tell me how to get to Ridgeland Cemetery, he gave me a startled look, saying, "I can tell you more than that, I can tell you exactly how to get to her grave. We buried someone there in the next plot just a week ago. I remember seeing the stone with Nell Davis's name on it. Don't know why I noticed it. But here, this is what you do."

Following Clark Lowther's directions, I easily found my way to the Ridgeland Cemetery and, once there, to Nell's grave, which is located near the property boundary, just a few paces from a wooded area. I could see the pink granite marker from where I parked the car, my heart pounding as I opened the door and got out, holding my rose. It almost felt as if I had come to talk to Nell and I was afraid—a feeling I did not understand. I approached the stone and knelt down to place my plant, with its small red blossoms that I knew would soon be dead, a thought that brought home the futility of my gesture.

In front of the marker that bears her name, her birth date, and the date she died, a sun-bleached spray of pink plastic daisies lay upended on the grass. I plunged their central spike into the soil and spent another few minutes tidying the stone, brushing away pine straw and leaf litter. The ground was lumpy with mole tunnels and fire ant mounds, as I discovered when they started stinging me, sending me running back to the car to remove my sandals and brush them off.

For a while I sat on the car fender, listening to the sound of a marching band practicing in the distance. Vultures circled in the sky overhead, and four of them came to light nearby, spreading their gigantic black wings as they touched down. A crow cawed, though I couldn't see it. I tried to speak to Nell, telling her I'm sorry, so, so sorry, and felt the sobs rise up from deep inside, gripping my chest, contorting my face until tears ran down, bringing no relief, only a deeper sense of loss, and more than that—of a desolation that has nothing to do with me, but speaks to the horror I feel whenever I think of what her last moments must have been like—of the betrayal she must have felt, watching her daughter stand by as she was struck, of the physical pain she suffered as she struggled valiantly, yet hopelessly to defend herself from the blows that, had she not died, would have made her life a living hell.

■ ■ ■

When Nell Nickel became engaged to Mike Davis in 1993, it caused quite a stir among the single women who knew him, many of whom had supported him through the awful bereavement he suffered following his first wife's death from bone cancer. Mike was handsome, well educated, and still on the younger side of middle age when his first wife died. Following a decent period of mourning, he was considered to be one of the most desirable eligible men in the small town of Ridgeland, South Carolina. Main Street Pharmacy, which he owned, was for years the only drugstore in Ridgeland, and so Mike was known and respected by practically everyone in the community. Nell didn't know him because she didn't live in Ridgeland, or Hardeeville, or Bluffton, or any of the other small towns that clustered in the area. She was a transplant to the area and lived in Hilton Head, besides. So when she snatched Mike out from under the very noses of the women who had labored long and hard for his attentions, she did not immediately become the most popular new wife in town. That she had two children by a previous marriage didn't make her more appealing. The gossips of Ridgeland watched Sarah and Willie like hawks, well aware that although their mother might have bewitched Mike by her intelligence, her beauty, and her sharp wit, the children, if they proved unable to fit into the small-town culture that was so unlike Hilton Head, that so-called millionaire's playground, might prove the undoing of this hasty alliance. In this they were to prove correct, though not exactly in the way they had imagined.

When I first visited the Main Street Pharmacy in 2004, it was still popular with locals, despite competition from a new Eckerd's. It was a small, old-fashioned drugstore with a brick front and off-white interior. The display windows featured home-care appliances such as walkers and four-pronged canes. The old-fashioned doors had brass handles. Inside, the shelves carried items like Tylenol and Motrin, bandages and antiseptic ointment. There were few items not related to health care, yet even those, such as the barbecue sauce packaged like a patent medicine, were in keeping with the pharmaceutical theme. To my query the cashier responded that Mr. Davis was out of town. I bought some Old Fashioned Rock Candy and left the store, recalling the conversation I'd had with Mr. Davis several weeks before, when, responding to a letter I'd sent, he had called me on the phone. The first thing he had said to me was that he couldn't help me much with the book because he was ready to move on with his life and couldn't do that if he had to keep rehashing what happened to Nell. He mentioned his upcoming marriage, saying it was especially important to put this part of his past behind him as he embarked on this new era in his life. But he would, he said, talk to me just this once.

I had already suspected, based on what was reported in the newspapers and what I'd heard from Sarah's family, that Mike held Sarah responsible for what had happened to her mother. He quickly confirmed this suspicion, some of the old anger and frustration, the stuff he was trying to put behind him, creeping into his otherwise well-modulated voice. "Rosalyn," he said, "Sarah had *so* much potential, but she ALWAYS made bad choices. If you put her in a room full of people she would always gravitate to the worst ones." When I asked if this was behavior that had begun when she hit puberty, Mike said no, Sarah was always a "pathological" liar. "She would lie about ridiculous things like whether she had brushed her teeth or not. Willie would tell on her for stuff like that."

When I asked Mike to tell me what Sarah was like in the months and weeks before Nell's murder, his answers seemed disjointed, and I got the feeling that he had too much to say, that each pronouncement was the beginning of a paragraph that would never be developed.

"Sarah was out of control. We knew something was going to happen, and we knew it would happen soon because she had violated her probation so many times. I thought maybe she would burn the house down. Nell said maybe if we could just hang in there and keep her alive until she turned twenty, maybe she would see the light. One of the last things Nell said to me was, 'The only thing we haven't tried is an exorcism.'" He gave a mirthless laugh. "Sarah had a split personality, Rosalyn. She was one of those people who cut themselves. She never said she loved her mother, never sent her a Mother's Day card." Nell's own words testify to this fact, as she wrote in a letter to Sarah shortly before her death: "It would be nice if someday you gave me a birthday card or told me happy Mother's Day or something—for all the years I have taken care of you."

There was silence for a moment, and when it persisted, I tried to get the discussion back on track by asking Mike why, in his opinion, if Sarah was guilty of conspiring to murder her mother, she had run away from Ridgway and Bergin when she had the chance. "Do you think it's possible that she was originally just planning to run away with Ridgway, as she claimed in her statement to police, and didn't know that the boys were really planning to attack her mom?"

Mike admitted that it was possible, but he didn't believe that's what happened because when the trio had stopped at a gas station shortly after leaving the murder scene, she stayed in the car while the boys went inside. "She could have run away then," he insisted.

"So why, in your opinion, did she drive to her dad's and then run away?"

"She changed her mind, Rosalyn. Sarah's a smart girl. She started putting two and two together and decided she wanted out of the situation. Let those thugs take all the blame."

"But her plan didn't work," I countered, hoping to prompt him to say more on the subject, but he grew silent again, then began recalling the crime scene.

"I got a call from Willie at the store," he said, his voice dropping so low I had to strain to hear. "He said there were police all over the place, that I needed to come home. I remember walking around in the rain with Willie and Haley and the police. Sarah called me on my cell phone. She said, 'Whassup?' just like nothing had happened. When I then asked her what was going on, she replied, 'Well, Kevin and John came over, and they hit mom with a baseball bat and stabbed her and stuffed her body in the compost bin.'"

Suddenly I felt awful, knowing I was causing this man, whom I'd never met, to relive what must have been the worst experience of his life, worse, even, than losing his first wife to cancer. I tried to change the subject, just a little.

"I understand Sarah lived with her dad off and on for several years prior to the murder. Do you think it would have been better if she'd stayed with Joe?"

Mike sighed. "Who knows? Sarah and Willie loved to go to Joe's house because Joe was always stoned and drinking and would pass out, and the kids could do whatever they wanted. But the judge wouldn't let her go back there, not after she ran away with John Ridgway the first time. That happened while she was living with Joe."

I would discover later that, despite the judge's order, Nell had let Sarah return to live with Joe, in the summer before the murder. And once again she had gotten into trouble and run away.

There was another silence, longer than any other, and I sensed the conversation coming to an end. Mike sounded tired, and it was late, and I felt sure he had a lot on his mind. He was getting married in less than a week. I thanked him for taking the time to talk to me and asked if there were anything else that I should know. He didn't respond right away, so I hoped that he was giving it serious thought.

"You know, I hate to say this, but I'm going to anyway," he confided. "In a way, you could say Nell helped bring about what happened to her." He paused, and I wasn't sure, for a moment, that he would continue. Then he said, "OK, the truth is, she wasn't firm enough with those kids, with Willie and Sarah. On the one hand she would complain all the time about Willie wearing black, looking like a hoodlum. I told her, '*You* buy the clothes for him. Just refuse to buy him those black clothes. Dress him up like a nerd and maybe those bad kids will refuse to hang around him anymore and we won't have a problem.'"

The idea is so logical, yet so outrageous, I couldn't help laughing, a reaction I immediately stifled. "I'm sorry," I said lamely and then, quickly scanning the list of questions I had created for my planned interview, asked the final one.

"What do you think of Sarah's sentence?" I queried, sensing the futility of the question, but knowing that I had to ask. "The lawyers I've talked to, both defense attorneys and a couple of prosecutors, think it's pretty harsh, considering her age and the circumstances. I mean, basically she got the same sentence as the two boys who pleaded guilty to the actual murder."

He didn't answer my question directly, and I could sense that he was drifting away, that this would be the last answer of any kind that he gave me tonight.

"When I was growing up," he reminisced, "it was a time when blacks were basically treated like dogs. They weren't allowed to eat in restaurants with whites, weren't allowed to use the same bathrooms or drink from the same water fountains. I didn't like that. There were black kids that lived around where we did and I wanted to play with them, but my parents wouldn't even let me sit on the front porch with them. Now blacks have civil rights and that's good. But civil rights have gone too far. Rosalyn, the bad people have more rights now than you and me."

A little confused by this connection he was drawing between the civil rights movement and the rights of criminals, I said, "Yes, but in Sarah's case . . ."

He interrupted me, still adrift, now musing. "You know, although she never sent me a card before she was incarcerated, Sarah now sends me birthday cards and Father's Day cards. The last one said, 'To the Best Dad Ever.' I heard that mirthless laugh again, and this time it made the hairs on my neck stand up. "I'll say one more thing," he offered, "And it's this. If Sarah would just admit that she planned the robbery, that she was in on that and planning to run away again, I might be able to believe that she didn't really want her Mama to die. But she'll never say that. Never."

Scribbling frantically in my notebook, I quickly thanked Mike Davis for calling and offered my good wishes for his coming marriage, hoping that his third wife, who must be a brave woman indeed, has a better future as Mrs. Mike Davis than the first two.

5

Digging Up the Past

The first time I drove out to Knowles Island Road, where Sarah Nickel jumped out of the car and ran from John Ridgway and Kevin Bergin, and where Sarah's father, Joe Nickel, still lived, I was tense with excitement and worried that I would be late. In Bluffton I got onto Highway 170 like I was going to Beaufort but then turned left onto 462, which would take me out to Roseland, the plantation-derived name of the area also known as Coosawhatchie. It had begun to seem as if every location I visited had at least two names. On the way to Joe's I was driving the same route taken by Lieutenant Michael Thomas the night he responded to a call for backup at the Knowles Island Road crime scene and, shortly thereafter, apprehended Bergin and Ridgway as they were walking on the shoulder of a side road.

For five or six miles, Highway 462 was lined with dense vegetation— palmettos, scrub pines, live oaks draped with Spanish moss. Then I came to a caution light at an intersection with a gas mart known to locals as Cooler's, which is the surname of the people who have owned and run it since for-ever. If I turned left, I'd be on my way to Ridgeland where Mike Davis's Main Street Pharmacy is located. I kept straight, instead, for another five miles, scanning the roadside for a yellow billboard advertising desirable home sites at Palm Key. When I saw it, I made a right, onto Knowles Island Road.

Like many of the dwellings in this area, Joe's house was a double-wide mobile home, hidden from the road by a screen of trees. A small banana plant grew all alone in the middle of the grassy front yard. I heard a rustling in the wooded area to my right, and when I turned I saw chickens, swoop-ing down from their roost in the pines, perhaps thinking I was going to feed them. A bantam rooster with mahogany feathers strutted aggressively to-ward me, then abruptly turned away. To the left of the driveway sat a rusting Porsche 911. The driveway itself was occupied by a blue 1968 Mercedes se-dan, which appeared to be in mint condition. I recalled that, for most of his adult life, Joe had made a living as an auto mechanic. Now, since suffering a stroke that had left him partially disabled, he did occasional repair work, most of it for former customers down in Augusta where Nell and I grew up, and where Nell and Joe met, fell in love, and got married back in 1982, the same year that Nell graduated from the Medical College of Georgia's program in x-ray technology.

Joe met me at the door dressed in dark blue jeans, a woven Native American–style belt, and a black t-shirt that looked as if it had been ironed. His thick, wavy hair was inky black with a few strands of gray. His eyes were dark brown, hooded, and deep set above high cheekbones. I remembered Nell telling me once, long ago, that some of his ancestors were Native American. I found myself wondering if that heritage is what gives his face its craggy melancholy. Joe shook my hand in greeting then led the way in-side, warning me of the mess I was about to encounter. "This is a bachelor pad, you see," he explained. "Just me and Willie living here now." Willie is the son Joe had with Nell. Thirteen at the time of his mother's murder, he moved back in with his father following the tragedy.

Despite Joe's warning, the house, or at least the part that wasn't covered with tools and auto parts, was quite clean. I found a seat on a plaid sofa. Joe took the leather easy chair. Folding over the pages of my note pad, I glanced around me once more, taking my bearings before I started asking questions. One object on the paneled wall behind Joe's computer leapt out at me. It was a framed *Life* magazine cover featuring Katherine Hepburn, a glamour shot of the young actress in profile, looking back over her shoulder. Though I had never realized it before, I could see now that the actress hauntingly resembled Nell. My eyes scanned the rest of the room, looking for photos. The only ones I saw were recent, fanned across the coffee table in front of the sofa. They showed a group of musicians. Noticing my interest Joe picked up one and extended it to me. "That's David, one of my boys from my first marriage, before Nell. He's in a band that played at the G-8 conference down in Sea Island. That guy there in the middle with the really red cheeks is Gerhard Schroder."

"Gerhard Schroder?" I asked, bewildered. "You mean, the chancellor of Germany?"

Joe grinned lopsidedly, a lasting effect of the stroke. "Yeah. Schroder liked the band so much he went out drinking with them after the show."

I didn't know how to respond to this surprising bit of information, so I just said, "Wow, that's pretty cool," and set the photo back on the table. Joe leaned back in his chair, hands splayed on his thighs, his face fallen back into melancholy.

"So you want to know what I think about this whole mess," he said, and though his face was sad, a hard glint came into his coal-black eyes. I perceived anger simmering below his poised and watchful demeanor.

I said, "Yes," and waited, pen resting on my pad.

"Nell Davis killed herself," he announced, watching me, assessing my reaction. I was shocked, but not only for the obvious reason. He was telling me the same thing, only stated more emphatically, that Nell's husband Mike had told me over the phone two weeks ago.

"Why do you believe that?" I asked, wondering if his explanation would be the same as Mike's—that Nell brought her death on herself by being too soft on Sarah. But Joe's understanding of the situation was somewhat— though not entirely—different. Before he shared that with me, however, he told me a story. Its purpose was to fill me in on Nell's life after she left Augusta, and our friendship had begun to drift into the realm of "used to be" and "former."

Reaching back into the past to retrieve memories that were obviously painful, Joe described how, in the year after he and Nell were married, they decided to leave Augusta because Nell and his first wife, who both worked at University Hospital, couldn't seem to make peace. He recalled one particular incident that took place in downtown Augusta, at the corner of Greene Street and the Calhoun Expressway. After spying each other in traffic, the two women had parked their cars and begun fighting in the street. Police came and charged them both, which meant they had to appear in court. This incident, Joe said, was the straw that broke the camel's back. He and Nell decided to leave Augusta in an effort to leave the past—specifically Joe's past—behind. They chose Hilton Head because both of them had always dreamed of living on the coast (another dream Nell and I had shared in high school). Hilton Head was still close enough to Augusta for Nell to visit her family and friends, and for Joe to maintain his old client base while trying to build a new one. Hilton Head also had a hospital where Nell could apply for a job as an x-ray technician.

Despite the fact that there were no official openings in x-ray at the hospital when they moved into the area, Nell found a job quickly, probably on the basis of the sterling recommendations she received from her supervisor in Augusta. Her performance continued to be outstanding. More than one person has told me that patients whose x-rays indicated a need for emergency action would be referred to the surgeon on Nell's advice, if the staff radiologist wasn't available.

During the years that they were married, Joe continued to work as a mechanic, specializing in foreign sports cars and sedans, like the Mercedes that currently sat in his driveway. Despite the fact that she only had a B.S. degree plus her training as an x-ray technician, Nell's career advanced rapidly. She would eventually become administrative director of the Radiology Department at Hilton Head Medical Center.

Nell Crowley was nineteen and fresh out of school when she married Joe Nickel, a thirty-year-old divorcé with two children from his previous marriage. Many of Nell's friends predicted that the marriage wouldn't last a year. They were right about the not lasting part, but wrong about the duration. Nell and Joe remained together for seven years, during which time they had two children, Sarah, born in March 1983, and Willie, three years after Sarah. Sarah was, Joe recalls, "Mommy's little girl." She was doted on and loved in the way that southerners fondly refer to as "spoiled." When they were not working, the Nickels went out on their sailboat or to the beach. Joe remembers calling Sarah his "beach baby." Joe's unmarried sister, Anita Belding, cared for the children while their parents were at work.

Joe was unable or unwilling to tell me about how his marriage to Nell fell apart. The memories, he said, were simply too painful. Anita, who'd moved in with Nell and Joe after Sarah was born, remembers a lot of yelling and some objects being thrown about, sort of like Katherine Hepburn and

Nell with Sarah as a baby on the beach at
Hilton Head. Photograph by Joseph Nickel.

Cary Grant in *Philadelphia Story*. Only this wasn't a movie with a happy
ending. Recalling some of the scenes she witnessed, Anita told me how she
would try to distract Sarah, visibly upset by the arguing, by getting her to
play Candy Land, one of the little girl's favorite games. Sometimes the distraction worked, but oftentimes Sarah would just cry and demand to play
with Mommy and Daddy.

It wasn't all bad, though. There were plenty of happy, "crazy happy"
times, too. Joe laughed as he remembered Sarah's birthday party when she
turned two, which had been held at the home of Mary Ellen Crouch, one
of Nell's close friends from the hospital. At the end of the party, which had
been "huge, with tons of people," Joe and Nell and Mary Ellen had gone
around gathering up all the trash in black plastic garbage bags. On the way
home, Joe dropped the bags in a trash dumpster, only to remember, when
they arrived at their destination, that Sarah's presents had also been packed

into a black plastic garbage bag to take home. That bag, like all the others, had gone into the dumpster. "And guess who had to go dumpster diving that night?" Joe asked. I didn't have to guess. I had known Nell well enough to know that it wasn't her.

And the good crazy times weren't limited to Sarah's babyhood, either. Recalling Nell's love of animals, a love shared by her daughter, he told me about an episode involving the family cat that occurred when Sarah was in kindergarten. Shortly after the family had moved into their house at the Gatherings on Hilton Head, Sarah and Nell had come home crying hysterically, saying that their cat was dead, that it had been hit by a car and squashed out on Highway 278, one of the busiest roads in Beaufort County. "They begged me and begged me to go get it, and I knew I wouldn't get any peace until I did," Joe said. "So I went out with a shovel and scraped that dead cat up off the road and brought it home. We put it in a box, I dug a hole and buried it, and the two of them had a little funeral. Well, just about the time they were crying and remembering all the wonderful things that cat had done in its life, here it comes, trotting up out of the bushes, alive as

Sarah Nickol at Christmas, circa 1988.
Photograph by Joseph Nickel

you or me sitting here today." This time the chuckle was accompanied by a knee-slap. I laughed too, relieved that the heavy mood of his narrative had been relieved by some lighter moments.

But such moments were not enough to sustain a marriage.

Finally, in 1989, the relationship between Nell and Joe became too volatile for either one of them to feel safe. The couple decided to call it quits. Joe moved out of their house in Hilton Head, but his sister Anita stayed to continue helping Nell with the children. Sarah was six years old.

Joe recalled suffering a serious depression following the divorce. He said that although he wanted to be involved in the lives of his children, it was, for a time, nearly impossible. Every time he and Nell saw each other, a new fight would break out.

For the next part of the story, once Sarah's parents were living separately, I would have to depend on other sources. Anita, who spent more time with Sarah than anyone else during these years, slowly realized that the emotional distress Sarah felt in the wake of her parents' divorce was gaining in intensity. The child started to have bizarre mood swings, would sometimes burst into tears for no apparent reason. On one occasion, when she was in first grade, Sarah packed a suitcase and tried to run away on her bicycle. Fortunately the weight of her suitcase kept her from getting very far.

Initially Nell didn't seem to pick up on the distress signals that Sarah was sending out. Anita, who had an intimate relationship with both Sarah and her mother, speculates that this may have happened because Nell was working so hard, and for such long hours. And when she did realize that something was wrong, it was easy enough to explain what she observed as the "normal" difficulties experienced by a child of divorce. Sometimes Sarah's moods spiked with an intensity that was frightening, but they were usually short-lived, passing away like a summer storm, leaving a buoyantly happy little girl in their place.

Proud of her daughter's natural grace and beauty, Nell encouraged Sarah to enroll in ballet and gymnastics classes, and the physical activity seemed to stabilize her moods somewhat. Having scheduled activities in the afternoons also kept her from brooding. Anita, who suffered from bipolar disorder, worried that Sarah was showing early signs of the same illness, but since Sarah seemed to be doing better, she kept her thoughts to herself, though now, she admits, she wishes she hadn't. Then, when Sarah was seven, Nell began dating a man named Chris, whom nobody, but Sarah, seems to remember anything about. Lieutenant Bukoffsky had told me he thought Nell's murder may have had, as its root cause, some kind of abuse, that Sarah fit the profile of a sexual abuse victim. I had not mentioned this to Sarah when she wrote the following, in a letter dated July 28, 2004:

The next thing I remember is Mom's boyfriend Chris. I don't remember his last name and I don't want to. He molested me and I don't think Mom knew about it because I never got up the guts to tell her before she died. He took us to Disney World, came to my birthday party (there's a picture of us somewhere from that day), and generally made himself at home. I don't know why he and Mom didn't work out but I was glad he didn't come over anymore.

When I asked Sarah why she didn't tell her mother how Chris climbed into her bed and "touched" her while Nell was asleep, she said he'd threatened that if she did, she would be taken away from her mother.

Nell's next serious romantic relationship stirred more positive memories for Sarah:

Mom met Mike at someone's wedding. I can't remember who was getting married, but I think the reception was at Sea Pines on Hilton Head. I was running around with my shoes off and cut my foot on a piece of broken glass. They took me to a little room with a sink and that's how I met my future step-father. He looked at my foot and cleaned it, then sent me off to play with his son, Justin, who was 3 years older than me. He seemed like a pretty nice guy, but after Chris, I was wary about the men who came around Mom, especially the ones who showed any interest in me.

Nell and Mike were married in July 1993 on the dock at Mike's place in Lobeco, a small community north of Beaufort where the streets have quaint names like "Backache Acres" and "Polite Family Lane." Sarah, who was ten, acted as a combination bridesmaid–flower girl for the small, informal ceremony. Sarah remembers that she was excited about having a new stepdad and a new big brother, but the move from Hilton Head to Ridgeland, a much smaller, more insular community, came as quite a blow, particularly when she started school. Many of Sarah's friends at her former school on Hilton Head had been black, and her mother had taught her to hate the word "nigger" and the racism it conveyed. At her new private, all-white school, the Thomas Heyward Academy, she heard the racial slur often and felt her cheeks burn with anger each time. "But what can you expect," she comments now, "from a school whose football team was called the Thomas Heyward Rebels? Their mascot was a Confederate officer who would wave a Confederate flag at the games." Sarah had a hard time fitting in at Thomas Heyward for other reasons as well. It was a small school where nearly everybody knew everybody else (and had since kindergarten or before), and most of the kids' families had lived in Ridgeland, or the surrounding area, for generations. "Plus," Sarah says, describing her misery, "I was all knees and elbows, I was in the 5th grade and didn't have my period and Mom made me get those god-awful body waves put in my hair, which made it frizzy and unmanageable." Sarah stayed at Thomas Heyward, and stayed pretty miserable, through seventh grade.

■ ■ ■

As any child or adventure story will tell you, one of the most efficient ways to cope with present misery is a change of scenery. That is why things promised to get better for Sarah when Mike decided to build Nell a new house out in Okatie, on a beautiful parcel of land overlooking one of the tidal creeks of the Chechessee River. When they moved in, Sarah went back to school in Hilton Head, looking forward to spending more time with her old friends, particularly her best friend, Amy Heath, who would later testify at Sarah's trial. Unfortunately it wasn't as easy as she had expected to readjust. She was now in eighth grade, and her adolescent hormones had kicked in big time, creating another element of distraction. Although she had inherited her mom's quick mind and scored high on both aptitude and intelligence tests, she was finding it increasingly difficult to concentrate on her school work. She started getting interested in boys, and they returned her interest. She started smoking marijuana occasionally, and drinking alcohol, which seemed to take the edge off her mood swings, and enabled her to forget, for a brief time, how "perfect" her stepbrother Justin was. Justin made all As on every report card, had a wonderfully even temperament, and was, according to Sarah, "the golden child who always did everything right." Compared to him Sarah says she always felt like a failure. An excerpt from a letter Nell wrote to Sarah shortly before she died confirms that Sarah felt this way: "Nobody can be like Justin and nobody expects you to be." Besides Justin's grades, there was also his temperament; even if Sarah did manage to do well in school, she knew she would never be even tempered like her stepbrother, and the belief that her parents couldn't seem to love her for herself fueled her anger. Another sentence from Nell's letter contradicts this perception of Sarah's. After stating that nobody expected Sarah to be like Justin, Nell writes, "That is just something you made up in your own mind." Perhaps the preference for Justin was "made up" in Sarah's mind, but her perception that her mother and stepfather loved and/or respected Justin more was both a cause and a product of dangerously low self-esteem.

Despairing of ever being the kind of child Nell seemed to want, Sarah began to identify more and more with her father, Joe, because she knew that he lived a different life, by a different set of rules. Proud and independent, Joe had experience and ability as a mechanic that allowed him to work for himself, unlike her mother, who sometimes seemed like a slave to her job at the hospital. Nell would compensate for her absence by buying Sarah nice things, something else that Nell's own words, again in a letter to Sarah, confirm. She writes, "I'm sorry I would buy you things. I thought doing it would give you pleasure but as usual you turned it into something negative that I did. I won't buy you anything else unless you ask for it."

Although Joe earned considerably less than Nell—to the point that he was often broke, *he* called the shots. *He* decided to be broke. Or not, because sometimes he was flush with cash. On a whim, Sarah asked her mom about moving in with Joe, who was living in a small cottage at Honey Horn Plantation, a historic site on Hilton Head Island. To Sarah's surprise Nell appeared to give the matter serious consideration. What Sarah didn't know was that, according to Joe, Nell had already been to see him, had dropped by unexpectedly on her way home from the hospital one afternoon.

Nell was still wearing her work clothes, and visibly upset when she arrived, but this time, Joe claims, he'd done nothing to provoke it. When he asked Nell what was wrong, she got right to the point. "You have to take Sarah," she had said, standing on the uneven boards of the front porch. Joe thought he could see tears welling up in her eyes, something he'd rarely seen before. Nell typically kept her emotions (except when she was angry with him) under tight rein. "If you don't, it's going to ruin my marriage." Joe knew then what he had suspected for a long time—that Nell's husband, Mike, and Sarah were as compatible as fire and water. "If you take her," Nell continued, "I'll never ask you for child support again." Joe explained that he had a roommate at the time, so he'd have to get that person to move out first, but yes, he would take Sarah and Willie.

Sarah began living with her father in a cottage at Honey Horn Plantation in the fall of 1998. Although times were lean, and there were days when Joe could barely afford to put food on the table for himself and his two children, for a while life seemed to flow along pretty smoothly. Living at

Honey Horn, Sarah appeared happy, being "out in the woods," as Joe called it, and taught herself to drive by tooling around the plantation in an old Volkswagen bus. Joe remembers that he was happy, as well. He speaks of it as an almost idyllic time, filled with the sense that, when they came home each afternoon, they entered a kind of sanctuary. Acres of meadow and pasture stretched out before the collection of houses and outbuildings that had previously serviced a working plantation. The cottage they occupied, built in the 1930s for Miss Millie, a former postmistress, had a tin roof, polished wooden floors, and a large fireplace in the front room with a stucco-covered wooden mantel. Some things were in disrepair (like the vintage linoleum in the kitchen that was peeling up at the corners), but at $220 a month, Joe felt he had little to complain of.

Then bad luck struck. No sooner had the three of them gotten settled than Joe received a notice that Honey Horn had been sold to the Town of Hilton Head. Part of the land was to be used for a cross island expressway, a toll road that would cut right through the plantation's acreage to ease the traffic congestion coming on and off the island. The remaining sixty-eight acres were to be leased to the Coastal Discovery Museum, which would give tours of the plantation house and outbuildings to educate residents and visitors about the history, culture, and natural environment of the low-country. When Joe broke the news to Sarah, he says, she was devastated. As he remembers it, the three of them—he, Sarah, and Willie—had just begun to feel like a family again, and Honey Horn was home. Now they had to move *again*.

Yet life at Honey Horn had not been the blissful idle that Joe imagined—at least not according to Sarah. By October 1998, just one year before her mother's murder, Sarah's mood had nearly bottomed out. She found herself spending a lot of unstructured time alone while Joe worked long hours at his shop, trying to get back on his feet financially now that it was beginning to look like he'd be bringing up Sarah and Willie by himself. She especially missed her four-year-old half sister, Haley, whom she hardly ever got to see now that she was living with her dad. Distractedly searching for ways to relieve her loneliness and boredom, Sarah started messing around with her dad's tools. Her favorite was a mini blowtorch, which she occasionally turned on the fire ants whose sandy mounds dotted the plantation grounds. Whenever a bare foot happened to land near one of their nests, these tiny pests would swarm up to deliver stinging bites that left large red welts on her feet and ankles. On one occasion she accidentally burned herself and was surprised to find that the resulting pain felt "good, in a weird kind of way." The weirdness of it made her feel guilty, but she couldn't ignore the revelation that hurting herself had brought more pleasure than pain.

Another item her father kept among his tools was a box of straight-edged razor blades. Sarah took a few of them from the box and stored them in her room, thinking that if anyone asked, she would say she was going to use them to cut pictures out of magazines. After hiding the blades, though, she forgot about them, at least for a while. Then one afternoon while she was reading in her room, the telephone rang. She picked it up, said hello, and heard her mom's voice saying, in a singsong voice, "Someone wants to talk to you." According to an essay Sarah wrote several years later, this is what happened next.

My little sister, Haley, came on the line and asked when I was coming home. She missed me. I started to cry and told her that I missed her too, but I didn't know when I was coming home. We talked a little longer and then hung up. Right before I ended the call she said, "I love you, Sissy." My voice choked with tears as I told her I loved her, too. Then I pushed the button that broke the connection.

Searching the top of her messy dresser for some tissues to wipe away her tears, Sarah found her hands come to rest on the smooth pink surface of her jewelry box. She opened the box and listened to the tune that played while the plastic ballerina performed her endless pirouettes. Beneath the ballerina, among the tangle of necklaces and earrings, lay one of the razor blades she had stashed away.

Slowly, I eased the razor from its cardboard sheath and watched it gleam in the light of my lamp. I took the blade over to my bed and sat down. I held it in my palm and looked at it. Would doing this make me feel any better? I've always taken pride in being a "try anything" type of person so I figured, what the hell?

I knew Daddy wouldn't notice if I cut myself because he never noticed ANY-THING I did, good or bad. My only problem was, my pain was my pain and I didn't want anyone to notice how I dealt with it. The weather was starting to get cooler so I knew I could hide it with long-sleeved shirts.

I chose my left upper arm.

I'm a weenie when it comes to pain but I found out that's not true when it's self-inflicted. As I raked that razor over my skin, my pain turned to euphoria. I felt like I was controlling my pain for once. As the blood dripped down my arm, I cut myself about three more times. Not deep enough to leave permanent scars, but deep enough to let the blood flow freely. I felt that with every drop of blood that left my arm, a little bit of hurt left with it. I felt a little guilty because, deep down, I knew that what I was doing was wrong, but it felt so good! It was one thing I had control over. People had hurt me all my life so hurting myself made it feel better. That's how twisted my conception of reality was.

Sarah goes on to describe the methodical cleaning and dressing of the wound, after which she put on clothes, including a long-sleeved sweatshirt, and joined her dad for dinner. She half-expected him to ask her why she looked so guilty, but he didn't. They ate in near silence, and after dinner she watched a program on the History Channel, then went to bed.

Sarah's life followed that pattern for months. In addition to cutting, she would stab needles into her skin until she bled, and burn herself with cigarettes and lighters. If someone hurt or upset her, she would hurt herself as compensation.

Cutting herself wasn't the only mode of venting Sarah found. By 1998 she was regularly keeping a journal where she recorded her crushes and romantic fantasies, as well as her inexplicably shifting moods. On October 6, 1998, the day her mom called and put Haley on the phone, the same day Sarah discovered the release offered by self-mutilation, she recorded the shocking journal entry that would later be read in court at her trial:

Haley just called me and asked me when I was coming home. She was about to cry when she asked me. It broke my heart to see her like that. I hung up the phone and I cried so hard. I love her and Willie to death and I would never let anyone hurt them but I know I'll end up hurting them both when I kill mom. She deserves to rot in the fiery pits of hell. I'll take her there myself.

Contemplating the juxtaposition of that phone call from her sister, the cutting incident, and the disturbing journal entry, my understanding of what Sarah wrote that day suddenly shifts. The shift reminds me of an experience I once had while looking at *Ranger Rick* magazine with one of my sons. The article I am remembering featured close-up photographs of one small part of a plant or animal or other object taken from nature. It was impossible to decipher the photo until you turned the page and saw the rest of the picture, the object whole and entire, and suddenly what looked like a shiny button became the design on a butterfly wing. A tiny metallic hook was really a hair on the leg of a housefly.

Thinking about the bigger picture afforded by my new knowledge, I find myself wondering . . . would the jury have felt any differently about Sarah's journal entry had they known the circumstances under which it was written? Maybe. Maybe not. But I do know that if I had been on that jury, I would have wanted to know. Because without knowing, I never could have understood the meaning of what she had written, and the immediacy of its relationship to what was happening in her life at that time. In contrast there were no entries in which she talked about hurting or killing her mother during the months and weeks leading up to her mother's murder, those who believe in Sarah's innocence are quick to point out. Those who believe her guilty, like her stepfather, Mike Davis, say it just shows that Sarah was planning her mother's death for at least a year.

■ ■ ■

Faced with eviction from the cottage he was renting at Honey Horn Plantation, and determined never to be forcibly removed from his home again, Joe Nickel decided to buy some property that he could put a house or mobile home on, out in a relatively undeveloped part of Jasper County called Roseland. In order to pay for the land and construction, Joe, who had not been working steadily, had to stay with friends until the new place was ready. Sarah returned to her mom's house, but that situation quickly deteriorated. Her stepfather, Mike Davis, seemed to get angry at Nell all the time for not being strict enough with Sarah and Willie. Nell responded by laying down more rules, but Mike was more consistent about enforcing them than she was, which led to further battles. That is why, Sarah says, one spring evening when the family went to see her brother Willie in a school production of *The Wizard of Oz* (Willie played the Cowardly Lion), she sneaked out of the performance and made a phone call to Joe's third wife, Tracy, from whom he was now separated. Tracy, Sarah has often said, had made her feel loved and welcomed in her home, even after it became obvious that she and Joe were never going to be able to put their marriage back together.

Nell, understandably, was hurt by Sarah's desire to live with her stepmother. She felt that it wasn't right for her to have the responsibility of caring for Sarah, especially when Sarah could be so difficult to handle. At the same time, she knew that the current situation between Sarah and Mike was untenable. Everyone needed a break. Sarah and Tracy seemed to get along with a minimum of friction. So perhaps Nell thought that the best thing was to wait a while, work on strengthening her marriage, and let well enough alone as long as Sarah stayed out of trouble.

The weeks drifted by, the weather cooled. The color of the marsh grass faded from bright green to yellow to winter brown. Sarah spent Christmas with Tracy and Joe, her Aunt Nini, and cousin Mary. Because it was both faster and less expensive, Joe ended up getting a mobile home for his new property. In February 1999 he and Sarah were moving her belongings into what was to be her new room when Nell stopped by to invite Sarah to attend a funeral. Her maternal grandfather, Jack Crowley, had died of a heart attack. Gran Gran was, in a sense, the last person in her mom's family to whom Sarah had felt a strong connection. For that reason, despite the tension that, Sarah said, hung in the air "like a million tiny bombs waiting to explode," she agreed to go and was ready when one of Nell's friends came to her school to pick her up on the day of the service. She remembers pulling down the sleeves of her navy blue dress, hoping no one would notice the stab marks she had made in her arms the previous night to relieve her anxiety. She had never been to a funeral before, and, estranged from her mother and stepfather, she felt like an intruder.

John Crowley had served the military in both the army and the navy, during World War II and the Vietnam conflict, retiring at the rank of lieutenant colonel; thus he was given a military funeral at the National Cemetery in Beaufort, South Carolina. He had been cremated, and his ashes were enshrined in an elegant bronze urn engraved with the silhouette of a man playing golf, one of his favorite pastimes. Uniformed soldiers stood off to the side, at ease but ready to be called on, after the eulogy, for the twenty-one-gun salute that was Lieutenant Colonel Crowley's due.

Listening to the record of her grandfather's distinguished career, Sarah found herself drifting off into memories of the past. She remembered the thrill of pulling into the driveway at her grandparents' house, being the first one out of the car, launching herself through the side door and into her grandfather's waiting lap as he sat watching television in his leather recliner. John Crowley loved plants and had a beautiful garden, plus a greenhouse full of exotic flowers. One of his favorite activities was to take Sarah and her brother Willie into the garden or the greenhouse, where they would be enveloped in the rich smells of fertile soil and burgeoning plant life as he pointed to and named the various species, showing particular pride in the ones that were difficult to acquire or required special care in order to thrive. On Sundays before the family left for the drive back to Hilton Head, he would load Sarah and Willie into the back of his Chevy Blazer for a trip to Krispy Kreme out on Washington Road. Sarah loved the ritual feel of it, the way they would always park and go inside instead of using the drive-thru, even though the children invariably selected the same kind of dough-nuts, Sarah the lemon custard or crème-filled with chocolate on top. Still, it was a delight to see all the pastries lined up so neatly side by side in their sparkling clean display cases.

I too have fond memories of Sarah's grandfather, Nell's father, Jack, as he was called by his wife and those who knew him well. In addition to the pancake breakfasts he cooked on the weekends I spent at Nell's house, he would sit and watch goofy TV shows with us when he got home from Fort Gordon—shows like *Gilligan's Island* and *Tom and Jerry*. I remember that he especially liked *Tom and Jerry*, and would sometimes whistle the theme song after the show ended. Unlike Sarah, Nell and I were kept on a relatively loose leash, often left to our own devices, and even expected, I think, to indulge in such minor vices as smoking marijuana and underage drinking. I vividly remember one afternoon when we went for a walk with Nell's dad around the neighborhood, and he asked Nell and me if we had any "pot." We said yes (I'm not sure why), and then he told us he would like to smoke some. So we lit up a joint, right there in the middle of Sussex Road, passing it back and forth and acting for all the world as if we owned it. When we had finished, he started humming a little tune and then pro-ceeded to execute several perfect cartwheels just before we reached their driveway and turned in to go to dinner.

At Jack Crowley's funeral, Sarah recalls, her grandmother Julia sat in a chair in the row in front of Sarah, her shoulders shaking with silent sobs as the eulogy continued. Noticing her grandmother's distress, Sarah slipped out of her chair and crept forward on her knees, putting a hand on her grandmother's arm. She had never felt close to her grandmother, but the love they both felt for Gran Gran seemed to bring them together for a sin-gle moment. The soldiers folded the American flag with their white-gloved hands and presented it to Julia. Sarah scuttled awkwardly back to her seat. Taps were played, then seven soldiers raised their rifles and fired, three times, in perfect harmony. As the service wound down, Sarah found her self feeling increasingly out of place. She looked at her mom's back, as Nell sat ramrod straight in the front row, and wondered if she had observed the interaction between her daughter and her mother.

The sense of being connected to her mother's family, so strong only moments before, faded like a dream. She was an outsider once more, the girl who had broken her mother's heart, who had disappointed her grandmother, who felt so ill at ease living in her mother's house that she'd spent several months of the past year living with her dad's ex-wife.

Later, when Sarah was dropped off back at her dad's and left alone with her grief, she felt that grief turn into frustration and then into something else. Even cutting herself didn't bring the necessary relief. She needed something stronger.

6

The Future in an Instant

When Sarah met John Ridgway she was in ninth grade at Hilton Head High School. She was on her way back to class from a bathroom break, and he was getting a bottle of water out of a drink machine. They had seen each other and said "Hi" many times, but the conversation never went further. This time, just as she was about to pass on by, John said, "Hey, can I call you sometime? Maybe we could hang out or something?" Sarah said yes and paused long enough to give him her phone number. The number she gave him was her dad's. She was still living at Honey Horn Plantation at this point, but the initial sense of freedom and relief she had felt upon moving in with her dad had worn off. Her life seemed hollow, even with an endless string of boyfriends and all the sexual attention she could stand.

She had started using her self-mutilation to test the boys, to see if it would scare them off. It worked for some, but not for John Ridgway. But then John wasn't a boyfriend anyway. He was a friend, her best friend she began to think, once he had introduced her to a drug that seemed capable of transforming her world. That drug was crack cocaine.

I know that people with mood disorders are more susceptible to drug abuse. Cocaine is especially appealing to depressives like Sarah because it stimulates a massive release of the neurotransmitter dopamine, thus un-leashing a momentary surge of blissful energy and exuberance. When the high wears off, depleted neurotransmitter reserves cause the user to come crashing down into a chemically induced agitated depression. When the user is already operating at a baseline of depression, such a crash feels in-tolerable. Yearning to rekindle the supercharged bliss of intoxication, Sarah quickly found herself on the treadmill of addiction.

But there was more to John than just the drugs. He was smart and witty and would do the most outrageous things, like wearing a skirt and eyeliner to school, not caring what the other students thought about him. He read philosophy and thick novels and knew enough about music to be consid-ered a bona fide audiophile. He was probably as smart, Sarah soon realized, as her stepbrother Justin, but unlike Justin he wasn't a nerd, and he didn't look down his nose at Sarah for her wild behavior, sexual or otherwise. Furthermore, unlike the other guys she knew, he never pressured her to have sex with him. He seemed to care about her as a person, a friend, even, rather than a "piece of ass."

■ ■ ■

Despite all the moving around she did during 1998–99, Sarah continued to develop a relationship with John Ridgway, who, like Sarah, wasn't happy at home. The two often fantasized about running away, and before long that fantasy became real. The first time, in November 1998, they stole a car and made it all the way to Connecticut, where Ridgway's family had lived before moving to Hilton Head. They were picked up when they ran out of gas, attracting the attention of a police officer who noticed the stopped car. He ran a check on the license, which revealed that it was stolen. They had also taken some money and a Colt .45 automatic pistol from Joe Nickel's house. They had used both to finance their trip, selling the gun to a friend of John's. The Connecticut authorities sent the teens back to Beaufort County on a Greyhound bus. John's parents picked them up at the station and would have taken Sarah directly home, except that neither of them had eaten for two days, so they stopped at a fast-food joint before returning Sarah to her mother.

After taking one look at her daughter, who was so skinny, strung out, and sick that she looked like a walking skeleton, Nell drove her directly to Charter Hospital in Savannah, where she would receive psychiatric care and be monitored for signs of drug abuse or addiction. Diagnosed with depression, she was put on Paxil and released into her mother's custody after a five-day stay. She was to continue attending counseling sessions with a licensed therapist. At first Sarah says she felt good about returning to her mother's house. Desperate for a change, she decided to try and make the best of it. She would even try to get along with her stepfather. Nell and Mike both said they wanted to help her get better, and she knew that they would pay attention to what she was doing, even if they did try to rein her in with rules and restrictions. Living with her dad, she'd begun to realize, she'd had a little too much freedom. Too much freedom had begun to make her feel invisible.

Charged with grand larceny (for the car theft), petty larceny (for the money they took from Joe), and running away, Sarah soon appeared before a judge in family court. Partly because Sarah was already in treatment, and partly because she had the support of her family, the judge let her off with probation. Feeling that Sarah needed more supervision than Joe was able to provide, Nell determined that her daughter needed to live with her again, despite the strain such an arrangement might put on her marriage. So she talked to Mike about her love and her fears for Sarah, and they both prayed about the situation and ultimately decided they wanted Sarah to come home. Sarah, hoping against hope that things would be better this time, felt that this was a chance for a new beginning. She became determined to make things work.

At first Nell seemed happy to have her daughter back, and the relationship between mother and daughter improved dramatically. Nell appeared more relaxed, more willing to let her daughter make some of her own decisions. This was especially important for Sarah when it came to choosing her wardrobe. Mike, however, when he saw some of the clothes Sarah appeared in, refused to let her out of the house, and so the battles began again.

Part of the family routine was for Nell to take the kids to school. One particular morning, when Nell had Willie and Haley in the car ready to go, Sarah walked out of the house just ahead of Mike. It was a cool morning, and she wore a long-sleeved shirt with a black t-shirt layered over the top. She had her hand on the door handle of Nell's Tahoe, just about to open it, when Mike grabbed her, saying, "You can't wear that." "That" was a t-shirt with a picture of Ozzy Osbourne on front, holding a dove and smiling. On the back of the shirt he held the same dove with his mouth open as if about to bite its head off. The images are a visual allusion to an incident early in

Osbourne's career when he did actually bite off a dove's head to get attention from the media.

In response to Mike's demand, Sarah recalls saying, "There's nothing wrong with this shirt. Mom let me wear this shirt." According to Mike's memory of the incident, however, Nell had also argued with Sarah over the shirt, trying, unsuccessfully, to get her to change it before they left. Opening the door and throwing her books on the car seat, Sarah prepared to climb in. Mike grabbed her arm and pulled her out, forcing her to turn and face him.

"It's disrespectful," he said, and she could see that he was angry.

But she didn't care. "It's not disrespectful," she spat back. "It's a joke."

Sarah could hear Haley start to whine now and remembers her mom saying, "Mike, we're gonna be late." That's when she tried to pull away, hoping it was all over. But it wasn't. Mike grabbed her other arm, tightened his grip, and shook her hard, then banged her against the side of his truck. Somewhere in the course of the argument the shirt came off and Sarah got in the car.

Later, at school, one of her friends grabbed her arm and she flinched. Rolling up her sleeves to see if Mike's grip had left any marks, she found vivid blue and purple bruises. She showed the bruises to the school nurse. The school nurse, of course, sent her to school guidance counselor Lisa Pulice, the same Lisa Pulice who would testify against Sarah at her trial. Pulice called the Beaufort County Department of Social Services, which sent someone to make a home visit. The social worker did not find anything that would indicate abuse or neglect at the Davis home, and things continued as they were.

Almost before she knew what had happened, Sarah found herself hauling all her stuff back over to her dad's trailer on Knowles Island Road. Mike took her there in his truck. Sarah tried to keep her mouth shut during the trip but finally couldn't let Mike go without saying something.

"Mom's a bitch." Mike didn't take his eyes off the road, but a half smile played at the corner of his mouth.

"You're both bitches," he said, and Sarah could detect the grim humor that signaled a truce. "When one of you has got PMS, there's no living with you."

Living with Joe she continued therapy for a while, but when her medication ran out and her dad couldn't afford to pay for the expensive prescription drug, she stopped. The school year ended, and she once again found herself with time weighing heavily on her hands, a situation that always led to trouble. In late June 1999 Sarah got caught cooking hallucinogenic psilocybin mushrooms with one of her friends who, Joe suspected, was also dealing more dangerous drugs. Fed up, both with Sarah's behavior and with Nell accusing him of being too lenient, Joe called the police. Two officers from Jasper County picked Sarah up and kept her overnight at Jasper County Jail, where she had to sleep in the visiting room because the jail didn't officially house juvenile females at that time.

The next day, after going home with her mother, Sarah eavesdropped on a conversation between Joe and Nell. She heard Nell say, "We've got to do something with her, Joe. I'm afraid she's going to run away and we'll never see her again."

Afraid of what that "something" might be, Sarah started planning her next bid at escape. Joe took her to work with him the following day so he could keep an eye on her, but she managed to use his cell phone to call an older man named Anthony with whom she had partied in the past. She told Anthony she needed a place to stay, and they made plans for him to pick her up at the Taco Bell down the street from the shop where Joe worked. They went to Joe's mobile home first and stripped Sarah's room, taking her clothes, her boom box, even the posters from her walls. She stayed at Anthony's for nine days. They partied almost continuously, and, according to Sarah, Anthony asked her to marry him.

Anthony, Sarah said, had a plan of sorts, which involved going to Jacksonville, Florida, where they would secure a marriage license. But before they could put the plan into action, Detective Joey Woodward spotted Sarah at a pizza place in Bluffton and confronted the couple in the parking lot. He took Sarah into custody, explaining that her dad had filed a missing persons report. Furthermore she had violated her probation by running away. Woodward drove her back to the Jasper County Jail. It was less than a month since her last visit. The next morning, instead of being released into the custody of her parents, she was transferred to Beaufort County (since that was the county of her mother's residence, and her mother had legal custody) for an emergency hearing. The judge, knowing the futility of sending her home again, sentenced her to six weeks at Midlands Reception and Evaluation Center, a juvenile detention facility located in Columbia, South Carolina. There a team of social workers and psychologists would evaluate Sarah and attempt to decide the best course of treatment for her behavioral and substance abuse issues.

While Sarah was in Midlands, Nell visited her every Saturday, and Joe came on Sundays. Her maternal grandmother, Julia Crowley, sent her books, and her mom made sure she had stationary and stamps for letters.

The first time Nell visited Sarah, she cried and asked Sarah why she hated her. Sarah insisted that she didn't, then felt the tears well up in her own eyes. Nell asked, "Do you want to get clean?"

Sarah said, "Yes, more than anything," and promised to give it her best effort when she got out. When it was time for her mom to go, Sarah hugged her hard, then turned away and walked back to her room, where she scratched her wrist with a staple until the blood came. This time, she felt, the pain was a form of punishment, for hurting her mother, for disappointing Nell over and over and over again.

Nell's second visit was more upbeat, at least to start with. She came bearing bags of fast food. Mother and daughter stuffed themselves while Nell told Sarah about the plans that were being made for her future. The case worker who was shepherding the case through the juvenile justice system had told Nell that the judge was considering a group home in Orangeburg, South Carolina. Nell wasn't thrilled with the idea, and Sarah was appalled. She immediately announced that if her parents allowed her to be put in such a place, she would run away, and they'd never see her again. Nell agreed to give her *one more chance* to make things work at home. Sarah promised that she wouldn't be disappointed.

In August 1999 Sarah was released from Midlands just in time to get ready for the next school year. She went home with her mother, once again vowing to get along with her stepfather, and to stay off drugs, but her record of failure in both of these endeavors was too weighty to overcome. Before long she was smoking marijuana every day yet was buoyed up by the fact that she had somehow managed to stay away from hard drugs like cocaine and crack, which seemed to be what had put her over the edge during the summer.

■ ■ ■

As for John Ridgway, his life had gone on pretty much as it had before the first runaway episode. Although he was scheduled to appear in court four times over the nine months following the runaway, for the grand larceny and petit larceny charges, each time his attorney filed a continuance requesting more time to prepare his case. And each time the request was granted. Nearly one year later, in October 1999, Ridgway still had not gone to court. But he did have a court date: October 21.

In the weeks leading up to this date, two significant events occurred. First, while attending classes at Beaufort-Jasper Academy for Career Excellence, Ridgway attacked a classmate with a kind of razor-knife used to open boxes. Although he was taken to the Jasper County Detention Center, authorities released him into the custody of his parents the next day.

Then, on Friday, October 8, thirteen days before Nell's murder, Sarah went missing. Sliding inexorably down into depression, she had become frantic to secure relief. Rather than telling her mom what was happening and asking for help, she set out to score some coke. John Ridgway, who had always found a way to supply her with the drug before, had nothing, and no money either, but that only made her more determined. She broke into her sister Haley's piggy bank, emptied it, and ran away to John's house with her tiny stash of cash. It wasn't enough to buy any coke, so they purchased two twenty-four-packs of Dramamine, went to the house of one of John's friends, Adam Thomas, and swallowed a handful each. A night of weird hallucinations ensued.

Later, when he was interviewed by police, Thomas confirmed that John and Sarah had spent the night at his house, noting that his mother kicked them out the next morning. Thomas also stated that the two of them were planning to run away and had invited him to go with them. They did not, in his presence, discuss any sort of plan to harm members of Sarah's family, or rob them, but he did say that he believed Sarah was running away because she hated her mom.

When John and Sarah left the Thomas house, one of the security guards at Hilton Head Plantation drove them back to John's parent's house, located in the same development. John's mother discovered Sarah hiding out in John's room and insisted that the girl call Nell, who met them at a halfway point between Bluffton and Hilton Head.

Mother and daughter had yet another one of their talks, but this time, Sarah recalls, it was Sarah begging her mom to send her to rehab. "I said if I didn't get help then I would end up dead sometime in the near future. I was scared. I was tired. Tired of everything. I wanted to be put away, far away from everything and everyone so I would be away from temptation. I wasn't strong enough and I knew it."

Nell agreed and began making arrangements to send Sarah back to

Charter, the private Savannah hospital she had entered briefly after the first runaway attempt. There were no beds currently available, so Sarah returned to the house on Bellinger Bluff Road. This house soon came to feel like a prison, as her mother and stepfather increasingly tightened restrictions on her movements, hoping to keep her from using the drugs, which, they knew, were destroying her life. As Mike Davis would say at Sarah's trial, in the weeks before her mother's death, "Sarah was caged. She did not have any privileges and I know she probably disenjoyed living in our house but she never could gain any privileges because she would not try at school, got into all sorts of trouble."

When Joe Nickel learned of Sarah's latest runaway attempt, in addition to Ridgway's arrest for assault, he immediately called Sergeant Chris Sankowski, who worked on the juvenile justice squad for the Beaufort County Sheriff's Office, and asked him for help. Joe wanted to have John Ridgway served with a restraining order requiring him to stay away from Sarah. Sankowski, when I spoke to him, confirmed Joe's calls and said that he had been unable to offer the kind of assistance Joe needed.

When Joe spoke about the days leading up to the crisis that would culminate with Nell's murder, his voice became harsh and insistent, as if he was once more trying to convince someone to do something before it was too late. "They told me I had to wait for Ridgway to go to court before they could do anything, at least on my behalf, because I wasn't the custodial parent. So I called Nell. I said to her, Nell, please have the SOB arrested now." Nell didn't think this was feasible. What, exactly, was she going to have Ridgway arrested for? "For contributing to the delinquency of a minor," Joe had suggested, insisting, almost begging. "He's dangerous. Something's going to happen. Have him arrested."

The line went dead. Joe assumed that Nell had hung up on him, something she had done in the past when they argued over the phone. At wit's end Joe called the solicitor's office, trying to get through to Dan Breen, who was taking the case before the court on the twenty-first. Maybe Breen could do something about the restraining order. Joe left urgent messages for Breen on Monday the eighteenth and then again on Tuesday the nineteenth. On the morning of Wednesday, October 20, Joe called his own attorney, who managed to get through to Breen with Joe's message. The message that was relayed back to Joe from Breen was, "We'll do it [get the restraining order] tomorrow when he goes to court."

Tomorrow, it turned out, would be too late.

Hell Is Murky

Brent Kiker, Sarah Nickel's court-appointed attorney, didn't especially want to talk to me about Sarah's case but finally agreed to give me a few minutes of his time one Thursday morning in late October 2004.

I raced to Hilton Head, climbed the stairs two at a time, then found myself sitting in the waiting room. His secretary said he'd had to go out to an appointment, which entirely flattened my hopes. Nevertheless, obeying the secretary's instructions to have a seat, I sat, gazing around me at the sleek modern furniture, which suited the triangle-shaped room with its taupe walls and its highly lacquered pine floor. There was so much natural light coming in that it felt, ironically, unnaturally bright.

Morosely I watched the hands of the clock opposite me as they crawled inexorably toward the end of what anyone would call morning. I forced myself to stop looking out the window each time a car drove up. I had finally drifted off into a hazy kind of daydream when I heard footfalls pounding up the stairs. The door swung open, and, even though I had seen him in photos, I was surprised by his apparent youth—or maybe it was just his boyish features, his wavy, slightly mussed, sandy-brown hair, his slightly rounded face. One look at him was enough to confirm that he would be more convincing, more real somehow, dressed in a t-shirt and jeans, rather than the dark suit, red tie, and blue Oxford shirt he was wearing now.

He guided me to a spacious office and took a seat behind a large, ornate wooden desk. The walls here were slate blue, an Oriental carpet covered the shiny pine, and prints of sailing ships and a black Labrador in a salt marsh adorned the walls. The only furnishing that hinted at an individual personality was a Hank Williams memorial plaque. Remembering with a jolt that I had only "a few minutes," I asked if he minded my taking notes. He shrugged and said he couldn't really tell me much about the case because it was in appeal. I told him that the decision of the appellate court had been handed down the previous week. He leaned back in his chair, eyeing me doubtfully. "Really?"

"Yes. The guilty verdict was affirmed."

He seemed surprised, so I proceeded to talk, hoping that my knowledge of the case would persuade him to speak more openly.

"Did you know the court-appointed attorney who was handling the appeal?" I asked.

"Savitz, wasn't it? Joseph Savitz?"

"Right. Well, I'm not surprised by what happened," I confided. "When I spoke to Savitz on the phone, he told me he didn't think thirty years was that harsh of a sentence for murder."

Kiker looked puzzled for a moment, then said, "But she wasn't convicted of murder."

"Exactly. When I reminded Savitz of that, he said, 'Oh well, yes, but everybody thought she was in on it.'"

Kiker said nothing this time, just shook his head. In disbelief? I wasn't sure, so I forged ahead. "The appeal was based on a claim of illegal search and seizure—the idea that the police shouldn't have been able to search Sarah's stuff."

"We argued that at the trial. And her journal, the one that says she's going to kill Nell, was ruled inadmissible, at least it was until she decided to take the stand." He sat musing for a moment, so I waited. "I think that's the only motion in the whole trial where the judge ruled in our favor. Though it came out anyway, once Sarah decided to testify."

He began to seem more relaxed. Perhaps, I thought, now that the appeal had been decided, he wouldn't feel such a strong need to be circumspect. I crossed my legs and leaned back in my own chair, trying to catch his gaze, which had wandered to his desk. When I spoke he looked up abruptly. "What was your general impression of Sarah during the time you worked with her?" I asked, pen poised to take down his response.

"She was a naive child," he said, without a moment's hesitation.

"Do you think she was in on the plan to kill her mom?"

"Honestly? She obviously knew Ridgway. They had run away before. She was certainly unhappy at home. Maybe when Ridgway called, she said, 'Yeah, come get me. We'll scare mom and get the keys to the car.' But did she plan for her mom to be murdered like that? No, I don't believe it at all. Bergin killed her, and John orchestrated the whole thing because he wanted to get out of town. You know, the whole trial was a fiasco, really," he continued, warming to the subject. "There was so much misinformation in the press—first this big story in the papers about an electrician who supposedly called the house while the murder was in progress, and who later reported to the police that Sarah answered the phone and sounded 'giddy,' like there was a party going on. There was no electrician, by the way. No phone call, no party atmosphere, nothing. Then there was Sheriff Tanner's response to Sarah abandoning the boys and initiating the 9-1-1 call."

I knew that already, having read it in the *Carolina Morning News*. Tanner had said, "It's my opinion that she was either having second thoughts about what was happening or trying to create her own alibi." I knew already what weight the sheriff's opinion could have in a community as close-knit as Bluffton. Still the jury pool had been pulled from Beaufort County. Presumably there was some diversity. I said as much. Kiker chortled at my ignorance, then set me straight.

"When the judge asked the jury how many of them knew about the case through the media, or had discussed it with anyone else, practically the whole lot of them stood up. That right there should have been reason enough for a change of venue, but no, he asked each one of them to stand up individually, and then asked each one of them couldn't they lay aside what they had heard in the media and bring in a fair verdict based on the evidence presented. So of course most of them said yes."

Later I would indeed learn how doggedly Judge Brown had pursued each juror. Speaking to juror number 239, Marleen Peritz, who'd read about the case in the newspaper, the judge had said, "Keeping in mind what I told you, do you feel that what you read would keep you from giving either the state or the defense a fair and impartial trial?"

Juror 239: "I don't think so but I can't say a hundred percent. I mean—"

Judge Brown: "Well, I would be telling my jurors, when you're sitting over there, what I told you awhile ago. I say you can't base something on what somebody told you. Or what—unless you were an eyewitness, of course. I would say could you listen to those jurors and lay aside what you had heard or read? If you found it to be different?"

Juror 239: "I don't know."

Judge Brown: "And bring a verdict that spoke the truth?"

Juror 239: "I don't know."

The judge finally let Juror 239 sit down, but not before making her look somewhat foolish.

Plunged back into his memories of the trial, Kiker was on a roll now, recalling, with a frustration that apparently still rankled, how much the massive press coverage seemed to hurt Sarah's case. "I think the worse thing," he said, "was when a statement I made in front of the TV cameras was taken out of context. Commenting on all the misinformation that had been put out there by the press, I said that, given the negative pretrial publicity, I didn't see how I could put up a defense that would be believed by the people in this community. The only part of that statement that made it onto the news had me standing on the courthouse steps, saying, 'I don't know how I can put up a defense that can be believed.'" He stared at me incredulously, reliving the frustration of the moment.

I responded, "So the implication was that, even in her defense attorney's opinion, Sarah was so obviously guilty, there's no point arguing."

"Exactly."

"So what is he like, Judge Brown?" I asked, remembering photos I'd seen in the paper of his bird-like visage, his intelligent eyes crowned by a thick shock of flowing white hair. I already knew he'd been in his seventies and semiretired when he took the case.

Kiker smiled and fiddled with a letter opener, and I could sense that this was an area he'd not be going into very deeply. "Uncle Luke," he said, and the smile turned into a smirk. Maybe I would get something after all. I fished some more.

"Some people have suggested that the solicitor was 'judge shopping,'" I said, "and that's why it took so long for the case to go to trial." It had taken more than a year, from October 1999 to January 2001. For much of that time, because of her age, Sarah had been locked up in a cell by herself at the Beaufort County Detention Center. Until she had turned seventeen, she had had to be segregated from the other inmates.

Kiker put his fingers together, a series of steeples, when he answered. "All I can say is that the solicitor can try a case any time he wants to. The case was scheduled to go to trial several different times during 2000. Each time we'd get ready, Sarah would get ready, and then the solicitor would ask for a continuance. The last time a date was set, well, it just happened to be when Judge Brown was on the bench." He smirked again. I interpreted his words in light of the smirk and asked another question, based on another rumor I'd heard.

"Joe Nickel told me that Mike Davis was seen going out with Judge Brown's daughter during the year that passed between Nell's murder and Sarah's trial. Do you know if that's true?"

The smirk vanished. His face closed like a door slamming. There was an embarrassingly long pause, after which he seemed to relax just a little before he finally said, "No comment." I considered the various reasons he might have for refusing to comment. Did he know something that could have changed the outcome of the appeal? If so, why hadn't he spoken up? Later several local attorneys would share with me their opinion that Kiker had been "woodshedded" by Judge Brown at the beginning of Sarah's trial. So-called woodshedding occurs when a young, inexperienced lawyer approaches a judge in chambers to discuss a concern he has over, let's say, a potential conflict of interest, perhaps even going so far as to suggest that the judge recuse himself from the case. When the young, inexperienced lawyer has finished, the judge smiles and tells the lawyer exactly what will happen to him (nothing good) if he makes such a statement in the courtroom where, technically, it ought to be made. So the question always is, in such cases, why didn't the young lawyer, in this case Brent Kiker, go on the record asking the judge to recuse himself? The judge could always say no and give his reasons for doing so. Could it have had anything to do with the fact that this was Kiker's first criminal case, a case he took on at the request of the local bar? Gene Hood in the public defender's office couldn't represent Sarah because he was representing her codefendant Kevin Bergin. Was Kiker unsure of the facts surrounding the potential conflict of interest? Or was he just afraid to step on the toes of someone who had a lot of power and influence in the circuit, and who might, if provoked, throw a monkey wrench into the political machinery of an ambitious young attorney's career?

Kiker cleared his throat, as if he sensed that my attention had wandered, and offered an explanation for his reticence on the subject of Judge Brown's daughter.

"Even though the appeals process is exhausted," he said, his composure fully recovered, "Sarah still has one last chance to get another trial." He was referring to the application for PCR (postconviction relief) that she would file in the coming months.

I remembered learning a little about this when I spoke to Joseph Savitz at the state appellate office. "The postconviction relief," I said. "What exactly makes that different from an appeal?"

"At this stage Sarah can seek to prove that her trial lawyer or the appellate lawyer was incompetent in handling her case, or that there were other errors proving the trial to have been unfair. If she wins she'll get another trial." He paused, then added, "If the decision of the judge who rules in her favor isn't overturned by the South Carolina Supreme Court."

I made a mental note that if she did get a new trial, she would be tried only for armed robbery, because of the rule known as "double jeopardy." Double jeopardy guarantees that a person found innocent by a jury cannot be retried for the same crime. Now I had to ask, "If she gets a new trial, will she be likely to get the same sentence?"

"Let me just say I've never seen one like hers in my experience. Giving the maximum sentence—thirty years—to a juvenile offender when there was as much doubt about her involvement as there was in this case. . . . It was a shock to a lot of people. Hell, they wouldn't even have had a case if those boys hadn't testified against her."

I asked him if he had any insight into why the boys decided to make a deal with the solicitor, rather than going to trial. As soon as the question was out there, hanging in the air between us, I could see how simple-minded it sounded.

"Well," he began, "they'd already confessed, in their statements to the police. Whether they went to trial or not, they were likely to get life without parole. Bergin could've gotten the death penalty. So the solicitor, that's Randy Murdaugh, goes to the public defender's office, presents this deal: 'You two stand up, plead guilty. We'll delay your sentencing. I will recommend thirty years. . . . I will guarantee thirty years if you testify against Sarah and we get the result we want in that case.'"

"The result we want?" I echoed, seeking clarification.

"The truth as determined by Randy Murdaugh. Then—and this is just what I *think* happened, because Mike Davis sat at the solicitor's table throughout the trial—Murdaugh goes to Mike and says, 'Do you want to make this deal?' Because it would be letting these two, especially Bergin, get off pretty light for what they had confessed to doing. So Murdaugh had to make sure it was going to be OK with the victim's family."

"So," I commented, "Davis really must have believed Sarah was guilty, if he was willing to see those two back on the streets after thirty years in exchange for putting her away."

"Well, he probably knew that was the only way Murdaugh was going to get a conviction."

"Not a very good choice, either way," I said, feeling a sudden flash of sympathy for Mike Davis. But I could certainly buy the idea that the solicitor was worried about getting a conviction. I told Kiker a story that Lieutenant Bukoffsky confided about a young man who had killed his mother back in 1991 and then "walked," receiving a suspended sentence and probation. I was told that Luke Brown had also been on the bench for that case.

"There was some kind of mental impairment, is what Bukoffsky said. The woman was a single mom and known to have been abusive. Also, there wasn't anyone to wage a campaign against him like there was with Sarah. Do you think Mike Davis's position in the community, and his desire to have Sarah kept behind bars for as long as possible, had an effect?"

Kiker nodded, then elaborated, "One of Mike's friends presented the judge with a petition signed by one hundred people asking for the maximum sentence. Maybe that had an effect." I detected a note of sarcasm and observed that his face was closing down again. I searched my mind frantically, trying to think where I could take the conversation from here. Now he was checking the time. I could see I was losing him fast. Or maybe not. Because suddenly he turned in his chair so that he was facing me directly and looked me right in the eye. The boyish charm that had never left his face, even when he described the disastrous sound bite on the courthouse steps, was gone.

"I'll tell you this, and then I have another appointment. I do know for a fact that Sarah didn't know that Bergin kid, didn't know he was coming down, and that Mike Davis lied when he got up on the stand and said Sarah had pointed a knife at him in the kitchen a short time before the murder, saying, 'Kevin's gonna take care of you.' Sarah insisted this had never happened, so I subpoenaed the investigating officer who took Davis's statement. That was Sam Roser. He had to get up there on the stand and say that Davis never mentioned being threatened with a knife to him, which is certainly something the man should have recalled, considering what had just happened. He didn't recall it, evidently, until the case went to court, a year and a half later." He paused for a moment, and I began to think he was done. Then he added, "Poor old Roser. I heard he got a new nickname out of that deal."

"A new nickname?"

"D.W. For Defense Witness. Not something a cop wants to be."

"And what about Kevin Bergin?" I asked, hoping to get just a little bit more before he called time. "What was your impression of him?"

"He was crazy." Kiker's hands came up off the arms of his chair, palms up. "He came down here to do that murder because he wanted to perform some high necromantic ritual where you had to have a dead body."

I sat up very straight. I was hearing something entirely unexpected, and I wanted to make sure I got it right.

"Ritual with a dead body? But I thought . . . ," I began, remembering Ridgway's insistent claim, in his statement to police, that they planned to go to the Davis home to commit a robbery, but then things got out of hand, that Bergin just sort of freaked out.

"Yeah, he freaked out all right. In his backpack he had a book called something like *The High Art of Necromancy.* The book described a ritual for achieving oneness with the Angel of Death. You were supposed to *somehow* come across a dead body. The body was supposed to be in a quiet place, abutting water, at a certain time of the day and year. There were certain stones you had to put around the corpse's head, and goat's milk, I believe it was, to pour in the corpse's mouth. There was even a part in the book that said you should give in to your sexual urges, while plunging a knife into the heart. Well, in that backpack we found the stones, the goat's milk or whatever it was, and a special kind of knife that he was supposed to use."

I was scribbling madly as he talked; the shock would register later—but not much later as he continued talking, relating Ridgway's comment to Bergin, "Do what you gotta do," as Ridgway and Sarah went into the house, leaving Bergin alone with the body. "I hate saying this—it's so crude, but somebody who was in prison with Bergin said Kevin skull-fucked her. And if you could see the pants he was wearing, the way they were soaked with blood at the crotch. Sarah and John both said he had his knees over Nell's shoulders when they came back out of the house."

I felt as if I was going to vomit right there on his Oriental rug. It would probably splatter onto the shiny pine floor. I had to get out of there before I was sick.

I literally remember nothing else about the interview. My notes record that Brent Kiker said he "would be delighted to see Sarah retried." Back at home I searched through old newspaper articles, looking for his comments following Sarah's sentencing. I found them in a story by Stephanie Ingersoll, who wrote for the *Carolina Morning News.*

"Thirty years for this little girl is a travesty. She got the same sentence as the two monsters who did this."

■ ■ ■

On my last day in the Beaufort area, I decided to go to the beach. It's not that there wasn't more for me to do; in fact just the opposite. There were still so many people I needed to talk to—most crucially the Nelsons, the first people who saw and spoke to Sarah after the crime—that I knew I would have to make another trip down there. So I dug out my map of Hilton Head, the island that first attracted Nell and Joe to the area, and scanned the grid of streets lining the south side of the island, looking for Dreissen Beach Park, which has a public parking lot and showers. Because the season was over, had ended Labor Day weekend, payment for parking was on the honor system.

I put my money in the box, took a ticket for my dashboard, and made my way across the boardwalk that led through the dunes to the shore. The sun was at two o'clock, slanting and golden, warm as summer, with thunderclouds in the east, far out over the sea. There were a few people on the beach, mostly in small clusters in front of a nearby high-rise. I spread my towel on the sand and slipped off my shorts, looking out over the water. It was low tide, and the sluggish waves were a strange color somewhere between brown and gray, a color I remember from childhood vacations in Savannah and Saint Simons Island, Georgia. Now that I had seen the Caribbean, and swum in the emerald-green waters at Wrightsville Beach in North Carolina, I felt inhibited by this color reminiscent of dirty dishwater. Fat gulls littered the shore, some of them sitting down, pouting like pigeons. The breeze was still in a midday lull. It seemed as if the wind, and everything else, was holding its breath. Even the gulls were quiet. Large silver-bodied dragonflies came in off the ocean. Despite the proximity of a gigantic piece of sludge, which looked like it could be the turd of a whale, I was desperate to get in the water. Swimming is like an addiction for me, and spending the previous week out of the pool hadn't helped my nerves.

I picked up my goggles and walked to the shore, wading in up to my ankles, then found it nearly impossible to continue. I was afraid, I suddenly realized. If I surrendered my body to that murky water I would be pulled under so quickly that no-one on the beach would even notice my disappearance. I knew the fear was irrational, that it had much to do with what Brent Kiker had told me about Kevin Bergin, and nothing to do with the sea, but I couldn't shake it. So I walked back and forth, shaking my head at my folly, when my mind was flooded with sudden memory:

I am fifteen years old, standing in the bathtub of a hotel room, wading back and forth in lukewarm water that just covers my ankles. Unlike today, I'm not alone. Two other pairs of legs pace with me. They belong to Nell and Kathy Kinson, my two best friends. We're sharing the hotel room with my mom, my Aunt Dot, and Uncle Fred, who, after endless nagging about our wanting to go to the beach, brought the three of us to Jekyll Island for Thanksgiving weekend. The adults have gone to bed, but the three of us are wide awake. We had gone out walking on the beach, where I cut my foot on some oyster shells. We came back to the room to clean my cut and now we walk in endless circles in the hotel bathtub, talking and giggling and trying to keep our voices low so as not to wake the adults. We are young and silly and irresponsible, but we are happy, delirious with the kind of joy that is particular to our age. Despite evidence to the contrary, provided by my foot's gaping wound, we share a conviction of our own invincibility, our immortality—a belief that, in too short a time, will be gone forever.

Why, I wondered, as I finally waded out to deeper water, does that memory have such force? Why does it shine like a beacon of happiness among all the myriad memories of my adolescence? Is happiness to be found in such inconsequential moments? Can the power of such a moment survive, when set next to the image of Kevin Bergin straddling Nell's shoulders, his pants soaked with her blood?

Amazingly, it can.

This realization helped to quiet my mind as I lowered myself into the water and stretched out for a few strokes, feeling my body glide through the languid waves, seeking just a few moments' peace, just a small rest from the sense of dread that, over the course of the past week, had become my constant companion.

8

The Role of the Press

My interview with Brent Kiker had made me want to investigate a number of different things, most of all the court records having to do with Kevin Bergin. But those were not immediately accessible, so I decided to look further into his complaint about the way that press coverage had interfered with his ability to be effective counsel for Nickel. I had read some of these accounts myself at the time they were published, but they were not vivid in my memory, so I decided to take another look.

"Sarah Nickel began planning her mother's death at least a year before Nell Davis, 36, of Okatie was beaten and stabbed to death on Oct. 20, said Staff Sgt. Jim Bukoffsky of the Beaufort County Sheriff's Office."

"Bukoffsky said Nickel lured her mother from their home, knowing the two other teens would be waiting around a corner, ready to bludgeon her with a baseball bat."

"Her stepfather, Mike Davis of Okatie, said Davis' death was an act of premeditated murder and asked Judge Gerald Smoak to keep all three teens behind bars."

These quotations are taken from an article printed on the front page of the *Carolina Morning News* on Friday, October 29, 1999, the day after Sarah Nickel's first bond hearing. The judge, siding with police officers and Sarah's stepfather, denied bond.

On November 4 the same paper reported Sheriff B. J. Tanner's response to the newly revealed fact that Sarah had initiated the 9-1-1 call for help after she had abandoned Bergin and Ridgway on Knowles Island Road: "If it was her, then it's my opinion she was either having second thoughts about what was happening or trying to create her own alibi."

This article also states that, according to investigators, Nickel "allegedly began planning her mother's death a year before the attack and wrote about wanting her mother dead in diaries and letters found in her room."

The sidebar for the article features a "History of Events" leading up to the murder. For the morning of October 20, it notes, "Sarah doesn't show up for classes at Hilton Head High School."

The *Carolina Morning News* also covered Sarah's second bond hearing, in July 2000, after she had been incarcerated at the county detention center for nine months. Jim Bukoffsky was replaced by Lieutenant David Randall as spokesman for the investigation. Of Sarah he said, "Someone like this does not belong on the streets and in the community."

Mike Davis, Sarah's stepfather, agreed, telling Judge Jackson Gregory that Sarah "told me she wanted to kill her mother. She's told friends and church members that she wanted her mother dead."

The article furthermore reported that Sarah had "allegedly put on her mother's earrings after helping stab, beat and stuff the woman into a compost heap at the family's Okatie residence."

The *Beaufort Gazette,* reporting on the hearing, included a statement by the solicitor's office that "an electrician telephoned Nickel's house after the murder. Nickel answered the phone and was "giddy" during the conversation." In *The Carolina Morning News,* it was not an electrician, but "a friend" who reported Sarah sounding "giddy, like there was a party going on."

A number of these statements are simply untrue. Attendance records at Hilton Head High and testimony from witnesses would show that Sarah was at school all day October 20. There exist no phone records or testimony from an electrician, or anyone else, who phoned the Davis residence and spoke to Sarah while the crime was in progress. No church members ever testified that Sarah told them she wanted her mother dead. If she had done such a thing, surely the prosecution would have called them as witnesses. As for Sarah's friends, Amy Heath did testify that Sarah said, "I wish I could kill her," referring to her mother, but denied that she ever heard Sarah speak of a plan. Much of the information published in the press, such as Sheriff Tanner's speculations regarding Sarah's motive for initiating the 9-1-1 call, or Bukoffsky's statement that Sarah had been "planning" her mother's murder for more than a year, is simply specious, or very biased, often, interestingly, using the same language that Mike Davis would use, years later, when he told me his opinion about what had happened, language that would be echoed by Judge Luke Brown when I interviewed him. It's also worth noting that the information reported in the news was geared toward the sensational. A story about a girl who hated and killed her mother is, after all, much more titillating than a story about a girl whose mother was killed by a stranger from Connecticut.

Examples such as these illustrate the difficulties faced by Judge Brown in seating a jury whose members had not been affected by what they had read in the paper and seen on TV. When he asked for those who "know anything about this case through any of the news media, radio, TV, newspaper, or have discussed it with someone else" to please stand, fifty-seven members of the seventy-member jury pool rose from their chairs. This meant that Judge Brown had to go through the process of questioning each one, asking if they could set aside what they had seen or heard, and base their verdict on the evidence presented in court. Thirteen jurors said they could not. Seven of these said they knew or had spoken to a member of the family. One Beaufort County citizen summoned to serve on the jury, Lisa Pulice, was dismissed because she would be testifying for the prosecution. She was Sarah's guidance counselor at Hilton Head High.

Once the process of jury selection was complete, Brent Kiker, who believed that Nickel was convicted in the press before she ever went to trial, made his motion in court for a change of venue. He reminded Judge Brown of his own words to the jury, when the judge acknowledged that in "this little town, everybody knows everybody. Everybody's been talking." Kiker continued, adding his own impression of how this small-town phenomenon was actually playing out, "I can't go anywhere without people saying, aren't you the lawyer that represents that girl, oooooh, you got your hands full, like, you got an uphill battle. I've heard it so much I, I don't know how I can—I can put up a defense that it can be believed by the people in the community."

Ironically, thanks to the TV cameras that were in the courtroom that day, the last part of this statement, "I don't know how I can—I can put up a defense that it can be believed by the people in the community," appeared on the evening news, fueling the very fire of negative publicity that he was attempting to put out. And the effort was wasted, anyway. Judge Brown denied the motion for a change of venue. He also denied Kiker's request that the jury be sequestered to prevent their exposure to media coverage, and to discourage them from talking about the case with family or loved ones.

9

Conspiracy to Kill a Goose

Later, perusing court documents, I learned that Kevin Bergin had a complicated history pointing to mental illness aggravated by drug abuse. Adopted at birth by John and Patricia Bergin, he had an apparently normal childhood, growing up in an affluent neighborhood in Darien, Connecticut. He was a quiet child and generally performed well in school until seventh grade, when he began acting out in class. This started with harmless clowning and escalated to more disruptive behaviors, including pranks such as setting off a smoke bomb at school. Around the same time, he began smoking marijuana and, shortly afterward, drinking alcohol. These behaviors were accompanied by a decline in his academic achievement.

Although his grades improved with his enrollment in a private Catholic school, his mood continued to deteriorate. He experienced frequent, extended periods of lethargy punctuated by bursts of intense energy. His moods were undoubtedly affected by a developing cocaine habit that, when he could afford it, had him using up to a gram a day. During this period he also told his parents that he believed God did not like him but refused to elaborate with details or explanation. As if reacting to this feeling of rejection by God, he stopped going to church with his family and became much more interested in supernatural topics such as UFOs, aliens, and extrasensory perception. He began reading books about satanic and other cult worship and started buying black candles and herbs, studying their use in "magic" rituals. During this period Bergin also began displaying symptoms that would, in hindsight, suggest paranoia, such as making comments about being followed and suggesting that unknown "others" were trying to entrap him. He recalled seeing a particular car in different locations about town and told his parents that he felt government agents were following him. He also professed to hearing "clicks" when he talked on the phone, which led him to believe the line was tapped.

In the fall of 1997, shortly after returning to public school, he became very intoxicated at a "drug-free" teen hangout known as the Depot. When his father came to pick him up, Kevin attacked him so violently that it took several men, including police, to pull him off. Court records show that he was charged with criminal domestic violence, and remanded for diagnosis and treatment to a series of mental hospitals and treatment facilities. At the Stamford Hospital, where he resided from September 26 through September 30, he received a diagnosis of conduct disorder, alcohol intoxication, alcohol abuse, cannabis abuse, and rule out major depression. From there he went directly to Silver Hill Hospital in New Canaan from September 30 through October 22. At Silver Hill, a private psychiatric hospital distinguished by its success treating dual-diagnosis patients (those with substance abuse disorders in addition to psychiatric illness), he received a diagnosis of major depression (single episode), cannabis abuse, alcohol dependence, and oppositional defiant disorder, a diagnosis specific to children and adolescents. He was presumably treated with therapy and medication, though the records do not specify the latter. Kevin then went home for about a month before being readmitted to Stamford Hospital on November 22, where he stayed until November 26, his diagnosis containing the now familiar terms, major depression, conduct disorder, and alcohol abuse, with the addition of antisocial personality traits.

Antisocial personality traits (ASPT) are actually a cluster of personality traits that have a strong association with criminal behavior. By definition they are any actions that oppose legitimate social order that promotes "the common good." Three core antisocial behaviors focus on challenging authority, breaking rules, and violating the rights of others. These behaviors are sometimes covered by what are termed "disguising behaviors," which consist of superficial charm, duplicity, and deceptiveness. When people with ASPT are caught engaging in criminal activity, they typically respond evasively. They rarely feel guilty but often go to great lengths to justify their behavior, denying personal responsibility and blaming the victim for their offense. Prior to recent revisions of the diagnostic terminology, people who exhibited such behaviors were classified as "sociopaths."

It would be useful to know what Kevin said to his doctors at Stamford Hospital. Whatever transpired there his parents were concerned enough for his welfare to transfer him to the Yale Psychiatric Institute, a small private hospital affiliated with Yale University, where he remained from November 26 through December 3, 1997.

Conduct disorder and antisocial personality traits are diagnoses that overlap one another to some degree, the primary difference being that conduct disorder is more commonly applied to juveniles. In the *DSM-V* (*Diagnostic and Statistical Manual*), the manual that mental health clinicians use when assigning official diagnoses, conduct disorder behaviors are broken into four main categories: (a) aggressive conduct that causes or threatens physical harm to other people or animals, (b) nonaggressive conduct that causes property loss or damage, (c) deceitfulness or theft, and (d) serious violations of rules. Fundamentally conduct disorder consists of a repetitive and persistent pattern of behaviors in which the basic rights of others or major age-appropriate norms or rules of society are violated.

Because neither Kevin nor anyone in his family had been willing to talk to me at this point, I didn't know if he was engaged in theft or the destruction of property, but I did know that, on at least one occasion, he was cruel to an animal, and that he violently attacked two human beings, one of whom he stabbed ten to twelve times after she was dead.

One thing is for certain: Kevin Bergin was a young man with a serious substance abuse problem, one that wasn't just limited to one or even two substances. When interviewed by the forensic unit of the William S. Hall Psychiatric Institute for the purpose of determining whether he was competent to stand trial, Bergin candidly informed clinicians that, in addition to the fifth of liquor that he ordinarily consumed on a daily basis, he smoked approximately $50 worth of marijuana a week, and by the age of sixteen was using about a gram of cocaine per day. Although he did not mention crack by name, he did say he "would wake up and smoke it first thing in the morning," suggesting that he ingested the drug in that form. He confessed to feeling addicted.

The quantities and combinations of drugs mentioned above already sound toxic, but add to them the variety of inhalants Bergin was abusing, and you have a mix that has, in many cases, proven lethal. In other words it is a wonder he did not kill himself before he had the chance to kill someone else.

From aerosol air fresheners to bug sprays to spray paint to gasoline, Kevin "huffed" them all, even to the point of blacking out. An old friend of mine who huffed gas in high school describes the high as being "kind of foggy, but also very intense, almost psychotic—much more potent that what you get from smoking weed or having a few drinks." He said it made him feel both carefree and powerful. The medical literature shows that the short-term psychological effects of huffing gas include emotional volatility, paranoid delusions, passive-aggressive attitude, memory loss, impaired judgment and coordination, severe mood swings, and both auditory and visual hallucinations. Long-term effects are more severe: they include ongoing hallucinations, psychosis, lowered intelligence, and antisocial personality disorder.

Although Bergin did not admit to huffing gas, or any solvent, in the hours before Nell's murder, by the time he was arrested and interviewed by Sergeant Woodward, it appears that some of these "effects," such as blacking out for periods of time, may have begun to occur spontaneously. When Woodward finally told Bergin that both John Ridgway and Sarah Nickel had said that *he* killed Nell by hitting her with the baseball bat, Bergin said, "I didn't go crazy, but if I did go crazy . . . I must have lost it, I must have lost it at one point, because I blacked out and I don't remember half the shit that happened." Certainly, emotional volatility and impaired judgment were evident in the violent attacks on both his father and on Nell Davis.

Without access to the medical history of Kevin Bergin's biological family, it would be difficult to determine whether the paranoid delusions he developed involving his supposed surveillance by the government may have manifested without drug abuse, and even having a family history of schizophrenia doesn't mean that a person is guaranteed to develop the disorder; however, the abuse of all these different kinds of psychoactive drugs, even without a genetic predisposition, put him at high risk and, at some point during his adolescent development, undoubtedly helped push him over the edge into severe mental illness.

The final drug in Kevin Bergin's arsenal of self-destruction was Dramamine, the over-the-counter motion sickness drug, which he would take in massive doses, up to twenty-four tablets (1200 milligrams, twelve times the recommended adult dose) at a time, according to court records. On the streets Dramamine, or dimenhydrinate, is known for its ability to induce euphoria, as well as pleasant visual and tactile hallucinations. It is often referred to as "poor man's heroin," and a user whose case made it into the *American Journal of Psychiatry* referred to it as a "cheaper alternative to cocaine." Dramamine also has a mild tranquilizing affect.

Taken as a whole, the pharmacopoeia of Kevin Bergin appeared to be one that would create a variety of different moods and psychological states, ranging from being hyperalert (cocaine) to mildly intoxicated (marijuana) to entirely "fucked up" (inhalants). One only has to cruise the Internet to see that many people have experimented with one or more of these drugs, even with huffing gas, and not gone on to become full scale drug addicts or criminals, or society dropouts. So it certainly isn't fair to put all the blame for what happened on drugs, but they surely played a part. Kevin Bergin perhaps had some underlying mental illness that the drugs made worse. All of them, alcohol, cocaine, marijuana, inhalants, and dimenhydrinate, have the effect of lowering the user's inhibitions, making it easier to say or do things he or she wouldn't without the drug. All three of the young people charged with Nell Davis's murder denied being high on the day that she was killed, but all of them had a history of drug abuse, and of increasingly uninhibited behavior, the kind of behavior that led John Ridgway to cut a schoolmate with a knife for refusing to share answers, the kind of behavior that led Sarah Nickel to have sex with just about any man who wanted her, the kind of behavior that led Kevin Bergin to lure a Canadian goose into a gazebo at a place called Tilly's Pond, where a friend of his stabbed it until it died. Following this incident, Bergin was charged with "Conspiracy to Kill a Goose." One of his friends who was present when the incident occurred described to me how the goose lurched away after the attack, stumbling back to the water where it flipped upside down and spun around in circles until it died. Most of the kids thought it was hilarious, but someone in the group "told," which is how Kevin got caught.

The psychiatrists who examined Kevin for the State of South Carolina came up with a new diagnosis to add to the litany of those he had accumulated from his previous stays at various inpatient units in the state of Connecticut: "Schizophrenia, Paranoid Type." In their narrative these doctors noted that Bergin "expresses a complicated delusional system related to the government," adding, "He feels the government is out to control all of its citizens through the use of a supercomputer." They also made a note of his "abnormally intense affect," that is, facial expression, something that comes across with considerable force in the videotape of his police interview, and even in his photographs, including the one on the South Carolina Department of Corrections inmate identification website. The only other new findings are not mentioned in their diagnosis but are included in a paragraph headed, "Results of Psychological Evaluation," where Bergin is described as showing "significant indication of borderline and antisocial personality traits." This section concludes with the statement, "Overall, Mr. Bergin did not evidence significant cognitive deficits which would affect his ability to follow and participate in legal proceedings."

Bergin's "Mental Status Exam," which took place on May 19, 2000, yields further information about his perception of himself in relation to the world, information that would be echoed in court, when he would take the stand to testify at Sarah Nickel's trial. His mood he described as "sometimes up and sometimes down," adding, "I go through the day trying to figure out the world, but it's like I don't exist—I can't find the central point of my consciousness." The psychiatric team's primary objective, however, was to determine Bergin's competency to stand trial. Finding him able to read Miranda and restate it in his own words, they go on to note the many different occasions upon which, during his evaluation, Kevin exhibited behaviors demonstrating that he understood the legal procedures he was undergoing, that he was aware of the serious nature of the charges, and that he knew the name of his attorney and understood his attorney's role. He furthermore demonstrated his understanding of the role of the solicitor, the judge, and the jury, and an awareness of the pleas available to him, as well as the concepts involved in plea bargaining, and the desired outcome of his case. For all these reasons, the team determined, Kevin Bergin was competent to stand trial. Although there was evidence of mental illness predating the murder, they could "find no evidence that his mental illness would have prevented him from distinguishing legal or moral right from legal or moral wrong." Curiously they go on to say that he initially stated he had "committed a murder because he needed to release sin into the world and that spirits were commanding him to commit a killing and make it look like a murder. The purpose was to release sin into the world because without evil there can be no good." He had also initially reported that he "was hearing spirits commanding him to do this," and added, in a stilted manner, that "although he knew the legal wrongfulness of what he had done, he did not believe it was morally wrong because of these delusions."

During a later interview, however, Bergin admitted that these delusions had been fabricated in an effort to secure an insanity defense. Fabricated or not, that he would consider using these ideas to rationalize his behavior brought me back to his preoccupation with "satanic and other cult worship" as it is termed in the psychiatric evaluation, and to what Brent Kiker had said about a book called "something like *The High Art of Necromancy*." This book, according to Kiker, had been found along with other ritual objects such as "certain stones" and "goat's milk," which were to be used in a ceremony involving a dead body. Just from the small acquaintance that I had with Satanism and Wicca, I knew that the idea of there being a necessary balance between light and dark energies (embodying the sense of other opposites such as masculine/feminine, active/passive, solar/lunar, fire/water, and yes, even life/death) was fundamental, so I didn't want to jump to conclusions, at least not without reading the book, and comparing its instructions and description of materials to evidence found at the crime scene. So I began to search for the book by title and soon realized that Kiker's "something like" was probably an indication that he didn't remember exactly what the title was. I looked for anything with variations of the words "necromancy" and "ritual" in the title, and my search eventually yielded a small book of some fifty pages, *The Necromantic Ritual Book* by Leilah Wendell, printed by Wendell's own Westgate Press and limited to five hundred copies. That I had found the right book was later confirmed by the trial transcript, where the correct title was on record.

For the time being, everything I had learned about Kevin Bergin suggested to me that his involvement in the murder of Nell Davis was precipitated by mental illness and drug abuse. One big question, however, remained unanswered: Why had he left his home in New Canaan, Connecticut, to travel all the way down to Hilton Head, South Carolina, in order to "run away" with John Ridgway and Sarah Nickel, a girl he had never met, when, according to statements made to police, they were simply going to turn around and head back north, to Detroit? If his goal was to be with John, his best friend from their days together in Darien, why not just take a train or bus and meet up with him after he and Sarah got to Detroit and save himself the expense of the additional travel to South Carolina? There had to be a reason for Kevin to come to Hilton Head, and certainly Brent Kiker's theory was worth pursuing. Maybe Kevin Bergin's purpose was to perform a ritual, a particular type of ritual that his friend John Ridgway would help him set up, a ritual that, if performed properly, would enable him to experience oneness with the Angel of Death.

10

The Solicitor's
Worthless Check Unit

Randolph Murdaugh, known to friends and enemies alike as "Randy," is the solicitor who prosecuted the case against Sarah Nickel. He agreed to meet with me at his office in Hampton, South Carolina, which lies along Highway 278 on the way to Columbia, where I would be seeing Sarah the next day. Hampton, population 2,837, bills itself as a "hunter's paradise" where people "yearning to escape from the hustle and bustle of the big city" can hunt for deer, turkey, hog, and quail. Visitors uninterested in shooting the wildlife are invited to engage in the more peaceful activity of viewing it at Lake Warren State Park, or they may wish to spend a day visiting the Hampton County Museum, or the Hampton Museum and Visitor's Center, which boasts a display of military artifacts. The town was named after Confederate Civil War hero Wade Hampton, who, following the war, went on to serve two terms as the governor of South Carolina and, after that, served as a U.S. senator until 1891.

Murdaugh was, at the time of this writing, the solicitor for the Fourteenth Circuit, the only one in the state that has five counties: Allendale, Hampton, Jasper, Beaufort, and Colleton. Accordingly Murdaugh was a busy man, and I certainly appreciated his taking time out of his packed schedule to see me. Although the directions he gave me to his office in Hampton were reasonably good, it still took me a while to find the place, mostly because it didn't look like a solicitor's office, at least not what I expected one to look like. In contrast to other government buildings I had visited over the course of the past several weeks, this one, lodged in what appeared at first glance to be an abandoned storefront, had no official-looking sign out front. I peered into the shade cast by a swooping navy awning. The only clue that I had reached my destination was a small, dirty sign in the window saying, "Solicitor's Worthless Check Unit." I stepped inside where a disheveled-looking man sat at a makeshift desk. I had a distinct feeling that this person was not an employee but stated my business nevertheless and was directed up a set of creaky wooden stairs with peeling vinyl treads. Entering a narrow hallway, I proceeded to a warren-like office area crammed with room dividers.

Randolph Murdaugh, who is every bit as tall as his photographs suggest, greeted me with a large handshake and led me through the maze of room dividers to his office, simultaneously offering me a cup of coffee. While he was gone to get the coffee I studied my surroundings, struck by their stark contrast to the relatively lush furnishings I am accustomed to finding in legal offices. Here, although the room was pleasantly spacious in contrast to the cubicles outside his door, its plastered walls were dingy and garlanded with brown water stains. A tightly woven carpet of faded brownish-pink, like dead rose petals, covered the floor. Wooden wainscoting and a large picture window behind Murdaugh's desk suggested that the building had seen better days. Perhaps, I decided, noticing the framed pictures stacked by the door, he was just moving into this place and the remodeling hadn't been finished.

Or maybe he was moving out.

Reentering the room and taking a seat behind his desk, clasping his hands on its surface, Murdaugh appeared bemused and self-possessed, 100 percent the country gentleman lawyer, dressed down for a day at the Worthless Check Unit. The fabric of his shirt was brown-and-white plaid—not a small, delicate pattern such as you might see on some of the more casual dress shirts with designer labels, but the broad hearty perpendicular stripes that most often appear on flannel. His wide desk was quite messy with folders and papers. More folders were stacked on the floor, in precariously high towers, threatening to spill their contents.

I began by asking him questions about what, exactly, a circuit court is. I know I must have learned this somewhere down the line of my education, probably in ninth-grade civics with Mr. "Ignorance of the law is no excuse" Jones, but I couldn't remember it just then, and the question seemed like a good icebreaker.

Murdaugh cleared his throat, leaned back, and started to fill this gap in my knowledge. "With the criminal courts, there are two levels. The first is the summary or magistrate's court, which tries every case that is punishable by thirty days or up to a $500 fine. Everything else goes to a circuit court."

"But the circuit court isn't just for criminal cases, is it?" I asked, feeling slightly stupid, but then I've only been to court twice, and that was more than twenty years ago.

"Oh no. In addition to its general trial jurisdiction, the Circuit Court has some appellate jurisdiction, but I don't think that's what you're here to find out about."

"No," I said, glad that he had resisted the opening I gave him to go off on a lengthy tangent.

To give me some sense of his background and experience, I asked him how long he'd been in the solicitor's office, which I understood is an elected position.

"Since 1987," he said proudly, "which makes it seventeen years. I'm the third solicitor in my family as well. My father held this office from 1940 to 1986, and his father from 1930 to 1940."

"So it's kind of a dynasty," I said, unsurprised because, after all, I grew up in a Georgia town where members of the same family had sat on the judge's bench for generations.

"You could say that," he said, smiling and taking a drink of his coffee. I noted that he drank from a Styrofoam cup just like mine. More evidence that he was moving? Maybe just on the move, too busy to be bothered with washing up.

"I understand you have five counties in your circuit. What's your caseload like?"

The smile vanished; his expressive eyebrows shot downward in a deep frown. "Now that's where all the trouble starts. Yes, it's the largest circuit, plus, this circuit has had the second-highest growth in the state for the past five years. Beaufort has about 50 percent of the population, and the caseload mirrors the population. And while I'm talking percentages, let me say that—and this is just a guess, but it's probably pretty close to the truth—65 to 70 percent of my case load is attributable to crack cocaine. I mean people buying, selling, stealing, and committing other crimes to get their hands on it or on the money to buy it."

His mention of crack sparked my interest because there was speculation in the community that two of the three teens involved in Nell Davis's murder, John Ridgway and Kevin Bergin, were strung out on crack when the crime was committed. But that is not something that made it into the trial, so I asked if he thought the teens were high. He answered in the affirmative but stated that no evidence was collected to that effect.

Wanting to get down to more particulars, I said, "Can I ask you some questions about the case now?" He nodded. "What can you tell me about it that I won't find in the records?"

He gave me a long, shrewd, assessing gaze before finally saying, "What you won't find anything about in the record is that young lady's intelligence."

"You mean Sarah?"

"Yes."

Actually there is plenty in the record about her intelligence, beginning with Sheriff Tanner's assertion, reported in the local papers, that she was so smart she figured out how to cover her butt by framing her accomplices for doing her dirty work. I decided to ask a less comfortable question. "What affect do you think Mike Davis's position in the community had on the outcome of the trial?"

"None at all," he answered quickly. Now his eyebrows shot up, nearly to his hairline, or where his hairline would be if it weren't receding.

"Was the trial postponed in order to get Judge Brown?"

Had it been possible, the eyebrows would have gone up another inch. I could tell they were straining to do so. This time he gave me one syllable. "No."

I pondered that single syllable, wondering why he didn't offer any other explanation for the delay, such as the need to prepare the case, to make sure they had all the evidence and witnesses ready to go, to make sure all the rules had been followed pertaining to mutual discovery. He, after all, had requested that the trial be postponed each time it was put on the calendar. Perhaps I should have asked some of these things, but realizing I was getting nowhere fast, I backed off, decided to go with my "heartfelt" question, the one fact about the trial's outcome that disturbs me more than any other: what will happen to Kevin Bergin after he gets out of prison. So I told him, "My biggest worry is what will happen when Kevin Bergin is released after thirty years."

Now he simply looks stunned. I've hit a nerve, a sore spot, it seems, and it's too soon to assess the damage. I wonder if he will suddenly and apologetically remember an appointment. I tried to soften the blow by continuing to talk, giving him a moment to think. "I've read his psychiatric report," I said softly. "It concludes that he's suffering from paranoid schizophrenia. He has delusions, and a history of violent assault prior to the incident with Nell Davis. What I'm wondering is this: is there any kind of safety net for a person like Bergin? Will he be connected with someone in social services or some kind of halfway house, some facility that will help him get job training and a job, make sure he has a place to live and that he continues taking his medication?"

"No, no safety net." Murdaugh shook his head, as if regretting this state of affairs. "If he's released on parole, a letter will go out to the chief law enforcement officer in the community where he'll be living. He'll have to check in with his parole officer. There'll be a record of where he lives, works, et cetera."

I reminded Randy Murdaugh that Kevin Bergin was serving what is called a "straight sentence." There is no parole, no chance of getting out early, on a straight sentence.

"Ok," he said, "then if he serves the full sentence, no, there isn't even that. Only notification of release."

"Well, doesn't it worry you that he'll be back on the streets, with no assistance, readjusting to the community?"

Murdaugh scratched his head, looking down at his messy desk. When he looked up, the expression in his eyes was completely different from anything I have seen there before. It reminded me of desperation, but not quite. I gave up searching for a label and simply listened.

"People like that, like Kevin Bergin, go in for thirty years, they don't come out."

I understood what he was implying, and it was my turn to be stunned. But the implication wasn't enough; I had to ask him precisely what he meant.

He answered, "He'll get beat up so much he'll be disabled, or he'll be murdered."

I wasn't sure what to say to this, so I sat there staring, wondering if he'd continue. He did keep talking, but the subject had changed. Or maybe he was just trying to provide a context for what he had said.

"Crack has changed our entire culture. When you wake up Monday morning, see the things I see, you can't help becoming a cynic. We had another girl; Sarah was her name, too. Tortured a paraplegic man. Tried to kill him for two days. Injected him with air, put him in the trunk of a car with the motor running for forty-five minutes, shut him up in a refrigerator, stoned him, and stabbed him. Then there was two boys came down from Pennsylvania, kidnapped a retarded girl, had sex with her every way known to God and man, then killed her. A Hardeeville man cut off his wife's head and put it in the bed with her, stuck it under her arm."

On and on went the catalogue of horrors.

I'm sure Murdaugh didn't intend it this way, but the stories he told me were somehow a comfort, reassuring me that, although Nell died a horrible death, it certainly could have been worse. Now, whenever I find myself paralyzed by imagining what her final moments must have been like, I dilute the terror by thinking of that poor paraplegic, or the retarded girl, or the beheaded wife, wondering if the wife was conscious when her husband started sawing. I can do this without a great deal of discomfort, for the same reason that other people can watch the nightly news without having nightmares. I don't know the wife who lost her head, or her benighted husband. I've never seen either of them. They are just characters in a story, and it might as well be fiction. But Nell, dead, cremated, and buried more than five years before I sat in Randolph Murdaugh's office, lives in me still, has somehow, through her horrific death, become as much a part of my conscious existence as she was thirty years ago.

Since Murdaugh seemed to prefer discussing other cases over the one I had come to see him about, I asked him if he remembered the case Lieutenant Bukoffsky told me about in which a nineteen-year-old boy killed his adoptive mother, a college professor living in Beaufort. This supposedly happened back in 1989, during Murdaugh's tenure as solicitor, so I figured he might have some memory of the case, even though, according to Bukoffsky, the case was pleaded out of court and the kid walked away with probation.

"No," he answered, looking slightly puzzled. Either he didn't remember, or he's good at feigning forgetfulness. Without knowing him better, it's hard to say which.

■ ■ ■

Later, when I went over the notes from my interview with Randy Murdaugh, I became aware of how successfully he avoided giving me information about the case. What is most significant, he offered no explanation for the numerous requests, issued by his office, for a continuance (that is, delay) each time a date was set for Sarah's trial. When I tried to reach him by phone to get some more answers, he was always, somehow, away from his desk or seeing a client, or otherwise unable to take my calls, which he also never returned.

His reaction to my questions about Kevin Bergin spoke more eloquently, however, than I had at first realized.

"People like that, like Kevin Bergin, go in for thirty years, they don't come out."

"He'll get beat up so much he'll be disabled, or he'll be murdered."

Prompted by these remarks, I launched a small, informal investigation of prison conditions simply by registering with Prisontalk.com, a message board used by friends and family members of incarcerated individuals. A registered user can post messages that can be accessed by all other registered users. Mostly people come on asking for help. A lot of them know or are related to someone who's just been incarcerated, and they're frightened and upset and want to know what the prison is like and what they can expect when they visit. Sometimes there's a crisis—a lockdown because of violence or contraband—and people get online to try to find out what's going on, because they can't get any information from prison officials. Sometimes they want advice for dealing with the prison system, or the legal system, and sometimes they just need to feel that they aren't alone. To my query regarding conditions at South Carolina men's prisons, every reply I received was negative, which is not surprising. Prison is not a country club or luxury resort. People go there because they have been convicted of a crime and now have to pay for that crime by serving time, by giving up the privilege of living a comfortable, free life. But surely they are entitled to inhabit a safe, clean, healthy environment.

Apparently not.

Many of the people who corresponded with me about the experiences of their loved ones in the South Carolina Department of Corrections' prisons were unwilling to go on record. They are afraid that doing so will have negative repercussions, affecting the way that their friends or family members are treated. One woman, however, decided that it was more important to tell me what she had been hearing from her family members and friends. Her name is Sherrie Allen.

Sherrie's cousin Frank was at Broad River when we began corresponding, the same facility as John Ridgway. Unlike John, Frank had HIV. When I first made contact with Sherrie back in 2006, Frank had been taken off the medication that kept the virus in check because he was not "in compliance" with his doctor's orders. "This is true," she wrote, "my cousin has not been in compliance. However, there is a reason. He must go to the 'pill line' 2 times a day for medication. The morning dose is given out at 4:30 A.M. SCDC [South Carolina Department of Corrections] turns their sprinklers on even in the dead of winter, water runs down the sidewalk and it creates a stream inmates must walk through. My cousin cannot wear regular shoes and even though he's had an order for new orthopedic shoes for almost 2 years, he is still wearing shoes with holes in the soles. Every day he'd drudge through the stream, get his medicine and drudge back to his dorm with his feet soak and wet. He developed pneumonia—something no one with HIV wants—and he couldn't get rid of it. My cousin stopped going for the morning meds because the wet feet were causing him to get sick. SCDC took his medicine away because he was found to be out of compliance with taking the meds 2 times a day." She goes on to say that they are currently reviewing his case, but that he has gone 3 months without any HIV medication. His tests show the HIV "running rampant" in his body, and she fears that "he will die waiting for the medicine to be given back to him." After being taken off the medicine completely, his physical condition deteriorated rapidly: "His skin is peeling off his fingers. His tongue is raw and he has an open sore—a hole—which we are told is the HIV getting worse and a condition that shows up in patients not on medications."

Sherrie and her family also fought to get better quality food for inmates with HIV. From her I first learned that every meat served to inmates is "processed," which basically means that the meat consists of animal parts, including snouts, tails, livers, brains, lips, ears, and so on, as well as the parts we traditionally think of as meat such as steaks, cutlets, chops, breasts, thighs, and such, all ground together and shaped into a loaf, patty, or meatball, or crumbled into a stew or spaghetti. As for vegetables, nearly everything comes out of a can—very large, institutional-size cans of course. When there is "fresh produce," it is rarely fresh; the lettuce is wilted or dried out; the carrots have black spots that have to be cut off. Sherrie told me she had contacted PALS, a local advocate group for people with HIV. The result? "Point blank they told me that they constantly try to get SCDC to let them help the HIV inmates but SCDC says they are doing everything for the inmates that they need. SCDC refuses to even let PALS send reading materials to the inmates."

Kevin Bergin, as far as I know, doesn't have HIV. He was diagnosed with a psychiatric illness, schizophrenia, which, if the diagnosis is correct, will require lifelong medication. And if he doesn't take that medication regularly, it's possible that he could become violent. After his evaluation by a forensic team of psychiatrists for the State of South Carolina, he had been placed on the antipsychotic Zyprexa, which alleviated his symptoms, greatly reducing his feelings of paranoia. Since Zyprexa is available in its generic form olanzapine, it is possible that he may have been able to continue taking this drug that seemed to be working for him initially.

If Bergin should become the victim of a violent attack, if his experience is anything like those reported by Ms. Allen, his survival will depend on the time of the attack and the severity of his wounds. In an e-mail dated June 9, 2006, Ms. Allen reported being contacted by Troy Roach, a man from her neighborhood serving a ten-year sentence for drug trafficking. Mr. Roach was at this time confined at Ridgeland Correctional Institute, a level 2, or medium-security, facility. The first time Roach called, he told Allen he had been waiting "at that time over 2 hours—for medical treatment. He had been stabbed in the proximity of his kidney. He was in extreme pain and was bleeding. He told me that he had been told he might have to wait for the day staff to come in at 7 A.M.—it was 11 P.M. when he called." Despite the lateness of the hour, Sherrie called a friend of hers, a nurse, who told her it was possible he was bleeding internally, or if a kidney or his spleen had been nicked, that toxins could be leaking into his body with potentially lethal results.

Mr. Roach and Sherrie's cousin Frank both fortunately survived their ordeals, but another inmate was not so lucky. I learned of this man's fate from a former CO (corrections officer), who asked not to be named, since he still uses his supervisor at SCDC as a job reference. This man says he left "in part because of inhumane medical treatment" of inmates. On one occasion, when he complained about the medical treatment of an inmate, he was threatened with being charged with "fraternizing with an inmate." After that experience he "personally watched an inmate die waiting for medical attention. The inmate had a heart attack, medical staff was called, 2 hours later while still waiting for medical the inmate had another attack and died." This man insists he is "*not* a hero of inmates" and asserts that he understands the institutional reasons for doing things in ways that may seem harsh to an outsider. But he also believes that just because someone is sent to prison doesn't mean they should be denied proper or prompt medical treatment. "A judge sentenced them to years for punishment, not death, disfigurement or a life of pain that could have been avoided with medical attention," he concluded.

In 2005 I wrote to the SCDC asking for statistical information on inmate assaults and was told that the information was being processed. A couple of years later, it was available, for the years 2004–7, under the "Research" link on their homepage, www.doc.sc.gov. A graph, which is based on Management Information Notes, showed the number of cases that resulted in assault charges, broken down into three groups: inmate on inmate, inmate on employee, and inmate on other. By far the largest number of cases, each year, involved attacks of inmates on employees; furthermore, for each year in the five-year span, the assaults numbered in the hundreds, averaging 862 per year, with a high of 987 in 2003 and a low of 765 in 2005. What should also be taken into account, of course, are fluctuations in numbers of prisoners. The number of incarcerated individuals increased by 310 between 2003 and 2007, though the trend was not consistently positive; for two of those years, 2005 and 2006, the numbers actually declined. The average daily number of inmates incarcerated in South Carolina prisons in 2007, when the number of assaults was 798, was 23,375, which means that approximately 3.4 percent were involved in a violent attack of some kind, unless some of those were repeat offenders. More recently the page has been updated with a new set of statistics, for the period 2006–10. The average number of assaults has gone up slightly, to 864 per year, though the high, 977, is slightly lower than before.

What seems most significant is that the numbers are being recorded, and posted, and that, in accordance with the Freedom of Information Act, any citizen now has the right to request further information about the conditions under which prisoners live. There is no guarantee that they will get answers, or that if they do, those answers will be entirely factual, but there does seem to be an increasing effort at accountability. Whether or not that will impact Kevin Bergin's ability to survive prison is anyone's guess. My own feeling is that when Randy Murdaugh responded to my concern about a person like Kevin Bergin being out on the street again without anyone or anything to prevent him from falling back into a world of drug abuse and violence, he was simply trying to assuage his own conscience. I am sure he assumed that I, like most people who loved Nell, would have wanted Kevin Bergin to be put to death, but that isn't what I want. I deplore violence of any kind, and especially institutionalized violence like the death penalty. So no, although I believe that what Kevin Bergin did was horrible as well as criminal, and that he certainly deserves to be punished (and, I hope, rehabilitated), I do not hope that he will, like his victim, be murdered.

■ ■ ■

On a more positive note, in the years that have passed since I first began observing conditions in South Carolina prisons, some very positive changes have begun to take place. Warden John Pate of Allendale Correctional Institution, where John was transferred in June 2011, has instituted a Character-Based Housing Unit program in which John has been able to participate. As part of this he has been able to create Art 4 Hope, a program in which inmates create various kinds of art, such as paintings, stuffed animals, quilts, and wooden toys, which are then donated to terminally ill children who are in treatment at the Medical University of South Carolina. He was also involved with a cat rescue program, Meow Mates, and the prison has one for dogs as well, Mutt Mates. Perry Correctional Institution, also a part of the SCDC system, has a more developed character-based program, which, on their website, provides a description of the program and testimony from inmate participants. In an overview of the program, the website states, that "the CBU Rehabilitation Program emphasizes the development of pro-social values, attitudes, thinking, and behavior above everything else," noting that it is available not only for inmates who are nearing their release date, but for all inmates who indicate a readiness, in one way or another, to make positive changes in their behavior. The program arose in part out of the recognition that inmates need to be trained in "emotional literacy—pro-social skills and personal development in their values, attitudes, thinking, and behavior—to navigate and cope with life in the free world." It is to be hoped that other SCDC prisons will follow the example of these pioneering programs that offer great support for the rehabilitation that is essential for inmates to succeed postrelease.

11

Meeting Sarah

The Camille Griffin Graham Correctional Institution sits on the highest elevation of an area called "the farm," on the western edge of Columbia, the state capitol of South Carolina. "The farm" is shorthand for the parcel of land where the state chose to build a prison complex, although complex is perhaps the wrong word, for the individual institutions located here are spread out, almost dwarfed by the sprawling acres of farmland by which they are surrounded. At the rather nondescript entrance to the compound, an entrance easily missed if you haven't been there before, stands a guard-house with stop signs on both the exit and entrance sides. The first time I visited Sarah, the building appeared to be deserted, so I drove on through, slowly, listening for sirens or some other indication that I had violated pro-tocol. Winding my slow way up the hill, I had to stop and ask a guard—one who had pulled over in his truck—for directions. There were, unsurpris-ingly, few signs. I wondered if this was a security precaution.

CGGCI is one of South Carolina's two level 3 (maximum-security) women's prisons. The notorious Susan Smith, who drowned her children and then claimed they had been kidnapped, resided here until she got caught having sex with a guard and was transferred to Leath, the other level 3 prison for women, located in Greenwood, South Carolina.

The main building at CGGCI is one story of faded red brick with a mansard roof. Seen from the parking lot, the roof appears to have a pale blue metallic finish. A gated yard protects the front door. In the control room to its left sits a guard who buzzes visitors into the yard. On the day of my visit, I found myself in the yard with other visitors who stood huddled in groups, waiting. Eventually the door buzzed, and one set of visitors went inside. I moved forward and put my hand on the door when a tall black man with loose shiny curls gently touched my arm. "Is this your first time?" he asked. I told him yes.

"They only let in one group at the time."

"Oh," I responded, embarrassed, feeling like I'd been caught trying to cut in line. "I'm sorry. I didn't know."

"That's all right," he said in a thick sea-island burr. "They don' tell you nothing before you come, even if you asks."

I concurred, because I did ask. I was just told to leave everything in my vehicle except my driver's license, car keys, and fifteen dollars in change for the vending machines in the visitor's area. What they meant, I would later find out, was fifteen dollars in one-dollar bills because there wasn't a machine that could change a five. But the first time I visited I embarrassed myself by carrying in two brimming handfuls of coins, all of which I had to dump in a small plastic bowl, along with my keys, so I could walk through the metal detector. The detector hooted at me so I had to remove my shoes which, unbeknownst to me, had metal shanks. The second time I passed. In the meantime the guard sitting at the desk by the door had checked my credentials against the information in her computer and filled out my visitor's pass. She stamped my hand with ultraviolet ink and gave me the pass. The pass had a number scrawled on it, indicating the table I was to sit at when I entered the visitation room. Next she buzzed me through another large green metal door into a hallway, where I faced a wall-to-wall, floor-to-ceiling chain-link fence, and another gate. I obediently looked toward the camera mounted near the ceiling and waited for the green light to go on, indicating that the gate was open. This one didn't buzz, so I had to watch for that light, which would stay on for just a few seconds.

Finally, I was in the visitation room, waiting for Sarah. The floor of the room was paved in asphalt tile, white with gray wisps like tiny cirrus clouds in an overcast sky. The walls were cinderblock, also white, and the doors and windows were framed with metal trim painted an assertive forest green, which could have been taken right out of a box of Crayola crayons. The tables were wood-grained Formica, about three feet square, with four tube-metal chairs upholstered in a vinyl that matched perfectly the forest green trim. Each table had a four-by-six-inch index card displaying a number taped to the top. I found table 4 and sat down to wait for Sarah, looking around at the other visitors: husbands, mothers, grandmothers, children, and friends. One young black woman, her hair in cornrows, had six at once. You could tell the inmates apart from the visitors by their uniforms: beige cotton button-up shirts and beige pants with a stripe down the side. Across the back of their shirts and down the side of the stripes on their pants they were identified as inmates of SCDC. Identification badges clipped to their shirt collars showed names, a photo, and their SCDC identification number.

After a few minutes the green metal door to the room opened, and there she was, the image of her mother. Sarah opened her arms, and I embraced her without thinking. The feel of her body was warm, light-boned, birdlike, just like Nell's.

I led her to the table and started to sit down, but she told me no—I would have to sit nearer the door, she at the far end facing the security camera.

At first I felt somewhat stunned, at a loss for words, even though we had developed the beginnings of a relationship through our letters and phone calls. Because I had such a limited time for the visit, every word I might say suddenly assumed a monstrous importance. I had to calm down, focus on Sarah rather than myself, and the task I had set myself, of getting to know her better. So I asked her to tell me about her life here in prison.

"We wake up at 5 A.M. for 'count' at 5:30, then go to breakfast," she responded, in a surprisingly low, throaty voice with a heavy southern accent. It was different, heavier or fuller than her voice over the phone. "After breakfast we go to work. I'm doing landscaping now. There's a second count, then lunch at 10:30, count at 12:30, then more work, until 3 P.M., when we come in for count and have dinner from 4 to 5. After everybody has eaten, we can go out in the yard and walk around for a while. Lights out is at 10:30, but we can stay up until 11:00, till twelve on weekends, but we still have to wake up at five no matter what."

I asked if she had access to TV or radio. She told me she had a portable radio, which was a lifesaver because, aside from reading, it was really the only thing that could make her forget, for a few minutes, where she is, though the noise usually keeps her from forgetting, no matter what. At the time of our first interview, she was living on an "open" building with forty-eight cubicles that have no doors, and walls that don't reach the ceiling. Her "cube" was five feet by nine feet. Inmates are supposed to stay in their own space after lights out, but the open doors invite an activity known as "creeping."

"Only inmates who've been here for a long time have their own TVs because some male prisoners were using TVs to smuggle in drugs," she informed me, adding that although there is a television in the common room, it's so noisy in there you can't hear anything. They don't get to watch movies, but there is a gym. And no, she responded, when I asked about arts and crafts, there weren't any classes, though prisoners could use their money to order handsewing kits like cross-stitch. They could crochet, with plastic crochet hooks, but weren't allowed to knit because knitting needles could be used as weapons. For the same reason, they weren't allowed to have silverware, or even plastic knives and forks, which could also, when modified, be made into weapons. What they did have is "sporks," those hybrid utensils popularized by the Kentucky Fried Chicken food chain, except the ones provided at the prison were school-bus orange and made of industrial strength plastic. "We call 'em our shovels," Sarah told me, and I began to see a glimmer of the tough-girl persona she has cultivated since childhood, a persona that has served her well during her stay in prison. "Only a few people, like me, have mouths big enough to get the whole thing inside." She smiled but raised her hand to cover her mouth. The tough girl was embarrassed by the width of her grin.

The meat served by the cafeteria was either cut into bite-size chunks, or tender (that is, overcooked or processed) enough to cut with a spork. To make sure no funny business happened with the sporks, inmates were given one and required to wash it and bring it with them to all meals. If they broke or lost it, they would have to buy a new one for twenty-five cents. This may not sound like much, but when you don't have any income—as is the case for the women incarcerated in Camille Griffin Graham—and depend on the kindness of family members for the money in your account, losing a spork can mean going without some other "luxury," like tampons, or a bag of Doritos to help you bridge the long calorie-free gap between dinner at 4 P.M. and breakfast the next morning at six.

Toilet paper, lacking the durability of a plastic spork, was distributed weekly. Inmates received one roll of toilet paper every Thursday, and heaven help them if they ran out before the next distribution. When I asked, incredulously, "What do you do if something happens . . . ? Do inmates ever steal toilet paper from each other?"

"People are pretty good about not stealing that. And if you do run out, there's always Kleenex," Sarah said but then added, "as long as you can afford to buy it from the canteen."

Sarah was wearing artfully applied makeup, with mascara and pale-blue eye shadow. I asked her how the inmates get access to cosmetics, and she told me that they are also available at the prison canteen, where a bottle of L'Oreal make-up costs $12. She thinks this is outrageously expensive, so I tried to remember the last bottle of makeup I bought. I wanted to tell her I don't think it's overpriced compared to a department store, but I didn't have the heart. I suddenly realized how much the world has changed, is continuing to change, since she's been locked up. She must know this at some level, but I'm sure it will be quite a shock when she reenters the other world, the one outside the boundaries of "the farm."

When Sarah talked I couldn't help staring. Although she looks a lot like Nell, her mannerisms are *exactly* like Nell's, especially the way she fiddles with her hair while she's talking, combing her fingers through it, pulling it back from her face, flipping it over her shoulder. Her eyes are an intense dusky blue, her mouth a Cupid's bow—if Cupid had used a longbow.

I asked her if she wanted anything from the vending machines, telling her I'd brought money and dumping a handful of change on the table where it clattered and rolled. "Yes!" she answered, speaking more emphatically than she had, thus far, about anything. Because prisoners aren't allowed in the vending machine area, which is outside the visitation room and on the other side of the gate with the green light, I took her order (a cheeseburger, chips, and a Dr. Pepper) and navigated my way through the process and back again. The cheeseburger looked awful, like a typical vending-machine cheeseburger, but at least she didn't have to eat it cold. There was a microwave in one corner of the room, which had a steady stream of business this afternoon. While Sarah was heating her sandwich, a prisoner came in with an enormous greyhound. The dog was greeted with a chorus of "oohs" and "ahs," just as if it were a new grandchild. Sarah explained that the dog is part of a program in which retired racing dogs are trained, by inmates, to be pets. This saves them from being euthanized, which, before the existence of such programs, was the usual fate of a retired racer. The tall, graceful dog seemed oddly at home among the inmates and their visitors.

Again reminding me of her mother, Sarah ate her sandwich delicately, but with evident relish, prompting me to ask for further details about the quality of the food served in the prison cafeteria. She pronounced it "gross," sounding for the first time as young as she is. "You like liver?" she asked. "They serve it three or four times a week here. Just the smell of it makes me sick. That's why I lost so much weight."

We talked for a while longer about how terrible it is to be served liver several times a week, and then I decided it was time to ask the hard questions, some of which she had already answered either on the phone or in her letters, but I had to ask them again because I had to see her face when she responded. I remembered Lieutenant Bukoffsky sitting in the deputy's room at the Beaufort County Sheriff's Office and telling me, with great assurance, that he would like to look her in the eye and have her say she didn't stab her mother. I suddenly realize that he's already had that chance, in the wee hours of the morning on October 21, 1999. This makes me wonder why he would want to do it again. Did he have some doubts? Or was it just that kind of wish familiar to every parent, even when they know their child is guilty of some misdeed, to have the child confess? I told Sarah I had to ask her some things about her mom's murder, and she said OK readily enough, though something inside her seemed to collapse.

"Did you help plan your mother's murder?" I asked, waiting to see if she would look away, pull at her ear, or display any of the other physical tics associated with lying. She didn't even blink when she answered me.

"No, I didn't plan my mom's death." Her answer was simple and straight to the point. She didn't attempt to qualify or embellish, but just sat there in an attitude of enduring what she must have endured a hundred times before.

"Were you planning to run away with John Ridgway when it happened?"

"No."

"Had you ever met Kevin Bergin before that day?"

"No."

"Why didn't you warn your mother that John and Kevin were behind the garage?"

"Because I was scared. I thought they were gonna kill me and my brother and sister." She suddenly became more voluble, as if aware of the inadequacy of her answers. "Have you seen how many windows are in that house?" she asked, referring to the Davis residence on Bellinger Bluff Road.

"Yes." It was my turn to be laconic.

"So there's John with a knife, Kevin with a baseball bat, they're both acting like they've gone nuts, and I'm gonna go in and tell my mom to call 9-1-1? What if she doesn't believe me and wants to go see for herself? What if she gets on the phone, but John and Kevin get suspicious and come to the house because I'm taking so long? What if the police can't find the house back there in the woods?"

We were still sitting there staring at each other when time was called, and I had to prepare to leave. Sarah had tears in her eyes as we embraced once and said good-bye. Then she joined the other prisoners who filed out into the hall to line up for count before they were allowed to return to their cottages.

Afterward I sat in the car, replaying the visit like a movie, frantically writing down the notes I wasn't allowed to write inside. When I got to the part where I was recording Sarah's answers to the questions about her mother's murder, I realized that, despite her answers, I still didn't have *the* answers. Although I had *felt* that she was telling me the truth about not planning her mother's murder, if I was honest with myself, I would have to admit that I really don't know—and the more disturbing possibility that no one, except Sarah and John Ridgway, and possibly Kevin Bergin—ever will know for sure. And with that realization, something inside *me* collapsed. I closed my notebook and drove away, down the winding road, past the big-eyed cows whose livers will one day grace the tables of the inmates living nearby, out through the gates, and onto the freeway, heading home.

Writer's Block

Back at home, waiting for the outcome of the 2004 presidential election, I found myself sinking slowly into depression. I had gathered volumes of information during my trip to South Carolina, but it remained packed in my briefcase, untouched, where I imagined it hardening into a stony, unreadable mass, as if transformed by the weight of my sorrow. There was another dimension to the problem as well, one revealed by my conversation with Brent Kiker, Sarah's defense attorney. I couldn't stop thinking about the rumor of what Kevin Bergin allegedly said, when he was locked up in the county detention center, about molesting Nell's corpse. I know that if I had died in such a manner, I certainly wouldn't want it publicized. But then, I argued with myself, it's already been publicized. It was in the newspaper, as I had recently discovered, mentioned by a journalist writing for the *Carolina Morning News,* Stephanie Broadbent (now Ingersoll), when she covered Kevin Bergin's testimony. She had written about the boys' possession of books having to do with voodoo and magic and even mentioned Brent Kiker's suggestion that Kevin Bergin may have molested Nell's body. So yes, it was already public knowledge. Except the details weren't. The newspaper can't print a term like "skull-fucked"; there isn't even an acceptable euphemistic phrase. I try to imagine one: He inserted his penis into the mouth of the corpse and brought himself to sexual climax. It's ridiculous, but this version does sound better, more sanitized, just the way a euphemism should sound. That's because what lies at the heart of this matter is the issue of shame, the strange fact that having something like that done to your body, even after you're dead, can somehow harm you, or your family. I suppose it shows how attached we are to our bodies, to this marvelous structure of blood, bones, muscles, and organs whose boundaries define the boundaries of selfhood, and contain the identity we forge through experience. This attachment to our physical selves explains why the desecration of corpses, even in wartime, is considered an atrocity. So I went round and round, unable to make up my mind and, when I did sit down to write about what I had learned, found myself spiraling into a depression so black that I simply could not do it, even if going through with it meant finding out the truth—the full story of what happened on the day Nell was killed. One night I got food poisoning after eating raw oatmeal cookie dough. The diarrhea and vomiting left me so exhausted I got the shakes. I couldn't sleep so I lay awake, cramps wracking my gut and thighs, thinking about Nell, remembering the crime scene photos, those gaping holes in Nell's chest, and worse than that, the autopsy photos of Nell, open-mouthed on a steel slab, the skull beneath her skin so clearly visible, her right temple obscenely swollen and bruised. Eventually, when I was sure I would not vomit it up, I took a sleeping pill and passed into oblivion.

■ ■ ■

Ironically, once I had accepted that I might not be able to write the book, I started writing it. The prologue and first chapter rolled effortlessly off the tips of my fingers, onto the keyboard and into my computer's memory. Reviewing my notes, which had not congealed into stone after all, I found that, to help complete my research, I would have to order the trial transcript, as well as talk to more people. Some of them were additional officers at the scene, whose names I had come to know by reading the police reports they filed. Others were friends of Mike and Nell Davis, who could give me another perspective on what conditions were like between Sarah and her mom in the weeks leading up to the murder.

■ ■ ■

Before long I had drafted several chapters and was making my way back down to Beaufort County, thinking about the days ahead of me and all the things I needed to accomplish. I had an interview appointment with Gene Hood, Kevin Bergin's attorney, and, most important of all, I was going to the Nelsons' residence. The Nelsons were, in fact, at the head of my list because of my growing awareness of their importance as the first people not involved in the crime itself to have seen and talked to Sarah following her mother's murder.

Someone else I had hoped to speak to was Scott McNair, a friend of both Mike and Nell who testified at Sarah's sentencing. McNair had asked the judge to give Sarah the maximum sentence for armed robbery. When I called Mr. McNair, he was initially quite friendly, even jovial on the phone.

He said he was not "set against" talking to me, but he must talk to Mike first, and get Mike's blessing, because this is, he says, "Mike's life." I promised to call back when I arrived in Bluffton and hung up, thinking that yes, that's certainly part of the problem of writing this book—Mike's life and the way I have to delve into it, laying parts of it open to public scrutiny. But it's also Sarah's life, I reminded myself. And Nell's death. And all these are interwoven so that I can't investigate one without trying to understand the other.

Several days later Mr. McNair would tell me that he could not speak with me, because Mike did not, after all, give his blessing. Considering Mike's willingness to talk to me, I began to wonder if there were things he didn't tell me that he doesn't want me to find out about by other means. Suddenly suspicious I determined that I must find someone who was close to Nell and Mike who would share their impression of what was going on. McNair did, however, talk to me at some length on the phone, giving me his opinion of the case's outcome. This he characterized as "unbelievable."

"It was so clear that she should have been convicted of murder," he said. "But Murdaugh just couldn't get his act together. He came off like a real idiot in the courtroom." How ironic, I thought, considering that those who believed that Sarah should have been found innocent on both counts also thought Solicitor Randolph Murdaugh was an idiot. Mulling it over, though, I realize that many prosecutors must find themselves in this unenviable position, despised by the victim's family because they couldn't get the conviction they wanted; despised by the accused because, even if found innocent, they will always carry the memory of having been hounded, pinioned, punished by the ordeal of going to trial.

Following his evaluation of Murdaugh's performance, McNair told me a "funny little story" concerning a "crazy old black man" who had squatted in some woods out in Yemassee near where the McNairs live. This man passed the time by making signs that he posted by the side of the road, signs that often criticized various state and local political or law enforcement agencies or individuals. One day while driving past the wooded area where the man lived, McNair noticed a sign saying, "Murdaugh passed the bar exam by drinking more than anyone else the night before." McNair liked the sign so much that he bought it from the guy, put Plexiglas over it, and now has it hanging in his office. *Still,* six years later, he had it hanging in his office, like someone else might have a poster advertising a favorite theatrical performance or sporting event. It is, I suppose, nostalgia's other, darker side.

Speaking of Sarah, McNair characterized her as a sociopath, saying she felt no remorse for killing her mother, an impression at least partly based on Mike's characterization of the phone call Sarah had made to him shortly after the murder, informing him about what had happened to her mother.

McNair never spoke to Sarah personally following her arrest, but his name appeared first on a petition of one hundred names presented to the judge at Sarah's bond hearing, a petition stating that people like her were a danger to the community and asking that she be denied bond. Bond was denied, for her and her codefendants. None of the three has been out of custody for one minute since they were arrested on October 20, 1999.

One of the reasons McNair found it unbelievable that Solicitor Murdaugh failed to get a murder conviction is the excerpt from Sarah's diary, the one written approximately a year before the murder, where she expresses regret that she will hurt her brother and sister when she kills her mom. McNair exclaimed to me, "She was planning this for over a year!" That is certainly one way to interpret the entry, which is shocking in its sparse brutality, and clearly supports Mike's assertion that Sarah wanted her mother dead. Yet there are many intervening entries in the diary over the next year, and none of them shows evidence of planning a murder. In its other entries, the diary primarily talks about sexual liaisons with various boyfriends, parties, school gossip, and sleepovers with girlfriends. It is the kind of embarrassingly gushy babble you would expect to find in a teenage girl's diary, if a bit heavy on the sexual activity. Stuff like this: "Dear Diary, God was today confusing! During geography, Austin was hitting on me, during Biology, Eric Fly was giving me a back massage and stuff and he was flirting with me a lot. Matt King gave me a ride home . . ." but then, inevitably, it gets sad. "I have a feeling that if I ask Matt out he'll say yes but only for the sex. That's all people ever use me for. Victor only went out with me because he heard I was a ho, Scottie only hooked up with me because of what he's heard. The same with Richie, David, ToGo, and Matt. Justin too. All they want is sex."

The overall impression is of a girl with an impoverished sense of self-esteem, someone almost entirely dependent on the attention of others for her sense of self-worth. The fact that she sought this attention through sexual activity is fairly typical of teenage girls experiencing depression or associated mood disorders. Anger against a parent is also typical. Even wishing a parent dead is not that unusual. A close friend of mine who is a psychiatric nurse working in an adolescent unit with teenage girls recently told me that he hears this kind of thing at least "once a week." He said the girls make threats against other staff, against their parents—basically whoever is making them angry. Writing "when I kill mom," is, according to several child and adolescent therapists with whom I have spoken, less common, but not rare, and is written about far more often than acted on; nevertheless I would be willing to bet it is that particular journal entry as much as any of the other evidence against Sarah, including the testimony of John Ridgway and Kevin Bergin, that turned Scott McNair, and most people in the communities of Beaufort and Jasper Counties, against Sarah Nickel, and kept them from believing her version of events when she took the stand to testify on her own behalf.

I found further evidence of Sarah's problem with low self-esteem in a journal she kept while she was locked up at Beaufort County Detention Center, awaiting trial. Joe Nickel allowed me to have this journal when I asked him if he had any papers belonging to Sarah that I could look at. In an entry dated July 23, 2000, she writes,

Dear Journal, I had another crying jag today. Just thinkin' about stuff, love in particular. I was thinking about the lack of it in my life. How all I've ever wanted is love and approval, and all I get is abuse. Since the first night Chris [a man her mother dated after her divorce from Joe] raped me when I was 7, I've never met anyone's standards, never matched up to what I should be, never made anyone happy. I've been a fuck-up all my life and I'll probably continue to be. I get support and encouragement from no one and that really hurts. Even my family, my own flesh and blood, don't love me. All anyone has ever done is put me down, tell me I can't measure up, scream at me, say I'm stupid and worthless, and I believe them. If they say it, why shouldn't it be true? Mom said it all the time. She didn't even realize how bad she was hurting me. She didn't understand that the reason I messed up so much was because I figured that since I couldn't have her approval, her disapproval was better than the nothing I was getting. She was ALWAYS too busy for me, never asked what I was feeling or thinking, never gave me any affection, never asked me if I was okay with Daddy gone. She never cared! Why? What did I do wrong? Am I that unlovable? If my own mother can't love me, who can? She was never there for me and I always had to depend on myself. Daddy wasn't there, either. I can't do it anymore by myself. I <u>need</u> someone to help me.

Where, though, can we go to hear Nell's voice, to hear her side of the story? Because I know, deep in my heart, that Nell must have loved Sarah, even if Sarah couldn't feel it, and maybe that stemmed back to the abuse. Mike had told me that Sarah was out of control, that she and Nell fought constantly, that their last, best hope was that they could just keep Sarah alive until she turned twenty, and that maybe, by then, she would settle down and see some sense. Why twenty? Maybe because that is when Nell and I both started to settle down and see some sense? Because yes, we were both a little wild, did our share of drugs and alcohol, though Sarah never knew this until I told her. To Sarah, Nell was always "the model parent," while Joe was the one who smoked, used drugs, drank alcohol. Admittedly, compared to Sarah, Nell kept her substance abuse pretty much under wraps, and, as far as I know, it ended when she and Joe divorced. But maybe it was this wildness in her past that made Nell fantasize that if she could only keep her daughter alive until she reached twenty, some rational inner self Sarah hadn't discovered yet would suddenly be activated.

I have often wished that I could speak to Nell myself, not in dreams, but that she would have left me some kind of message, something that would let me hear, in her own words, how she felt about her relationship with her daughter. Then one day when I was at the Beaufort County Sheriff's Office, looking at a statement that had been missing from the investigation files when I originally scanned them, I found something else that I had not seen before: a letter from Nell to Sarah that, I soon learned, was printed off the hard drive of Nell's computer. There is no date, and the file gives no indication of when it was last saved to the computer's memory, but I suspect that it was written not long before the murder. As I read through it, I got the eerie feeling that Nell believed she would never see her daughter again. But she thought that her daughter, not she, would be the one who was irrevocably lost.

Sarah,

By the time you read this letter you will already be gone but I just wanted to leave you with a few of my thoughts since we can't seem to talk to each other.

The first thing you should know and always keep with you is that I love you very much—always have and always will. I admit that I don't agree with your philosophy of life but I do find a lot about you that I like and I am very proud of you even though I may not express it as often as I should or you think I should.

Every relationship has to have the will to succeed by both parties. I feel that I have not done a good job as a mother in making our relationship work.

I have to deal with that myself. You then should take an honest look at how much you have tried and given so that you don't continue to have the feelings you have for me because it is very unhealthy for you mentally.

I hope you find your happiness and I am very sorry for not being able to give you the life you want. I can't help the way I feel about school, responsibility, helping around the house, and all the other things you hate about me. I feel a certain responsibility as your mother to assure that you will have the things in life that you can use to have a happy and successful life. I hope you can prove me wrong and you do what you want now and still make it later in life because I really do want you to be happy.

You are always welcome to come home but we have to resolve the issues that have ruined our relationship. I know you don't want to go to counseling so if you can think of some other way let me know. If you find that you don't want to come back home someday I understand.

I love you and if you ever need me you know where I am.
Love,
Mommy

In this letter I find a strong sense of Nell's love, but there's also a feeling of resignation. The battle is over, and she has, in effect, surrendered. It's a note she might have tucked into her daughter's suitcase, knowing that she was planning to run away, and having given up trying to stop her.

I also find Nell's true voice, the emotional intelligence and willingness to work out a conflict that has arisen in a relationship, taking responsibility for her own part in creating that conflict, but also insisting that the other person do the same—one of the things that made me love her. I read it, and my own wounds become fresh again.

13

The Nelsons

On my way back to Beaufort, traveling north on South Carolina Highway 21, I passed a sign for the Oyotunji African Village located in Sheldon. The community, established by Yoruban immigrants, was there when Nell, Ann Handy, Kathy Kinson, and I drove down to the Handys' Fripp Island beach cottage for a weekend, about twenty-five years ago. One of the girls had heard of the settlement before and referred to it as a "voodoo colony." Ann suggested we drive down the rutted dirt track to see the place for ourselves. Nell, who was driving, swung a hard left and brought us onto the road. It had been raining, so the tires slid a bit, kicking brown mud up onto the Mazda's fenders. The car, I remember, was a sporty little red thing that ran so quietly you would swear, sitting at a stoplight, that the engine had stalled.

I don't know what we had expected, but when we got to the end of the road there were a few primitively constructed whitewashed buildings, something that looked like a stockade made out of narrow pine saplings, and, standing beside the road, a tall black man in flowing white robes, his head topped by a white turban that looked like the swirled cap of a soft-serve vanilla ice-cream cone, a tall wooden staff in his hand. Anne said, "Oh my God, turn us around. Right now." And Nell complied, her movements, as always, calm and studied. We had gone about fifty yards back down the road, just around a bend so that we were out of sight of the watchful man in the turban, when one of the back wheels hit an extra-deep pothole. The car stuck, mired in the mud, wheels spinning.

For a moment we sat petrified, looking back over our shoulders, each of us wondering, I have no doubt, what advantage the inhabitants of the "voodoo colony" might take of our dilemma. We were young, racially insular, and had stayed awake far too late on many a Friday night, watching a feature called *Shock Theatre* on TV. Finally Ann and I got out of the car and tried to rock it while Nell hit the gas at strategically timed moments. When that didn't work, Ann and Nell decided to walk back up the road toward the highway. There was a mobile home at the corner of the highway and the dirt road where they were going to ask for help. While they were gone, Kathy and I sat in the car with the windows rolled up and the doors locked. I didn't mention it to Kathy, but I had a sudden fear that the people in the mobile home might pose a greater danger than the inhabitants of the village. The people in the village at least had a sign announcing who they were. The people in the mobile home could be anyone and were likely to be rednecks, the one class of people my friends and I feared even more than we feared Africans, who, really, were more unknown than genuinely feared.

My fear of approaching the Nelsons reminded me of the anxiety I had felt toward both the African Village and the mobile home on the corner. It was fear of the unknown coupled with a reluctance to intrude on the privacy of strangers. Before I headed over to the Nelsons', I stopped to talk to Joe Nickel, who made a phone call in the attempt to determine whether they still lived in the mobile home that stood several lots further down the road. The person he spoke to informed Joe that they did live there, or did the last he heard, so I had to be satisfied with that. I got back in my car and drove slowly, eyes searching for a black mailbox with the silhouette of a ship on top, relieved when I could see that it still bore the name "Nelson." I pulled into the yard, taking heart at the fact that there was no longer the NO TRESPASSING sign posted on the door, which I had noticed the first time I drove past the mobile home,. The rusted swing set that had sat in the front yard had been replaced by a new one, and now there was also a trampoline and various toys scattered across the lawn, showing this to be a house where children played. I walked to the door quickly, before I had time to think too much about what I was going to say. There was a truck in the driveway, and I could hear voices from a television show on the other side of the wall, so someone must be home. The door was answered by an elderly woman with a corona of fluffy white hair. She frowned at me suspiciously, but her expression gradually changed as I explained who I was and why I had come to see her. She seemed surprised but not dismayed by my request. She invited me in and asked me to sit down, offering me a glass of water.

We talked with the TV on, the serious, tender voices of *Guiding Light* turned to low volume. Later I would be reminded that Mary Nelson was watching the same show on October 20, 1999, when Sarah came running through her yard, screaming. Neither Heather, who is Mary's granddaughter, nor James, her grandson, was home today. I should really talk to them, Mary said, because they probably would remember more than she did about the day Nell was murdered. She would tell me what she did remember, though, and for that I was grateful.

Mary Nelson's eyes were hazel, and I noticed that they would change color, from blue green to green blue, when she warmed to her subject. She began her story by telling me about her various orthopedic surgeries.

"I've had two hip replacements and a knee replacement," she announced, gently patting one knee with her hand. "One hip was done just a couple days before this thing happened. I was sitting on the sofa watching

TV with Heather. The TV was on the other side of the room then, and Heather was sitting over there," she said, indicating the spot where the TV stood presently, "by the window. She looked out and saw Sarah running across the yard, and she yelled, 'The dog's after Sarah!' We had a German shepherd then who couldn't stand Sarah. We had to hold him whenever she came into the yard. So she jumped up, to go holler at the dog. And Sarah come busting in the door to us saying, 'They killed my mom, they killed my mom!' I guess I come up off the sofa and crossed the room before I knew what I was doing because I had forgot my walker, so I got it then, some way, and I saw out the window the two boys running behind Sarah. I screamed at Heather to go get on the phone and call 9-1-1. I told Sarah to grab the shotgun and hand it to me. And I jerked the door back open with the shotgun in my hand and the boys were at my doorstep. One was at the bottom step and the other one was, about, maybe ten foot behind."

"Wow," I said, my mind suddenly filled with the image of Mary, balancing on her walker, leveling the shotgun to get a good aim, and then holding it steady as the two men approached her front door. "So what did they do when they saw the gun?"

"They stopped dead. They looked me straight in the face and tuck and run."

"Did they say anything?" I asked, feeling shivers run up my spine as I thought about what might have happened had Mary Nelson not immediately demanded the shotgun, or had there been a moment's delay in Sarah's locating and passing her the gun.

"I think one of them said, 'Let's get out of here,' or something like that. James might could tell you better because he was outside where they were, working on his truck I think."

A black cat came padding into the room and rubbed itself against my legs. "That's Elvis," Mary said, smiling as if introducing a member of the family. I reached down to scratch the cat's head before asking the next, most crucial, question. "Tell me what Sarah was like, emotionally."

"She was very scared, very emotional. I'd never seen her that way before," Mary confided, patting and then rubbing her knee in a circular motion. I wondered if it was hurting now.

"Did she tell you anything about what had happened?" I asked.

"One thing... one thing that stays with me is her saying, 'They was only supposed to knock her out.'"

"They were only supposed to knock her out? Meaning Nell?"

"I suppose. Another thing she said was that the boys made her take her mother's earrings out of her ears and her watch off and put it on herself. And she had them both on when we was talking."

I remembered reading about this in the paper. One of the Nelsons, I had thought it was Heather, had testified that Sarah said John made her take the jewelry off her mother's body. Mary, apparently, had received the same impression.

For a moment Mary's eyes got a faraway look, and I wondered if she was getting tired. Suddenly she changed the subject, telling me that she has rheumatoid arthritis, Crohn's disease, and respiratory problems, but that she has been feeling a lot better lately. "Heather and me drove to New York a couple of weeks ago, and I helped her with the driving. Went to Niagara Falls, took her little girl, my great grandbaby." She pointed to some photographs stuck in the corner of a larger framed picture that hung over the couch where we were sitting. I took a few sips of my water and leaned back, looking around at the comfortably furnished living room, the clean wood-laminate floor, the pile of half-folded laundry sitting on the other sofa. The room seemed so peaceful. The laundry smelled so clean. It was hard for me to imagine the turmoil that had invaded this space five years ago.

"I couldn't believe Sarah was as bad as some of the things that came out," Mary told me as I carried my empty water glass to the kitchen sink. "She used to come up here all the time when she was staying with her dad, and we had no idea all this stuff was going on with her mom."

"She never said anything about it?"

"No, not once. Sarah was a little wild, but no more so than a lot of the other kids her age. You know, we knew her stepfather Mike Davis as good as we knew Joe. Mike had the only drugstore in Ridgeland for a long time. Until Eckerd's came. So we went there for everything."

Mary had started to breathe harder than sounded normal, and she told me she was getting tired. She also told me I should come back the following day between 4:30 and 5:00, when I could catch Heather and maybe James, too. I gathered up my belongings, and we said good-bye.

On my way back to Bluffton I found myself obsessing over some things that Mary had said. The first was Sarah's comment about how "they," that is, Ridgway and Bergin, were "only supposed to knock her out." Recently, going through the voluminous files I had copied when I was at the sheriff's office, I had come across a note Sarah had written to one of her friends, a girl with the unlikely name of Nicole Cocola, in the days before the murder. I remembered reading it the first time I went through the file, and I had been haunted by its significance. Dated October 7, 1999, just thirteen days before the murder, it reads as follows:

Hey chika! What's ↑? Not 2 much here. I'm gonna miss you a lot. Please DON'T TELL ANYONE WHAT I TOLD YOU! *If anyone asks, I told you I was going to rehab and then I disappeared. Okay? I promise I'll call you or write you as soon as I get the chance. I know I shouldn't go, but I have to. This is my big chance. I have to take it. Right now, my life is too restricted. I'm a bird trapped in a cage. Even though my song is beautiful, it will be even sweeter once I'm free. I'm a free spirit. I can't be tied down. I know this sounds really sappy, but it's the way I feel. I will really miss you a lot. Bye girl.*
,
Sarah

This note may of course refer to the runaway attempt Sarah made on October 8, a week and a half before the murder, but the note of desperation sounded by phrases like "I'm a bird trapped in a cage" and "This is my big chance. I have to take it" suggest a persistent need to escape, one that would not subside just because she was apprehended by her friend's mother and sent home.

I remembered Brent Kiker's response when I asked him whether he thought Sarah was in on her mom's murder. He had said he believed she was going to run away, but not that she had planned to kill anyone. The more I found out about the case, the more I tended to agree with Kiker, yet in Mary Nelson's memory of what had happened there was the suggestion that Sarah had at least agreed that some violence would be done. And in this Mary's testimony supported what John Ridgway had said about there being a plan to knock Nell out. I found myself wondering if any one of the three young people really understood the danger of trying to knock someone out without killing or seriously damaging them. I thought about all the TV shows and movies I have seen in which people are knocked unconscious and shortly afterward get up to resume their normal lives (well, normal for television). So maybe it's not entirely crazy to assume someone could be knocked out and not be killed or seriously injured, even in real life. But does that make it OK? Certainly not. Especially when the assault was premeditated. But, if Mary's memory was accurate, Sarah hadn't hit her mother. She had watched, acquiescent that Nell should be hit, as someone else swung the bat, only realizing, perhaps, after the second and third blow, what was really happening.

The other thing that bothered me was the jewelry. If Sarah was, like her mom, a victim, and not part of the plan, did it make sense for her to have taken her mother's jewelry? She had said John made her take it, but if John made her do it, why wouldn't he simply take it himself? On the other hand, if Sarah was colluding with John and Kevin, why did she only take a pair of earrings and a watch? Surely those weren't the only valuable pieces of jewelry her mother possessed, or the only items of value in the house. Why didn't she take anything else? Does it matter whether she took the items off her mother's dresser or removed them from her mother's corpse? Certainly it matters, and it was one of those questions that I would have to ask Sarah when I was once more sitting across from her in the visitation room at CGGCI.

■ ■ ■

The evening of the day I spoke with Mary Nelson, having received my copy of the trial transcript, I read the testimony of Kim Collins, the medical examiner who performed the autopsy on Nell's body.

Prompted by Solicitor Murdaugh, Collins went over the details of Nell's autopsy, stating that the "pertinent findings were predominantly over the head and neck area as well as the chest. She had nine and possibly ten stab wounds on the right chest." Collins said "possibly" because "there was one stab wound, which was jagged and was probably composed of two stab wounds together in one location." Nell also had "severe head trauma and neck trauma on the—all sides of the head, front, back, left, right and around her neck."

Murdaugh asked if Collins had been able to tell what caused the trauma to the victim's head and neck. She responded by characterizing it as "blunt force trauma . . . from being hit with a heavy object, enough to cause the damage we saw on the scalp, on the skin, fractures of the skull and bruising on the brain." She confirmed that these wounds would be consistent with those made by a baseball bat, and when asked if she had found, in conducting the autopsy, the cause of death, she explained that it was listed as "both blunt force trauma to the head as well as exsanguination." The latter is explained as "bleeding to death," from the stab wounds to the chest.

Relentlessly thorough in his quest to show the jury the extent of Nell's injuries, Murdaugh had continued with this line of questioning, now asking the medical examiner to detail the size and shape of the area covered by the stab wounds, which was roughly a three inch by three inch patch over Nell's right breast. Reading this information, even without the visual aid of the bloody t-shirt, which was displayed for the jury during Collins's testimony, I found myself growing increasingly nauseated.

Next Collins proceeded to describe a large bruise over Nell's right eye and cuts on the inside of her mouth—both the upper and lower lip, as if she'd been hit in the mouth and her own teeth cut into her lips. She also had "petechia," or "pinpoint hemorrhages" on both of her lower eyelids, caused by strangulation. On her right temple region, there was a laceration where the skin was lifted away from the skull, had actually peeled up. Surrounding the tear was a four by five inch bruise. Above this tear was another laceration on the forehead, and then a third in the scalp, which connected to yet another, each one about two inches long. The left ear was suffused with bruising. The right neck was bruised on the side and around to the front, affecting the thyroid, and there were contusions all over the scalp—on the front, back, and both sides. Hemorrhage was present over the skull on the right, left, and the back. There were six fractures of the skull, and then beneath the skull, evidence of hemorrhage over the brain in three different locations, with bruising of the brain on all sides. A dissection of the neck revealed additional hemorrhage around the thyroid gland, around the larynx, or voice box, and the right side of the larynx was fractured.

I had to stop reading here because I was remembering something Sarah had sent to me a couple of months after I had asked if she could write about the day her mother died, describing what she had felt during the experience. I already knew, from the police reports and her official statement, her version of what had happened, but those reports held no sense of the events' emotional impact. I wanted her to describe how she had felt, because I believed it would give me some insight into the level of her involvement.

She had balked at first, saying it was really hard to write about those events because, in order to do so, she had to relive them. Eventually, though, I received a fat envelope with no letter, just the pages of an essay that had no title, but that began with the words, "October 20, 1999, the day my mom died, is the day I descended into my own private hell." At one point in this harrowing narrative, Sarah describes Bergin and Ridgway standing over her mother's . . .

"moaning form, arguing about how to finish her off, when she used her last reserve of strength to sit up and look at me. One of her eyes was swollen shut, but the other was clear and brown and beautiful. She tried to speak my name, but she couldn't."

Couldn't, I now reasoned, because her larynx was crushed. Couldn't, perhaps, because her right frontal lobe was fatally damaged. Sarah's essay goes on to describe how Nell

"held her arms out to me, wanting to embrace her eldest child before she went to Heaven, but before I could take a step towards her, Kevin shoved her back into the mud and proceeded to choke her." Still, Sarah wrote, Nell had fought back, *"kicking the air in a futile gesture to save herself."*

Or kicking the air, I speculated, because she was being strangled.

Never in my life have I seen a more horrifying description of a murder—not in the many murder mysteries I have read, nor in the crime dramas I've viewed on TV, nor in the newspaper, or anywhere else. The extremely well-publicized murders of Nicole Brown Simpson and Ron Goldman in 1994 came close, with the description of Nicole's throat cut so deeply that her head was nearly severed, but surely, I rationalize, the rapidity of death following such an attack was more merciful than what Nell endured.

The questions Brent Kiker asked pathologist Kim Collins made him seem a bit tongue-tied. No doubt he was uncomfortable with their implications, but they had to be asked, in order to lay a foundation for what would come later, when Kevin Bergin would take the stand to testify against Sarah.

When given the opportunity to question Ms. Collins, Brent Kiker asked, "Did you—as part of your—did you conduct any other examinations . . . for instance, to determine if there was any sexual abuse? Of Ms. Davis? Did you investigate that possibility?"

The term "sexual abuse" seems odd here, at least in terms of its conventional use, but perhaps only indicates a southern gentleman's avoidance of a more graphic description.

Collins effectively dodged the question, saying, "We examined her physically. And then we—and we took nail scrapings. And we did toxicology."

Could she have been uncomfortable with the implication that the body should have been—but was not—evaluated for sexual molestation?

Kiker persisted, this time becoming more specific. "Did you conduct a search for any sort of biological evidence of rape?"

"I don't believe we did." And after a pause, "No, we did not."

Kiker's decision not to probe the issue further may have been confusing to jurors, but he had his reasons for waiting. Those reasons would surface when it was his turn to cross-examine Kevin Bergin.

The Nelsons after Dark

The next time I drove out to Knowles Island Road to visit the Nelsons, I realized it was almost exactly the same time of day that Sarah Nickel, John Ridgway, and Kevin Bergin pulled up in front of their mobile home. The weather was eerily similar, too. While it had been hot and sunny all day, thunderheads now marched across the sky, heading steadily inland on a northwesterly flow. James Nelson came to the door. He was a slender young man with strawberry-blond hair and a complexion to match, his skin sun reddened below the eyebrows—and stark white above—from wearing a baseball cap backward. His short hair came to a spiky point above his high forehead, like a widow's peak in reverse. Like Mary, James said he didn't remember much about the day Nell was murdered, but as we started talking, things came back to him.

When Sarah had stopped her mother's Chevy Tahoe in the middle of the road out in front of the Nelson residence, fifteen-year-old James had been out in the yard, working on his El Camino. He said that the whole thing was so unreal, he could hardly believe what was happening for the first few minutes, as he had watched Sarah come sprinting across the yard, the expression on her face "like she was scared out of her mind, screaming, 'They killed my mom! They killed my mom!'"

Flabbergasted, James had watched as Sarah ran up the steps and into the mobile home. Not entirely comprehending his own danger, he had accosted the two young men who came barreling toward the door in Sarah's wake. They hadn't seemed to notice him at first, even when he had yelled,

"What the hell are ya'll doing?" because they had kept going until the first one, "the skinny one," as James recalled it, reached the door and Mary Nelson, hip-replacement surgery notwithstanding, met him on the other side with the shotgun. At that point, James told me, the skinny one had turned around and said, "Let's get the hell out of here," which they proceeded to do.

Seeing his grandmother with the gun had jolted James into a new awareness of his own danger, as well as a need to protect his family. He had bolted into the house, taking the gun from his invalid grandmother and speedily loading the shells that would render the weapon more effective should the two strange men return.

Heather Nelson, a slender, attractive twenty-two-year-old with streaky blond hair and black rectangular-framed glasses that gave her a studious look, confirmed James's and her grandmother's impression of events and provided some additional detail. Seventeen in October 1999, and three months pregnant with her daughter Amára, Heather had gone to school with Sarah at Hilton Head High. Specifically, they had been in the same world history class the previous year.

Like her grandmother, Heather had initially thought Sarah was running through the yard screaming hysterically because she was afraid of the "shepherd dog," but as soon as she got inside, it had become apparent that this was not the case.

Sarah had also been wet; the tank top and sweat pants she'd had on were drenched with rain. But this was something Heather must have registered later, because she had felt pretty hysterical herself when she realized what Sarah's screams were actually trying to tell her.

"It was horrible. I was so freaked out. Sarah was saying, 'You've got to help me, they killed my mom.'" That was when Heather picked up the phone to call 9-1-1. "You should hear the 9-1-1 tape," she told me, pushing a streak of blond hair back behind her ear.

I told her that I had, and she blushed.

"It was so embarrassing when they played it in court. Every other word out of my mouth was the f-word."

In the moments after Sarah's arrival, safety had become the number-one concern for the people holed up in the Nelsons' mobile home, especially when Sarah had told them that Bergin and Ridgway possessed knives and a baseball bat, which had already been used to commit a brutal murder. It had seemed to take "forever" for the police to arrive, James recalled, but he also acknowledged that any lapse of time, under those circumstances, would have seemed long. When officers from the Jasper County Sheriff's Office, the Beaufort County Sheriff's Office, and the Department of Natural Resources (DNR) did arrive, however, they came in force, in James's words, "loaded down with enough guns to start a war."

"I've never seen so many guns," Heather agreed. "And they had the road locked down from here to Cooler's," she said, referring to the Exxon station and convenience store at the crossroads where South Carolina Highway 462 meets Old House Road. She drummed her fingers on the table, saying, "Yeah, I thought, 'We're gonna have a war in Ridgeland.'"

After determining that the fugitives had fled into the forested area across the road, the police were joined by two dog handlers, who, along with men who looked as if they belonged to a SWAT team, made their way into the woods. The Nelsons had had a long wait before a DNR vehicle drove up out front and disgorged the two suspects, but the atmosphere had changed remarkably since the police had arrived. They had all felt safe now and had little idea of what was to come when John Ridgway got out of the truck, yelling loud enough for James to hear him, "Sarah told us to do it. It was all Sarah's plan."

I asked James what he thought about Sarah's demeanor throughout the ordeal.

"Well, she was crying and, like, scared out of her mind when she come running up to the house. Then later, once the boys was caught, she had a jokey attitude, was smiling. That didn't seem right to me."

Heather said she remembered everyone, and especially Sarah, calming down once the police had come. "She sat right there at the kitchen table to write out her statement. They treated her pretty well, I guess, until they picked up the boys and they came out of the woods yelling about how Sarah had planned everything."

"Did you see how Sarah reacted when the police said they'd found the body?" I asked, still hoping for more evidence regarding her state of mind.

"Sarah was outside then, sitting on the hood of James's truck. I don't think she heard them, actually. I don't think they told her until later." This accorded with Sarah's version of events. Sarah said Officer Woodward—whom she, like everyone else, still refers to as "JoJo"—wouldn't tell her anything about her mom, even though she kept asking him about her. It wasn't until after Heather had told Woodward that Sarah was wearing earrings that belonged to her mother, and he had Sarah in the DNR truck, charging her with murder, that he had said her mother's body had been found.

"So what about those earrings?" I said. "They seemed to mark a turning point in the investigation."

Heather said, "Well, I was bothered by what Sarah had told me about them, you know, while we were waiting for the police to come. She was sitting here on the couch and she was playing with her ears. She said, 'They made me take my mom's earrings out. And her watch, too.' It freaked me out because it sounded like they made her take the earrings out of her mom's ears."

"After she was dead?"

"I guess."

"Did that make you think she was in on what happened?"

"I don't know. It just seemed weird. I thought about it a long time before I told the police because I didn't want to add to her troubles, but I finally decided I had to tell because I would feel too guilty if I didn't."

Heather's five-year-old daughter had joined her on the couch and was snuggling up tight against her mother, making me aware that I should probably leave soon, even though I could hear the rain roaring through the thin walls of the mobile home. I decided to ask a few more questions, and then I would have to take off, even if it was still pouring.

"So, did you know Sarah very well? Did you see her much when she stayed over at her dad's?"

Heather was caressing her daughter's curls as she answered. "Sure. We hung out all the time. Sarah was a little crazy, a little wild, but never did I hear her say anything about hurting her mother, or really anything out of the ordinary. She had arguments with her parents, but they were typical teenager arguments, you know what I mean."

"Typical like?

"Oh, 'my mom is such a bitch because she won't let me go out with this boy.' That kind of thing."

We were all quiet for a moment, and I noticed that Amára had fallen asleep, leaning against her mother. "She could be pretty wild, though," Mary chimed in. Heather looked suddenly alert, as if she had remembered something.

"You know Sarah was locked up over at the detention center for more than a year while she was waiting for her trial?" she queried. I nodded in affirmation.

"Right. She had to be kept in isolation from the other inmates because she was under seventeen." I remembered Sarah telling me they let her out of her cell for only one hour a day, to go to the library. The rest of the time, she says, she wrote in her journal, wrote letters, and read books from the library. She read 324 books during that period. I have the numbered list, kept on various odd sheets of paper, somewhere in my files.

"Well, I don't know about her being kept in isolation. All I ever heard was this story from someone else who was there at the same time. She stripped herself naked, covered herself with baby oil, and then ran all around the detention center, and the guards couldn't catch her because she was too slippery."

It was an interesting story and certainly added color to the portrait of Sarah that was emerging through my research, but it didn't do much to help me with the big question—whether or not Sarah played any part in her mother's murder.

As I thanked Mary and Heather once again for their help, it occurred to me to ask Heather if she knew how I could contact a couple of Sarah's other friends who served as witnesses at the trial. I had exhausted my resources trying to come up with phone numbers and was hoping she could help. The two people I most wanted to speak to were Nicole Cocola and Amy Heath, both of whom were in close touch with Sarah during the week preceding the murder.

Heather looked doubtfully at her grandmother. As her eyes traveled back to me, I saw her frown deepen. "Nicole Cocola is dead. Isn't that right, Gramma?"

Mary shrugged. "Sounds familiar. So many of these young people get killed in car crashes nowadays it's hard to keep track."

I sat there blinking in the lamplight, considering a world in which a grandma would make such a remark.

"Yeah, I think she is dead, Heather answered, but then added that Amy "is married to one of the Albee boys and lives over in Bluffton." She looked inquiringly at her grandmother again. "You remember which one it was married Amy?"

Mary raised her hands and shrugged, indicating that she did not, which inspired Heather to call someone, who called someone else, and then called back. "That's Wayne Albee? You sure about that? You got a number for them?"

She didn't get a number, but I added Wayne's name to the list and hoped

I would be able to find him. I thanked the Nelsons again and departed into the rain, which had now turned to a fine drizzle.

As the door closed behind me there was this strange lightning flashing, flashing, flashing all over the sky, and then it got really dark as I was trying to find my car. I seemed to have parked farther away from the house than I remembered. The car was almost in the woods. Once my eyes had begun to adjust, I could see fog rising from the ground, and I started thinking about what Heather and I had been talking about, and about how she had said she "thanks God every day that my grandmother wasn't here alone" when Sarah stopped the truck in the road and fled to their mobile home, because "who knows what would have happened, those boys had knives and a baseball bat."

By the time I got inside the car my hands were shaking so badly I could hardly fit the key into the ignition. I was experiencing the kind of dual consciousness that I have when watching a horror movie—on the one hand, I'm scared out of my mind; on the other, I know I'm completely safe—only it was much more intense. I locked the doors, took a few deep breaths, and started the engine. I found my way out of the driveway and onto the shiny black road. I had gone only a short distance down Knowles Islands Road when the windows started to fog up. I turned on the defogger but it didn't work at all until I adjusted the temperature to hot. Finally I was back on Highway 462, but the highway was deserted, and the weird lightning was going off all around me, and the rain was coming down harder, and visibility was terrible even with my brights on because of the fog rising off the road. I tried calling my husband on my cell phone, knowing that hearing his voice would calm me, and that talking would distract me. It seemed illogical, to want to be distracted in these driving conditions, but at the moment it seemed a necessity. Nothing happened when I punched in his speed-dial number. I looked at the phone. It said, "no service." So I turned on the radio to a bouncing oldies station, and that helped. Another car came up behind me and passed me, and that helped, too, because I could see his tail lights, which enabled me to keep my bearings, and eventually I got back to 278, and I was fine. Really. Never felt better.

15

Juror Number 13

Having the transcript meant I also had the names of the jurors. Using the phonebook and an Internet locator service, I tried matching names to numbers and got a couple of hits right off. The second person I called agreed to be interviewed. I couldn't believe my good luck. I was right not to believe it. It turned out that this person, a female juror with a soft yet firm voice, would be the only one who agreed to talk. Before our meeting was over, I would learn that the only reason she was willing to talk to me was because she and her husband were leaving the area, for good, within two months' time.

Juror number 13 and her husband welcomed me into their spacious ranch house located in the shade of the spreading oaks that shelter Oakwood Park subdivision from the southern sun. She immediately struck me as someone my mother would refer to as "a very lovely person." She was a tall woman—at least compared to my five feet two inches—with long slender fingers and an air of gracefulness that pervaded her smallest gesture, the turning of a doorknob, the gathering of a pillow to her chest as she described to me the experience of doing "the hardest thing I've ever done."

Her characterization of sitting on the jury as an active rather than passive activity grabbed my attention. I would eventually find out, as I learned about her life as a military wife and mother, that although she didn't work outside the home, she took the work of living quite seriously. Being on the jury was, for this juror, a job not to be taken lightly, a role not to be assumed passively. And so despite her willowy appearance, she showed a streak of moral toughness that ought to be welcome in any courtroom.

Ultimately, however, the interview was disappointing, partly because many of the things she said were things I already knew—what she remembered most about the trial were details that had contributed to the horror and stress of the experience: the crime scene photos, the testimony of the pathologist, the compost box that had been reassembled in the presence of the jury, the bloody clothes of both the victim and one of her assailants, plus the fact that the trial started early in the morning and frequently went on into the evening.

Perhaps she sensed my disappointment, because about a half hour into our somewhat desultory conversation, when I asked her to tell me about the deliberation process, she suddenly sat forward. "There was one juror," she said, two vertical frown lines forming between her eyebrows, "who was hanging up the whole deliberation process. The rest of us were ready to convict, on both counts, but this woman kept walking around the room, messing around with different objects and furniture in the room, saying, 'That little girl can't live without her mother. She's not guilty. I'm not agreeing to that.'"

The irony of this statement resided in the fact that, convicted or not, this "little girl" would most certainly live without her mother. If juror number 13's memory is correct, then it would appear as if this other juror's refusal to convict was based on emotion rather than the facts presented in the case, and probably represented her reluctance to see Sarah suffer what was, in her eyes, a kind of double punishment, as if being deprived of her mom were enough.

"So she was the only holdout?" I asked. "Everybody else reached a decision fairly quickly?"

She shifted sideways in her chair, hugged her pillow a little tighter. "Well, no. Earlier in the process there had been other holdouts on the murder charge, but they had all been persuaded to vote 'guilty' by the majority. The majority always believed the girl was guilty on both charges."

I asked this juror what convinced her, personally, of Sarah's guilt.

"Well," she said, considering the matter thoughtfully, "the girl's shoes were in the backseat of the truck. I kept thinking that if she'd been there against her will, if she'd been a hostage, she wouldn't have taken her shoes off."

Wow, I thought, you never know what's going to make an impression.

"Was there anything else?" I asked hopefully. Surely she hadn't voted to convict based on Sarah's bare feet.

"Well, yes. When Sarah was testifying, she seemed to be acting; she was sobbing but there were no tears."

But there had been plenty of tears in the jury room. Most, if not all, of the women were crying, and one of the men, as they finally reached a consensus, persuading the one holdout to vote "guilty" on the armed robbery charge, if the others agreed to vote "not guilty" on the charge of murder. It was what lawyers call "a compromise verdict," because, technically, under South Carolina law, if someone is guilty of armed robbery, and a murder occurs as a result of that robbery, even if that individual did not personally commit the murder, they are automatically guilty. This law, which goes under the shorthand name of "hand of one, hand of all" was repeatedly explained to the jury by the solicitor in the hope that this approach would gain him a conviction on both counts. And, according to juror number 13, it almost had.

Nevertheless juror number 13 admitted that she felt horrible when the verdict was pronounced, and the tears streaming from her eyes had rendered the courtroom, and the face of the defendant, a blur.

She shook her head, her straight, shoulder-length brown hair moving back and forth across her shoulders. "I felt horrible after, was depressed for a month, could hardly get out of bed or leave the house. But then we went to the sentencing over in Walterboro. When the judge gave her the maximum sentence—thirty years—that's when I knew it was over, that we'd done the right thing."

"You'd done the right thing because the judge gave her the maximum sentence?" I repeated, wanting to make sure I understood her.

"Yes. You see, the judge and the solicitor were such nice men, they were kind and were very careful and straightforward in explaining things. The defense attorney . . ."

"Brent Kiker?"

"Was that his name? I guess it was. Yes, well, he just tried to confuse people. I didn't like him at all."

I thanked juror number 13 for her time, asked to use her bathroom before I left, and found myself sitting on her lovely clean pale green toilet admiring the way the blue twilight poured in through the angled skylight in the bathroom ceiling. I didn't want to think, yet, about the implications of what she had just said, but I couldn't help it. I really didn't want to believe that this "very lovely person" believed Sarah guilty of murder, beyond a reasonable doubt, because she didn't like Sarah's lawyer. Surely it was more complicated than that. But wait, I reminded myself, there were the shoes in the backseat of the Tahoe. And the lack of real tears. I examined my memory, trying to determine if I have ever really cried without shedding tears. I know that sometimes, when I have been really upset, it has taken a while for the tears to come, following the wracking sobs, the dry convulsions on the bed or the couch, curled up in the fetal position. Like when I first heard about Nell's murder. But the moisture, the drops running down my face, would always, eventually, make an appearance. Would it be the same if I were in public, under scrutiny, with a group of men and women trying to determine whether I ought to be convicted of my mother's murder? I don't know. I can't honestly say.

As I drove back toward Bluffton and Vic's apartment, I weighed my reservations against my initial favorable impression of juror number 13. I reminded myself of her determination to do the right thing, to endure the ordeal of serving on that jury even though it put her through a personal hell. That was certainly something I could relate to at the moment. And surely it's unfair to judge a person based on a few randomly recalled details that stood out in her memory of an event that occurred five years ago. I also had to remind myself that she is not the only juror who, according to her memory of events, wanted to vote for conviction on both counts. That spoke volumes. Still, I think it is important to look at the matter from a broader perspective, because I know how thoroughly Sarah's chances were damaged by the local media's initial coverage of the crime. Our dependence on the media, and particularly television, for news, is one indicator, perhaps, of why our criminal justice system is broken and helps to explain why people who are smart and have power, like talented attorneys, are able to manipulate juries. Think about it—in a culture that ranks television shows like *Entourage* and *Shameless* as its most popular form of entertainment, is it really desirable to be tried by a jury of one's so-called peers? Isn't the very idea of being tried by a jury of one's peers misleading? If Sarah had been tried by her peers, that jury would have been full of high school students, many of whom would probably also have had problems getting along with their parents. I, under such a system, would be judged by a jury composed of college professors and writers, which might not be ideal, but would surely be better than having my future decided by a group of people who can't wait to see the next installment of *Empire*! But even that would not be as harmful, I soon discovered, as enduring the kind of bias practiced by the judge who presided over Sarah's trial, Judge Luke Brown, who, among inmates at Camille Griffin Graham Correctional Institute, has the nickname of "Lukewarm Brown." He earned this nickname, I have been told, by being especially lenient with female offenders. Sarah, somehow, failed to stimulate the "lukewarm" response from Judge Brown, and this was something, also, that must be looked into. When Sarah was convicted, as a first offender, of armed robbery, Judge Brown gave her thirty years. She must serve 80 percent, twenty-six years, before she is released. She will be forty-two years old, older than her mother was when she died, when she gets out of prison in April 2025. For a judge known for his leniency to hand down such a sentence, there had to be something he knew that I didn't. Yet.

16

The Public Defender's Office Weighs In

I was warned, by various people who make the rounds of the legal circuit in Beaufort and Jasper Counties, "Oh yes, Gene Hood might *talk* to you all right, but he won't *tell* you anything."

"We'll see about that," was my reply, more often than not unspoken.

The Beaufort County Courthouse is a solid pile of sandstone block with a ribbed tin roof painted red, bleached, like everything else, by the sun. On Ribaut Road, just off Boundary Street, it stands in the midst of a government complex that includes the sheriff's office, the public defender's office, and the county detention center, where Sarah Nickel, John Ridgway, and Kevin Bergin were taken after their arrests. The parcel of land occupied by this collection of courtrooms, jail cells, and office buildings is bordered to the south and east by a marsh fed by the waters of Battery Creek. Standing in the parking lot looking out over the marsh, I had the sense that the site was chosen for security reasons. Like a medieval castle, it is protected from approach on two sides by water; one of the remaining sides is fortified by the presence of the sheriff's office, its parking lot a hive of activity, police cruisers arriving and leaving regularly.

I had come here to meet with Gene Hood, head of the public defender's office in Beaufort County, who agreed to represent Kevin Bergin shortly after Bergin's arrest for the murder of Nell Davis. I rendezvoused with Mr. Hood in a small conference room to the rear of courtroom number 2, on the second floor of the Beaufort County Courthouse. It's a place where defendants can go to speak with their lawyers in private before entering the courtroom, and during recesses. Standing across from me after we had shaken hands, waiting until I was seated before he sat down, Mr. Hood was the epitome of the gentleman-lawyer, a man who was born and bred to have the letters *esq.* follow his name. He conspicuously lacked the hint of southern, good-old-boy scruffiness that characterizes many of his colleagues. A former JAG officer who served as an aide to Colin Powell during the first Gulf War, Hood was sleek and polished, impeccably dressed in gray wool, white dress shirt with French cuffs, and a gold silk tie; gold, but somehow not at all gaudy, with a subtle crosshatched pattern woven into the cloth. His thick, wavy hair, black streaked with just enough gray to add gravity to his presence, was combed away from his tanned face. A massive gold ring set with a blue-green stone encircled the third finger of his left hand. The hand rested heavily on the table between us.

My first question concerned how someone accused of a crime comes to be represented by a public defender.

"Every child accused of a crime is automatically considered indigent and has the right to an attorney," Hood offered. I reminded him that Kevin Bergin was eighteen, and from a wealthy family. "It always goes back to the individual," he offered, then added, "their individual situation, regardless of family. The clerk of court's office determines whether or not they qualify." As it turned out, all three of the young people arrested for the murder of Nell Davis were referred to Hood's office. None of their families, not even John Ridgway's, who would later spend thousands on the most expensive PCR (postconviction relief) attorney in South Carolina, chose to hire an attorney at this time. It was up to Hood to decide which one he should represent. He couldn't take on all three, because they were each telling a different story. He told me that his decision to represent Bergin was based on a review of the statements and evidence. "I always take the most culpable, the trigger man."

When I asked why he does this, he explained that the other two defendants, whose stories were in conflict with that of his client, would have to be represented by a member of the local bar, selected and appointed by a circuit court judge. "I don't want to pass off a difficult criminal case to a lawyer who may not have much experience in that area," he told me, leaning forward, his hands clasped, fingers curled around that heavy gold ring. "I can take the heat; I don't bend easily to pressure, and the details of a case like this—which are pretty horrific, I think you must know—"

I affirmed my knowledge of the horrific details, as he continued telling me about how hard it is for some attorneys to work with people accused of particularly brutal or grotesque crimes. "The worst are crimes against children."

I gave a wordless nod, taking note of how calm and rational he was as he continued explaining the process to me. I soon realized that if I were accused of a horrendous murder, I would much prefer to have this man, rather than Brent Kiker, representing me—because Hood is, in addition to being essentially a gentleman, essentially no nonsense, a distillation of the qualities implied by these descriptors, as if all the nonessential emotional ambivalence that colors the perception of most human beings has been stripped away. A defendant represented by this man, I surmised, has little hope of deceiving his lawyer, but every reason to believe that he will get the best deal possible, considering the circumstances of his crime.

When describing the process of negotiating a plea bargain, Hood said, "You have to be the first to get to the well. The first to get to the well is the quickest to drink." He means that the first defendant who approaches the solicitor's office with something to give—in Kevin Bergin's case, the testimony that could help send Sarah Nickel to prison—is often the one who gets the deal. Hood had been the first to approach Randy Murdaugh's office, but Murdaugh must have known that the state needed more than the testimony of this young man, who, in his own statement to police, had confessed to the murder. So Murdaugh had made deals with both Ridgway and Bergin, but not right away; not, in fact, until just before Sarah Nickel's case was to be tried. Why did he wait so long? Was it just to let Ridgway and Bergin sweat it out?

The irony is that if Hood had taken Nickel's case, from the beginning, she may well have been the defendant who, under Hood's guidance, first approached the solicitor's office. Is it likely that Murdaugh would have considered a proposal from Nickel? Hood thinks so. He believes this because of the increasing trend toward making deals rather than taking cases to court. In 2005, he informed me, "99.9 percent" of cases in general sessions court were bargained out.

"This is why I can spend the afternoon talking to you, instead of arguing in court," he explained. "Of course, I could be playing golf with the judge," he added, not with the wink I have come to expect from lowcountry lawyers, but with a glint in his eye. It was more an appraisal of my reaction than a qualification of what he had just said. But I have to wonder, did Brent

Kiker, who had never even tried a criminal case before, know about these percentages? If he had would it have made a difference in the way he handled Sarah's case?

"Truthful testimony," Hood said, changing tack, "is essential to the deal."

"But how do you know what that is? How do you know who's telling the truth, when you've got three different versions?" I asked, having wrestled with this question almost continuously since beginning my research into this case.

"Who knows?' he answered, and his large palm, the one that still rested on the table, turned upward. "If a person contradicts himself, things he said in his previous statement, I have to tease out the truth, look at the facts, decide what makes the most sense."

"So what do you do if they still won't come around? If they insist upon a version of events that you know doesn't make sense?" I was thinking of Sarah's statement, of its inconsistencies.

"Well, I get to know them, you see, as part of the process. I let them see the state's case, explain the law and how the scenario will play out in court. Once they agree, if the other side [the solicitor] hasn't come to me, at that point, I go to them, say 'we're willing to do this in return for this punishment.' If the state accepts, we're on."

And that was exactly what happened, for Kevin Bergin and John Ridgway, even though the state took its time in making the acceptance official.

John Ridgway has told me that, from what he remembers, the original deal was for ten to fifteen years rather than the thirty he and Bergin eventually got. Gene Hood said, placing both palms flat on the table so that his fingers were splayed, the tips of his thumbs touching, "I negotiated a deal for that boy to testify against Sarah Nickel in exchange for thirty years. I never heard anyone say anything about ten or fifteen." Again there is the matter-of-fact tone. Again there is the emanation of self-assurance.

When I told Gene Hood I was somewhat surprised that the state was willing to let Bergin get off with thirty years for such a brutal crime, just on the chance that they might get Sarah Nickel convicted for murder, he informed me that, under South Carolina's Victim's Bill of Rights, Mike Davis would have had considerable input on that decision. He explained that this Victim's Bill of Rights became a part of South Carolina law in 1996 with an amendment to the state constitution. Because of this law, the prosecuting attorney is now required to, among other things, "discuss the case and meet about the disposition of the case." He paused to see if I was following. I nodded to indicate that I was. He continued. "For instance, the victim can say, 'I don't agree with the plea bargain.' The prosecution doesn't have to do what the victims want, but they will often go along because they don't want bad publicity, which affects reelection. But the key is notification. That's what's required by the law."

No matter what he said, and even though Mike Davis sat beside Randy Murdaugh at the solicitor's table throughout the trial, I still found it difficult to believe that Davis had agreed to Bergin's receiving thirty years in exchange for testifying against Sarah, based on what I knew about Davis. At least that is what I thought then. But then, at that moment, I didn't have all the facts.

Several years later, when I finally met Davis face to face, he gave them to me. This is what he said: "Rosalyn, Julie [Nell's mom], and I *never* knew they were going to give those boys a deal for thirty years. We never would have agreed to that. The first I heard about it was when I read it in the paper the next day."

I couldn't believe what I was hearing. Everyone had told me—everyone, that is, except Randy Murdaugh—that the only way Murdaugh would have agreed to let Kevin Bergin off with thirty years in exchange for testifying against Sarah was if Mike Davis and Julie Crowley, Nell's mother, had agreed. I guess *everyone* was wrong, including Gene Hood, who made the deal and who, along with numerous other local attorneys who also spoke with me about the case, assured me that Murdaugh would have consulted with the family of the victim to make sure that the plea was acceptable before going forward, particularly in a case like this. According to Mr. Davis, Solicitor Murdaugh did mention that there was going to be a meeting to discuss a plea, but not that Murdaugh's office was prepared to accept one. Perhaps it was just a misunderstanding. I'm sure that is what Murdaugh would say. Only he was still refusing to take my calls. So why did everyone else associated with the case assume that Davis had been consulted, and that he had agreed with the plea? Presumably because he had sat at the table with Randy Murdaugh throughout the trial. But then, where else was he going to sit?

■ ■ ■

Looking back on my conversation with Gene Hood, I realized that, in spite of giving me quite a lot of information, he had, indeed, told me very little of consequence. I realized, also, that whatever his reasons for selecting the so-called trigger man to represent in this case because he didn't want to pass off a difficult defense to a member of the local bar, in passing off Sarah Nickel's defense, he had done just that. Kevin Bergin's case, really, was relatively straightforward. He committed a murder to which he confessed within twenty-four hours, and, should he have decided to retract his initial statement, there was loads of physical evidence that would have guaranteed a conviction, had he chosen to stand trial. The truth about Sarah's participation, the degree to which she was culpable in her mother's murder, was much more nebulous, and teasing out the facts would have been arduous and time consuming, not at all suited to the temperament of a matter-of-fact, no-nonsense attorney like Gene Hood.

17

John's Birth Mother

I knew about Cindy Frasier (pseudonym), John's birth mother, because she had written to Sarah, a very intimate and articulate letter in which she described her own troubled past and how she and John had found each other after he was in prison. At the time she wrote the letter to Sarah, in November 2004, Frasier said that she and John had been in contact a little over a year and stated that he had brought great happiness into her life, while at the same time being painfully honest about his past. This perception of John Ridgway was fascinating to me, and I wanted to know more, so I wrote to Ms. Frasier, asking if she would be willing to share more of her impressions of her biological son. Like John Ridgway, I was an adoptee who had been reunited with my birth mother and had found the love and acceptance in that relationship that I never felt with my adoptive mother. It made me wonder about John's relationship with his adoptive parents.

Cindy didn't write back, but just a week or so after I had written her, my phone rang late at night, just as I was falling asleep. I rolled over and groggily picked it up. The caller identified himself as John Ridgway. Being half asleep I misunderstood him and thought it was a wrong number.

Fortunately I realized who I had on the line before I hung up. My first thought was, how is he calling me? I had been required to go through an application process before being approved as a telephone contact for Sarah, who had to call me collect through a prison operator. When John called it was just him on the line, asking to speak to me.

It turned out that he was calling me on an illegal cell phone that his birth mother had smuggled in to him during one of her visits. I can say this now without harming either of them because he was later caught with the phone, and punished by losing many of the privileges prisoners value so much, such as visitation, for an extended period. Cindy, likewise, was barred from visitation for a time.

When John called the first thing he told me was that everyone he knows has told him not to talk to me. He has some friends at the prison who have had books written about them, and the books haven't been very kind, which is no surprise. "Basically," he told me, "I don't want to set myself up to further the idea that I'm some kind of monster or demon."

I told him I don't believe he is a monster or a demon, either. I don't think it's possible to characterize anyone by a single word.

We talked for a while about the genre of true crime and how my book is different. I told him that I want this book to be about my search for the truth about what happened to Nell—about me processing the event of Nell's death, me trying to figure out not just what happened, but how, and why.

John said he could tell me why, or at least part of why, and he reminded me that, of the three of them—himself, Sarah, and Kevin—he is the one whose story has been the most consistent from day one. I had to agree with that, at least in part. Recently I had been comparing his testimony on the witness stand to his statement following the murder and had found that they are remarkably similar. They are also very detailed, another sign that he was telling the truth.

"What happened that day was NOT what was supposed to happen," John said firmly and went on to explain that Nell wasn't even supposed to be at home, that they thought Mike Davis would be there instead. (*As if, I am thinking, they would have preferred confronting Mike?*) John continued, insisting, "I would never hurt a woman, or let someone else hurt a woman."

I wanted to say, "But you did. You let Kevin hurt Sarah's mother, you stood there and held Sarah, hugged her according to your own statement." I also wanted to point out that, in his testimony, he had said Sarah told him

NOT to come to the house if her stepfather's blue truck was in the yard. His exact words had been, "Sarah told us that her stepfather has a blue truck, I believe, and [if] it was in the yard, not to go in. So it wasn't there. So we went in." So much for consistency. I didn't say anything, however, because I wanted him to keep talking, and I was afraid that if I contradicted him, he wouldn't.

"Well, what was supposed to happen?" I asked, believing that I already knew what he was going to say.

"It was just going to be a robbery, that's why we were wearing masks. Why would we be wearing masks if the victim was going to die? Have you been to the house?"

"Yes."

"Then you know how it is around there. It's out in the woods, nobody near the place. Nobody would've seen us. Why would we have needed to wear masks?"

In his statement he had said they wore masks in case there were witnesses. But it's true he had maintained, even in court, under pressure from the solicitor, that their aim in going to the Davis residence was to commit a robbery, not a murder. "We were all strung out on drugs," he said, almost as an afterthought.

"Were you strung out that day?" I asked.

"No. We hadn't smoked any crack for seventy-two hours."

I was amazed he could be so precise. Surely the number must have some significance, legal or otherwise.

John was quiet for a moment, then said, softly, "But she wasn't supposed to die. And it does kill me every day when I think of what happened. But I still don't understand what Sarah did. Why she went out of her way to ruin my life."

I was looking hard, reading between the lines, trying to find some semblance of the John Ridgway that his birth mother had come to know, but it was difficult. I needed to meet him face to face, so I could see how he looks when he says something like he just said. First, he claims that it "kills" him "every day" to think of what happened to Nell; then he immediately bemoans the way Sarah ruined his life. It is as if he played only a minor role in the series of events that led to Nell's murder. Yet if what he says about planning only to rob the house is true, I have to wonder why he just stood there and allowed his friend Kevin to bludgeon Sarah's mother to death. Surely, if anyone could have intervened, John would have been that person. In terms of sheer physical bulk, he is nearly twice the size of Kevin, and Kevin told police that he thinks of John as a brother.

As if he were reading my thoughts, John said, "Kevin just lost it. That's what happened with him sometimes. He went off on his dad one day at the Depot. When he did that kind of thing, he just snapped, nobody could stop him."

I was confused by his reference to a depot. Does he mean a train depot? Home Depot? I explained my confusion.

"It was teen hang-out in Connecticut, supposedly drug- and alcohol-free." He laughed. "That's a joke. Anyway, Kevin's dad came to pick him up, and he was really fucked up, drunk, doing mescaline, I don't know, maybe he'd dropped some acid. He attacked his dad like he was going to kill him. It took four or five grown men to pull him off."

There was some noise in the background, and I was told to hold on one second. When John came back to the phone, he said he had to go soon. We established a day and time for him to call back, and I hung up the phone, Ridgway's message to Sarah echoing in my mind. "Please tell her she has nothing to fear from me. I would never hurt a woman."

Ridgway's awareness that Sarah was afraid of him seemed to confirm what she had written to me in some of her letters about being afraid of John. Yet, as I would find out later, she carried on a regular correspondence with him, facilitated by his birth mother, Cindy, even though to do so was against prison rules governing inmate-to-inmate communication.

John also told me that he and Sarah had been sat down and talked to by Sergeant Woodward when they got picked up for being runaways the first time. So both of them had been blips on Woodward's radar screen, two teenage juvenile delinquents repeatedly getting themselves into minor scuffles with the law. Did Woodward's previous encounter with the two of them, his knowledge of their prior runaway attempts, predispose him to believe Ridgway's story when he came out of the woods, yelling that Sarah "knew everything?" Possibly, knowing they had a prior history of engaging in criminal activity while in each other's company, considering the nature of their first attempt at flight. This had occurred in November 1998, when they had stolen a car from Sarah's stepmother and also a gun from her father, and made it as far as Darien, Connecticut, before being picked up by police.

The scenario that resulted in Nell's murder, if you subtract the murder, is essentially the same: the theft of a car, the intended theft of firearms, a runaway attempt. An even stronger parallel between the two incidents emerges when one considers the near involvement of Kevin Bergin in the first runaway. On the outskirts of Darien, in their stolen vehicle, John and Sarah had run out of gas. John had hiked to a pizza parlor, Upper Crust Pizza, and called Kevin to bring them a can of gas. When John had returned to the car, he had found a police officer waiting there with Sarah. The officer, who had stopped to offer assistance, had already run the license number and was ready to take him and Sarah to the station for processing. By the time Kevin arrived at the scene, his friend was nowhere in sight.

So there is a pattern, one that is triangulated by Sarah's runaway attempt only ten days before the murder, when she robbed her sister's piggy bank and went, without permission, to John's house to see if he could help her score some drugs. When John's mother found Sarah hiding out in John's bedroom, she had sent the girl home, so there was no car involved, but there was theft—this time from the little sister that Sarah loved "so much."

Looked at objectively the pattern does much to implicate Sarah in the crime that cost her mother her life, with one exception. On none of these or other occasions when Sarah was taken into custody for her various delinquent acts did she willingly turn herself in, or go screaming to the police for help. And this, Sarah's abandonment of Kevin and John in a vehicle full of gas, suggests to me that she may be telling the truth about one thing: that she was not part of any plan to murder her mother, even if she was planning to steal the car and run away that day. She did not, after all, physically participate in her mother's murder: she did not buy or carry the murder weapons or protective gear, did not bludgeon, strangle, or stab, or even help move the body to its hiding place in the compost bin. Sarah's crime was in failing to protect her mother. The question that remains is, did she do this out of fear of John and Kevin, or was it simple acquiescence that her mother should die, coupled with an unwillingness to bloody her own hands with the deed? The person I was scheduled to meet with next, Amy Heath Albee, claimed to have been Sarah's best friend from the time they were small children. I could not expect Heath's account to be unbiased, but I thought it realistic to hope that she could give me some deeper insight into Sarah's character, insight that, coupled with other information that I was able to pull together, might help me to determine the degree of her involvement in her mother's murder.

Later, perusing the trial transcript, I would come across John's statement, when he was on the witness stand at Sarah's trial, that Kevin went back and stabbed Nell's body in the compost box, "to make sure she wasn't alive anymore." Had John realized, I wondered, how this statement contradicted the idea that they had no intention of committing a murder when they went to the house on Bellinger Bluff? Why on earth, if you weren't intent on murder, would you stab someone to make sure she wasn't alive? But maybe he didn't mean what it sounded like he meant. When I search the transcript for further clues, I find John's statement about "the plan" that was so important for implicating Sarah in her mother's murder. After admitting that his conversations with Nickel and Bergin had taken place separately, John had stated, "We had eventually just about made up a plan, basically, to get money and it involved Mrs. Davis. There was—there was a bunch of different plans. A lot of them. Some involved killing her whole family, some involved killing Ms. Davis. Some involved killing Mr. Davis. But we weren't—when we went there we weren't really—we weren't exactly—had a set plan. Anything could've really happened but we didn't intend for what happened to happen like it happened. If I'm making any sense." He isn't, really, making much sense because we don't know who made what plans (John and Sarah? John and Kevin?) If we believe John, we know only that it wasn't Kevin and Sarah because, according to John, they never spoke directly to each other.

Kevin's testimony would also contradict John's. At the very beginning of Solicitor's Murdaugh's direct examination, when he asked, "And why did you come down [to South Carolina]?" Bergin had answered, "Purpose to commit a murder." Of Sarah he said he had only spoken to her on the phone once, and all that he recalled her saying about their plans was "She didn't want the kids harmed." He said nothing about Sarah asking him to kill her mother, or even to attack her, though he did say that his friend John Ridgway had told him about Sarah, mentioning that the two of them had run away together before, and that there was a safe in the Davis house with $20,000 in it.

As I lay in bed, staring at the ceiling and wondering if I would be dreaming about Nell again, I pondered the broader significance of Sarah's various attempts at running away, thinking how fortunate it would have been for Nell had the young people on their way to Darien not run out of gas. Had they experienced what it is like to live without parental protection, without the guarantee of food, clothing, and a roof over their heads, maybe the experience would have enabled them to appreciate what they so obviously took for granted, and the people who provided it for them. Maybe, like the prodigal son of the Bible, John and Sarah could have returned home to make new lives for themselves. But that probably isn't what would have happened. Both John and Sarah have told me that they are glad they got arrested (though not that they have such long sentences) because each of them knows, without a doubt, that had their lives continued along the trajectory they were on when Nell was murdered, they, too, would most likely be dead.

Mama; or I Digress

Nearly every time I traveled to Bluffton, South Carolina, I also visited my mother in Augusta, Georgia, where Nell and I grew up. Mama, as I still call her, no longer inhabited the house of my childhood, at 416 Kemp Drive, but, at the time of this writing, had moved into a senior citizen's high-rise called Saint John Towers. Visits with Mama were not and never have been easy. Mama would always ask me why I don't go to church and would still tell me I'm going to regret it. Even though my cousin James had been dead for ten years, she would still ask me, back then, "Can you believe that James, a man as upstanding and righteous as he was, turned out to be a homosexual?" and we would have the usual discussion, which always concluded with a question that I found impossible to answer, not because I don't know the facts, but because the facts are not at all what she wants: "Would you please explain to me how two men have sex?"

What bothered me most about these visits were the similarities I discerned between our behaviors—not that I condemn my cousin James for his sexual orientation. I am talking about my mother's personality traits of egocentricity, cantankerousness, and stubbornness, which sometimes surface in my relations with other people.

One particular time, when I was at my mother's just after visiting Beaufort, we were having an especially rough time. This was partly due to the fact that my children and I were, at her insistence and because of my inability to say no, staying in her one-bedroom apartment rather than at a hotel. One night we had an argument in which she accused me of stealing a hideous pink-and-maroon crocheted afghan when we had moved her from her house into the apartment. It was a ridiculous argument, not least because we had had it several times already. Before bed that night, I wrote the following words in my journal:

I feel I want to videotape myself during my waking hours to ensure that I spend most of my time not acting like her. Why, why, why did I have to get stuck with this mother? She is a black hole of horror, an emotional vacuum, an intellectual zero. How can I keep up this charade?

When I read this now, I remember, in particular, when I visited my mom for three weeks in 1995 to help her while she recovered from knee-replacement surgery. Because I was there, in Augusta, staying at her house, she was able to come home from the hospital instead of spending two weeks in a rehabilitation facility. The second day she was home a physical therapist arrived to demonstrate and explain the exercises she would need to do to get the full range of motion back in her knee. When he had finished, he gave me some papers outlining the exercises that also provided helpful diagrams. As he did so, my mother, propped up in her bed and looking splendid in a new pink nightgown and bathrobe, told him, "You're wasting your time giving that to her. She can't read."

At the time I had recently finished a Ph.D. in literature and was working at my first job as a college professor. When the man hesitated, I told him not to worry, I would manage, and ushered him out of the house. Later during that same visit, after giving me her credit card to buy a few nice dresses for work, I found her sitting at the kitchen table one afternoon with a dark scowl on her face and a paper with a bunch of figures on it. Beside the paper was the collection of receipts she had asked me to bring her for my purchases. When I asked her what was wrong, she answered, "I'm just trying to figure out how much it's costing me to have you here."

Once when I brought my ten-year-old son and my new husband (second marriage) to her house to visit, she announced in the presence of both of them that I had been on birth control since high school, since I was "nothing but a whore." These were typical examples of my mother's behavior to me.

Why did I keep going back? Because she was my mother. What else could I do?

Yet I am forced to admit that, on several occasions, I have found myself feeling an unnamable, unbearable emotion, the almost imperative feeling that both of us cannot, simultaneously, continue to exist, sort of like Harry Potter and Lord Voldemort. I suppose we are all, to some degree, "horcruxes" of our parents, the living repositories of their desire for immortality. For some of us this can be a good thing. For me it certainly is not.

So yes, like Sarah Nickel, I too had hated my mother. I had even wished her dead. Yet at other times I felt an outpouring of sympathy for her. Is that love? While she was still alive, I observed her frustrations at getting old, at being unable to accomplish what were for me simple tasks, like getting down on my knees to see if I could find an earring that has rolled underneath her dresser. I realize that, beneath her tough, cantankerous exterior, resided a fragility she didn't want anyone, least of all me, to comprehend. Yet without asking for my help, that precious clip-on earring—so hard to find these days, when everyone, even one of her friends, had had their ears pierced—would have been forever lost. When I am able to step aside from the anger that has lodged itself deep inside me since childhood, I can still see my mother more than ever making the effort to reach out, to find some common ground between us. If I said I didn't want to watch *Wheel of Fortune* on her television, she would search for something we both might have enjoyed, like *The Jeff Corwin Experience* on Animal Planet. These were the moments I clung to, the ones that helped me get through the rest, and that kept me coming back to visit, to ensure she was OK, to find the jewelry she'd lost under the bed, to scrub the mildew off the air-conditioning unit in her bedroom, and to clean the floor that hadn't been thoroughly mopped since my last visit. And it was during these visits that, after she had gone to bed, I ransacked the boxes of old photos in her storage closet, gazing with absolute wonder at the pristine beauty of her nineteen-year-old face, innocent yet of the suffering that life would bring with the loss of two husbands, one to war, the other to ravaging disease, leaving her with a child that her second, terminally ill husband had insisted on adopting so that she wouldn't be alone after he died.

■ ■ ■

In a recent letter, Sarah wrote, "I am starting to realize just how much Mom and I are alike. It's almost like she lives in me and through me, if that makes any sense. I notice, on an almost daily basis, how our mannerisms, speech patterns, and thoughts are alike. I look in the mirror and see her, but it doesn't bother me like it used to. I even walk like her! I'm starting to get comfortable with who I am and what I'm capable of."

What I'm capable of.

This phrase haunts me and sends me back, because I am still unsure of what Sarah is capable of. She, like me, was capable of, at times, wishing her mother dead. She was capable of standing by and watching while someone else killed her mother. I want to believe I could not do that; that I would have had no choice but to try to help my mother, despite my hatred and despite my fear. Did Sarah have a choice, or was she, as she claimed, too afraid of Ridgway and Bergin to go to her mother's aid?

I do not, cannot believe that Nell was anything like my mother, yet a letter that someone, Sarah suspects Mike Davis, sent to her shortly after she was incarcerated—a letter in Nell's unmistakable handwriting—shows me that she was, in some ways, like my mother, and it gives me chills to read it. In that letter Nell chastises Sarah for her "hateful and disrespectful" behavior (though she does say that she loves her), insisting that if Sarah would only find the Lord, that is, Jesus Christ, all would be well, as if Christianity were some sort of magic pill or bullet (which I suppose for some people it is): "Jesus Christ is the answer Sarah! He will put LOVE in your heart and everything else will follow. Yes! I will try to cram it down your throat because it is the *way*." My mother tried to cram Jesus down my throat as well. As a result, today I am a Buddhist who deplores the violence and misogyny of the Bible. But that is just me. I didn't know, at the time, how Sarah felt about Jesus. Later I would learn that, although she participates in things like "praise dancing" (dancing to worship the Christian God), she is more drawn to Wicca and Buddhism. As for her mother's attempts to get her to become a Christian, she, like John and Kevin, had hated Christianity at the time of her mother's murder, believing it to be filled with hypocrisy and lies.

19

Sarah's Best Friend

I met Amy Heath Albee, Sarah Nickel's "best friend" for many years, including the time of her mother's murder, in the café of the sprawling Hilton

Head Barnes and Noble bookstore. When I had asked her, on the phone, how we would recognize each other, she had told me she would be the petite blond, the one who looks like she's about twelve years old. I suspected that her description was an exaggeration, but it wasn't. At first glance Amy did look like a preteen. She was doll tiny, beautiful in a delicate, miniature way, like a fairy or a sprite, infinitely breakable. If I were a man, I would be afraid to touch her.

Initially she seemed reluctant to discuss the case, or her friendship with Sarah, so we talked about books and writing, which is one of Amy's passions. She has been writing poems and stories since she was little, almost as long as she has been friends with Sarah, and she said she honestly can't remember when they weren't friends. She had brought a photo album with her, filled with black-and-white prints of her and Sarah as teenagers. My favorites were those in which they wear Sarah's frothy, elegant pageant dresses, ones her mom bought for her to participate in the annual beauty pageants held at Thomas Heyward Academy. The photos show them dancing, then sitting on the lawn at the Bellinger Bluff house. Their dresses billow around them as they hold teacups in the air, two Alices in Wonderland, one of whom, in less than a year, would go crashing through the looking glass.

In a soft voice with an even softer southern accent, Amy told me about the good times, the tea-for-two parties on the lawn, carefree days spent at the beach during the summers, and one escapade that for some reason sticks in her mind when, stranded at Sarah's house and bored with make-believe, she and Sarah had used a jar of pennies for cab fare to go to Walmart in Beaufort. It wasn't enough to get them all the way there, though, so they'd had to walk the last mile. I could just imagine the cab-driver's face when the girls pulled out all their pennies to pay him. That is probably why they had to walk the last mile. When I asked how the two of them got back home, she said they just waited for Nell to get off work and pick them up.

I told Amy that is just the kind of thing that Nell and I would do when we were teenagers, though we would have hitchhiked, most probably. That is how supervised we were in the summers, which is one reason I find it so strange that Nell and Mike tried to put so many restrictions on Sarah's activities when she was a teen. I guess Nell and I earned our freedom by making good grades during the school year. We also did not live in a small community where everybody knows everybody, so it is doubtful that we would have gotten ratted out for hitchhiking.

Amy testified for the defense at Sarah's trial, something her father, then a police captain, has never forgiven her for. Her testimony was important because it helped shed additional light on testimony provided by Lisa Pulice, a school social worker at Hilton Head High, who had been called by the prosecution. According to Pulice's testimony, Amy Heath had come to see her on October 11, nine days before the murder, to express concerns about Sarah. Pulice summoned Sarah to join them in her office, then asked Amy to repeat what she had told Pulice. During her testimony Amy noted that she was worried about Sarah, and, during cross-examination, it came out that her worry stemmed mostly from Sarah's drug use. When Amy had repeated, in front of Sarah, what she had told Ms. Pulice, Sarah had become increasingly upset, her emotions flaring when Ms. Pulice picked up the phone and proceeded to call Sarah's mother to come to school and pick her up. "She thought she was gone [*sic*] get in trouble," Heath had testified. "And she said to Miss Pulice that she was gonna kill us."

Pulice had interpreted this statement as a threat, directed to all of them—herself, Amy, and Sarah's mother, who was on the phone. For Amy it was just words, something Sarah said because she was angry, but that she had no intention of actually doing. When Kiker had asked, "Did you think she was gonna kill you?" she had answered, "No, not literally. No." But when Randy Murdaugh had asked if Sarah ever made any other threats against her mother, Amy had admitted that on several occasions, after Sarah and her mother had gotten into heated arguments, Sarah had said something like, "I wish I could kill her."

When I asked Amy if she ever thought Sarah meant, literally, that she wanted to kill her mother, she said no, never; it was just a remark anyone might make, "I'm gonna kill you," if they were "pissed off." And that she hadn't actually taken the words as any kind of real threat to herself. It was just, Amy said, "Sarah's big mouth. She was always saying things she didn't mean and she always got in trouble for it." Sarah's "mouth," and her propensity for making outrageous and provocative statements, was, in Amy's eyes, a way of getting attention. It was the same with her promiscuity. "Any girl wants that kind of attention from boys," Amy said to me. "Sarah just took it to the extreme."

At the trial Kiker tried to use Heath to establish the tenor of Sarah's relationship with her mother in the days leading up to the murder. When asked to describe her observations, Heath had stated that there was some arguing, but that it was "like very rational arguing. I don't recall them arguing right after—right before the murder. They were, I thought, getting along." When asked to elaborate on what led to this assumption, she had stated, "I think a couple of days before they had baked cookies. Together." She had also mentioned Sarah being allowed to go to football games and a trip she had taken with her mother and grandmother to their house in the mountains of West Virginia.

The mention of the house in West Virginia (it's actually in the western part of the state of Virginia, on the Blue Ridge Parkway, not in West Virginia) called up a myriad of memories, all of them lit with the hazy glow of a perfect vacation in the midst of a perfect summer. Nell and her brother Jay and I had driven up to the mountains in Nell's little red Mazda, almost garnering a speeding ticket in, of all places, South Carolina, though Nell was smart enough to talk the officer into taking cash instead of giving us a ticket, which she would have had to tell her parents about. The mountain house was located in a small town called Meadows of Dan, and whenever I hear the John Denver song "Country Roads," I think of it because it was "almost heaven." I remember walking across the hills in the high country of the mountains, through meadows of wildflowers, smoking the weed that we had brought with us, and then lying on our backs, watching the clouds go scudding by in the sky. I remember visiting Mabry Mill, a famous landmark of which the Crowleys had a small painting in their house. Nell loved the painting for the memories it revived in her and always said she hoped she could take me there one day. The weather in the mountains was perfect, sunny days and cool nights, and because it was blueberry season we gorged ourselves on the wild fruit—my first experience of wild blueberries. One day as we were hiking we came across a little graveyard encircled by cedars, where it was dark and cool and spooky on the inside. We found a series of small headstones, one for each of ten or twelve children, most of them dated about one year apart, bounded at one end by a larger one for their mother, who apparently died in childbirth, along with the last of her children. Such a tragedy, we thought. We were quiet for the rest of the day and did not indulge our penchant for getting high.

■ ■ ■

A key moment in Amy Heath's testimony came when she spoke of letters she received from Sarah during her detention at Midlands Reception and Evaluation Center in August 1999, a little over two months before the murder. In one of these letters Sarah had mentioned John Ridgway's upcoming trial, saying that "she and her mother were supposed to testify against him." The letter also stated that "Sarah was afraid to do that, and that she was afraid of John." The letter was dated August 5, 1999. When asked if she had ever heard Sarah speak of Kevin, Heath had said, "No, never," and when I asked her about this, and whether she knew of Sarah having a plan to run away, either by herself or with John, Amy insisted that there is no way Sarah could have been planning something like this without her knowledge, because Sarah told her everything.

Even though Amy's only crime was that of being friends with Sarah, and telling what she knew about Sarah's state of mind and behavior in the weeks preceding the murder, she suffered considerably for these things. When a photograph of her hugging Sarah at the trial appeared in one of the local newspapers, people at school had come up to her afterward, saying, "How could you hug someone who just killed her mother with those arms?" Heath told me it didn't matter that the jury hadn't found Sarah guilty of anything yet, nor would it matter when she was declared not guilty of murder. Most of the teens at Hilton Head High had already decided that she was guilty because, according to Heath, they didn't like her. "My boyfriend hated her," Amy said. "I remember him saying, 'You watch. One day something really bad is going to happen to that girl.'"

Heath's parents, who couldn't understand her decision to testify on Sarah's behalf, felt the effects as well, more acutely because of her dad's position as a police captain. "Before the trial happened, Solicitor Murdaugh used to have dinner at our house all the time," Amy told me. "He and my dad were good friends. Since the trial, he hasn't been back. Not that I know of, anyway." She doesn't know whether her father suffered professionally because of what she did. He's retired now and doesn't wish to discuss it.

It's problematic when a long period of time, in this case more than a year, elapses between a crime and the trial. Witnesses' memories aren't always crystal clear. Of particular concern is the precise timing of events. Another friend of Sarah's who testified for the defense was Mistee McClain, a girl who claimed to have attended an awards banquet at Hilton Head Medical Center with her mom on the Saturday before the murder, which would have been October 15. Sarah, she said, was there with her mom, and the two girls made plans for the following weekend. "Either I was gone stay the night at her house or she was gone stay the night at my house. Like me and her and Amy were gone go like see a movie or something like that. We really—I mean all we really made plans for was to stay at each other's houses and we never really discussed what we were gonna do." Mistee's testimony was refuted by the last witness called by the state, a man named Stephen Campbell who lived in Ridgeland and worked at Hilton Head Medical Center. Solicitor Murdaugh simply asked him about the date of the awards banquet referred to in McClain's statement. Campbell answered that it took place on the twenty-fifth of September, and not the weekend before the murder, effectively destroying McClain's credibility.

When I asked Amy about John Ridgway, she told me he stood out at Hilton Head High for being on the edgier side of strange, wearing eyeliner, having his tongue and eyebrow pierced, being into gothic and death metal music. He wasn't the only kid into that stuff, but he stood out somehow, maybe because he was smart, maybe because he came from Connecticut and seemed like an outsider among outsiders. Other kids were a bit spooked by him; Sarah seemed to be mesmerized. Amy assumed it was a chemical romance. Ridgway was known for smoking crack. As for her own personal experience of John, Amy says she didn't know him that well, even though I know she writes to him in prison, or at least he says she does, and it was from him that I first got her address.

Someone who did know John well, if only in a clinical setting, was one of the witnesses Brent Kiker called, a child and adolescent therapist named Beth Wilson. Wilson had evaluated John Ridgway in September 1999, following the incident where he had cut a boy's arm in his vocational school cooking class. Kiker noted that "she expressed concerns in her report about John Ridgway's tendency to blame others for his actions." In response Judge Brown humorously confessed that in his fifty years of experience he "don't never have a client, practicing law, or a person standing up right there who doesn't blame somebody. Most of the time it's just I got with the wrong people but, you know, most everybody says I'm not really to blame."

Ridgway's attorney, Scott Lee, objected to Wilson's testimony based on client-therapist privilege. The judge decided to let the information go into the public record, yet it wasn't made accessible to the public until after the trial was over.

A mental health counselor with twenty-two years of experience in the field, Wilson received John Ridgway's case through referral from the Collaborative Organization for Services for Youths (COSY), a county agency that serves as a resource for case managers who are having difficulties with certain cases or clients. Wilson stated that she received documentation of

Ridgway's mental health information and affirmed her belief that she had sufficient contact with John to be able to form an opinion as to a diagnosis of his condition.

She explained that his previous diagnosis of "depression" complicated by "drug and alcohol abuse" was augmented, in collaboration with a physician who examined the young man, with the supplementary diagnosis of "conduct disorder," which she defined as "a juvenile disorder that basically violates the rights of others. It either involves intimidation of others, running away from home in a chronic manner, breaking the law, [or] doing a variety of things that fit a certain criteria within a certain amount of time."

When asked about the basis of the diagnosis, she explained that the criteria are based on the *DSM-IV*, shorthand for the *Diagnostic and Statistical Manual,* and stressed that "it is a repetitive and persistent pattern of behavior that violates the basic rights of others . . . manifested by the presence of three or more of the following criteria in the past twelve months, with at least one criteria present in the past six months: aggression to people and animals, police threats, intimidates others; two, often initiates physical fights; three, has used a weapon that can cause serious physical harm to others; four has been physically cruel to people; five, has been physically cruel to animals; six, has stolen from a victim." This was the same diagnosis Kevin Bergin had received during his hospitalization at Stamford Hospital following the attack on his father at the Depot.

At issue was the question of Ridgway's, in Judge Brown's words, "tendency to provide excuses for himself." The judge asked Wilson if she could recall "a particular example where John Ridgway gave an excuse for his misconduct."

"There was an incident that was alleged at the school where he allegedly carved something into another person's arm as well as his own and there was a minimization of that behavior, that it was no big deal, the other kid wanted him to do it. Just a lot of excuses."

The incident Wilson refers to here is in addition to the cutting incident that took place only eight days before Nell was murdered, on October 12, 1999. This second incident occurred at Beaufort-Jasper Academy for Career Excellence. This time Ridgway was arrested and charged with "assault and battery of a high and aggravated nature," in addition to possession of a weapon on campus but nevertheless was released into his parents' custody. These and other pending charges, such as the grand and petty larceny charges accrued during his previous runaway attempt, were dropped as part of the deal he made with the state to testify against Sarah Nickel. When I had asked Ridgway about the incident during one of our telephone conversations, he had told me that the kid dared him to do it. Even if he had, the fact that Ridgway carried out the threat, and was charged with such a serious offense, lends credence to the idea that he was, once again, engaging in this "tendency to provide excuses for himself."

I can't help wondering what effect Beth Wilson's testimony could have had on the jury in Sarah's trial, had they been given the opportunity to hear it. One remark of Wilson's struck me more after I had had the opportunity to get to know John Ridgway through conversations and letters, and to meet him face to face at Broad River Correctional Institution. It was Wilson's emphasis on one specific behavior, when Judge Brown asked her to state why she came up with the conduct disorder diagnosis for "this particular person."

Wilson answered, "The intimidation of others, often manipulating or lying or cunning to obtain favors or avoid allegations."

I would soon get to experience firsthand the experience of being intimidated by John Ridgway.

20

"A modern day Svengali"

Once I had begun to get to know John Ridgway and Sarah Nickel, something curious happened. The pervasive sense of dread that had, for months it seems, become my constant companion, pursuing me through my days, making my heart race, my palms sweat, my face flush with heat and color— driving me to become more and more dependent on Ambien for sleep— vanished. Although I had said I never believed it was fair to describe a person with a single word, such as "freak" or "monster," I'm not sure I really believed it until I'd gotten to experience two people who had been labeled as such, but who are, really, along with Kevin Bergin, complex human beings, who, over the course of their lives, have done both good and evil. The sense of relief I felt was darkened, though, by a shadow that I soon recognized as grief. Nell is still dead, and she always will be; her children, Sarah included, will never have their mother again. The youngest, Haley, will hardly remember her.

Grief is different from anxiety, a healthy rather than an unhealthy emotion. The process of grieving can in fact alleviate anxiety, but grieving is hard, painful work, and it's much easier, for a lot of people, to settle for the simpler, more immediately satisfying emotion of anger. Anger makes it easy to label people, to call them "demons" and "freaks," to say that they *are* evil, rather than to acknowledge the more complex fact that they have done evil.

John Ridgway and I had several more telephone conversations in rapid succession, and I began to understand why Woodward felt he was telling the truth, at the same time that I had comprehended Sarah's description of him as a "modern day Svengali." He answered all my questions, almost never hesitating in his response. He was intelligent, charming, even witty, but some of the things he talked about were, I will admit, vaguely disturbing. When I asked him to describe the sound of Cradle of Filth, one of his favorite bands, he said, "It's like listening to a horror movie. I don't mean it's like the soundtrack of a horror film. But if the images were sounds instead of pictures." He also appeared to be obsessed with people who have committed horrendous crimes, like Melinda Loveless, one of the teenage participants in the murder of twelve-year-old Shanda Sharer, who was tortured and burned to death in Madison, Indiana, back in 1992; and Crystal Sturgill, one of six teens involved in the 1997 so-called Satanist murder of Jehovah's Witnesses in eastern Tennessee. He corresponds with Loveless and says of her, "Mel doesn't talk much about her case. I've talked to her intimately for years. She's a college graduate training dogs and has a huge heart!" Of Shanda's murder he says, "It was a senseless crime that started with an entirely different idea. It went haywire, too far." Perhaps, I can't help thinking, he finds Loveless and her deeds compelling because of his own "senseless crime" and the way that it "went haywire." Or perhaps he, like me, is searching for the humanity in people who have committed such crimes.

When I talked to John's birth mother, Cindy Frasier, she told me how much grieving John has done over the past few years, how far he has come, how much he has changed since he was arrested on October 20, 1999. But what I want to know right now is not how far he has come, but how he got to where he was on October 20, 1999.

The second time we talked, I asked John how he started down the path that led to his virtual self-destruction.

"I did OK until I was ten years old. Then I started getting really angry." He told me he has no idea why he became so angry, but then recalled that it was around the same time that he found out he was adopted. Having been adopted myself, I believe I know exactly what he's talking about—the anger, the feeling that you don't know where it's coming from.

"Yeah," he continued, "so my parents took me to psychiatrists; they said I was depressed, bipolar, you name it. As I got older I just stopped caring about anything, about school, whatever."

Latching onto the adoption theme, I asked John if he felt alienated from his parents. I knew this wasn't a fair question, at least it was not fair for me to assume that adoption can be a predictor of teen or preteen alienation, but I can't help it. I've been there myself, and the son of a close friend, also adopted, was there right now, feeling, in his own words, that he's "in the wrong family."

John said yes and no. "My mom and I have always been tight. She's always been there for me. My dad and I were polar opposites back then. He'd fought in Vietnam, got straight As in school, did everything right. We didn't see eye to eye on anything."

"What about now?"

"Now? Now he's great. He's totally supportive, you know what I mean? And now I can see where he's coming from. They've been paying for me to take classes through the university extension at Ohio State. They buy me books, magazines, anything I need, basically."

Since our conversation seemed to be slipping fairly easily back and forth between past and present, I asked him again about Kevin. "How did you and Kevin become friends? Your testimony talks about how close you were . . ."

"Like brothers," John said, finishing my sentence for me. "Yeah. We met when I lived in Connecticut. I was hanging out with a group of weird kids, metal kids—you know, ones who like listening to heavy metal. We hung out at this place called "the Pits" over in Darien. It was this like broken-down area with abandoned buildings, a factory; no one lives there anymore, and kids would go there to get alcohol, drugs, whatever. Kevin was there, and we started talking, partying together, and then we found out we were both adopted from the same place in Texas, the Gladney Center, and both somehow ended up in Darien, Connecticut. I guess that's what drew us together."

One of the issues we discussed was the theory, presented by Brent Kiker, Sarah's defense attorney, that Kevin Bergin came to South Carolina to commit a murder so that he could perform the necromantic ritual that would enable him to become one with the Angel of Death. Even though John wasn't accused of taking part in this ritual, he is concerned because of its association with the case, and, as he said before, he doesn't want to be portrayed as a "freak" or "demon" anymore.

According to John, the solicitor's office was the first to introduce the idea of black magic and its involvement with the case when they had met with him during the initial stages of the investigation, while he was locked up at Beaufort County Detention Center awaiting trial.

"Randy Murdaugh wanted to make it sound like it was all some kind of cult thing involving all three of us and resulting in some crazed, insane satanic murder."

"And it wasn't?"

"No!"

"But what about the books, incense, and other paraphernalia?"

For the first time, he didn't directly answer my question but steered me in a different direction.

"OK. You've heard of Anton LaVey?"

"No."

"*The Satanic Bible*?"

No again.

"*The Devil's Notebooks*?"

It began to dawn on me who he was talking about. I had this vague memory of a Discovery Channel (or was it the Travel Channel?) show that investigated a site associated with Anton LaVey, whom, I now recalled, was referred to as the founder of something called the Church of Satan.

"So yeah, we were into that, but not into any kind of devil-worshipping thing, OK? LaVey's deal was that there is no god or devil, there's only yourself, you should be your own god. Do your own thing, basically. I am not into that anymore. Basically, now, I'm a Buddhist."

"Compassion and all that," he said, after a pause. "Karma—it really makes sense." (Most recently, John has informed me that he is practicing Anti-Cosmic Gnosticism/Chaos Gnosticism.)

"OK," I said, "But what about this book, the *Necromantic Ritual Book,* which describes having sex with dead bodies?" I asked, looking back over my notes to confirm that this was indeed the title.

"I don't know about that. That book belonged to Kevin. But I will tell you this. Kevin told me everything about everything. We had absolutely no secrets. And he never said anything about planning any ritual." There was a long pause and then a high-pitched "Kevin?" John's voice was drowning in incredulity. "He's *incapable* of forming and carrying out that kind of plan. When he killed Mrs. Davis it was just like when he attacked his dad. Impulsive. Freaky."

"So do you have any contact with him now?" I asked, hoping I could get an update on how Kevin Bergin had fared the last six years in prison.

"Well, in 2002 I think it was, he had a conversion experience. Now he's a Christian."

"Interesting," I said, understanding that becoming a Christian is one way to cope with the guilt that must arise from the memory of what Kevin did to Nell Davis. *Washed in the blood of the Lamb.* The phrase came back to me from my Southern Baptist childhood. I imagined the blood of Christ acting as a kind of spiritual Spray 'n Wash, washing away Nell's blood, leaving nothing behind but forgiveness and the promise of salvation after death.

John cleared his throat, reminding me that I was wasting precious time. I tried to collect my thoughts, remember where we were.

"OK, so what *was* Kevin thinking was going to happen when you went to the Davis house that day?"

"Same as me, far as I know. A robbery."

"But why did he testify that he went there to do a murder? That's what it says, right there in the transcript. Murdaugh asks Kevin how long he'd been in the area, and then, 'Why did you come down?' Kevin answers, 'For this purpose.' Murdaugh says, 'What purpose?' Kevin answers, 'Purpose to commit a murder.' Why did he say that if the purpose, his purpose, was armed robbery?"

It took a while for John to answer this one. He sighed heavily. "I don't know. I honestly don't know. It wasn't like that."

Then what was it like? I would ask, but he'd already told me, and the police, and the jury, and plenty of other people, no doubt, so he was not likely to say anything different now. So I said, "At Sarah's trial, during his cross-examination of you, Brent Kiker made a big deal of the fact that you and Kevin would not be sentenced until after Sarah's trial, that your sentencing was deferred, I believe was the word he used. He said this was unusual, because when a defendant pleads guilty, the judge typically hands down a sentence when the plea is entered."

"Yeah, I remember that."

"Well, it seemed to me that he was trying to make the point that unless your testimony satisfied Randy Murdaugh's own notion of truth, then there would be hell to pay, so to speak."

"Well, yeah, the deal was if I didn't testify truthfully, we'd start all over. I'd go to trial, and he'd seek life in prison."

"So did Murdaugh ever seem to be trying to engineer the truth, if you know what I mean?"

"No." John sighed heavily, then continued. "He never told me what to say. But I can't speak for Kevin."

Now that we'd opened up the topic of the plea-bargain agreement, John had just one more thing he wanted to tell me.

Without being terribly harsh toward Scott Lee, the attorney who handled his case, John did express his belief that Lee misled him, almost as if he were acting in concert with the solicitor's office. "He gave me the impression I was going to get twelve to fifteen years. That's the figure he kept throwing out. Twelve to fifteen years. It didn't sound great, but it was better than going to trial and facing life. Then, when I talked to Murdaugh face to face, he said he didn't care how much time I got—it could be five years, or it could be fifty—as long as the victim's family was satisfied."

It was nearly time for evening count, so John had to get off the phone. As I hung up, I thought, not for the last time, how I wished I could talk to Kevin Bergin and hear his side of the story.

21

Father's Day at Broad River

In a letter that he sent to me just after my visit, John Ridgway reminded me that his parents, his birth mother, his lawyers, and everyone else who cares about him had advised him not to write to me, speak to me, or to allow me to visit him. "But I did," he wrote, "because I felt that I had nothing to hide."

We talked several times on the phone in the weeks leading up to my visit, planning things out. His birth mother, Cindy Frasier, was flying in from Texas, as eager to meet me as I was to make her acquaintance. John's parents, Tom and Nancy Ridgway, were more cautious but, John assured me, would also make an appearance—at least his dad would. His mom was more, as he called it, "spooky," uncertain of the visit's outcome, not sure she wanted to be a part of something that, in her opinion, was certain to do more harm than good. Meanwhile Cindy and I had been in contact by both phone and email, and the two of us had decided to get together for coffee beforehand at a Ruby Tuesday's not far from the prison. Cindy felt that this would give her a chance to fill me in a little on John's biological background and, as I later discovered, help to prepare me, and John, for what was to come.

Cindy gave birth to John when she was thirteen years old and estranged from her own family. When we met she was in her midthirties, small of stature, her head adorned by a mass of brown curls stiffened by too much hairspray. Her soft, girlish voice had a charming Texas drawl, and there was something about the way she tipped up her chin, or sighed at the end of every other sentence that recalled the spirit of that thirteen-year-old, still wishing she'd had the guts or the wherewithal to keep her baby, even though she never could have provided him the material comforts that he enjoyed growing up with Tom and Nancy Ridgway. The Ridgways, she told me, have been wonderful, welcoming and treating her like one of the family.

Cindy and John "found" each other after he had been incarcerated, and they developed a very strong bond. They had both been diagnosed with bipolar disorder, and Cindy, unlike John, was taking medication to keep her moods under control. She told me that despite the medication, or perhaps because of it, she has terrible nightmares as well as visions. A particularly terrifying one was of her grandmother, beheaded. While Cindy and I were talking and fending off a waiter who appeared determined to take our order for lunch, her cell phone rang. It was John, who, Cindy had told me, was terribly anxious about the visit. She told me he wanted to speak to me and handed me the phone. When I answered he asked me how I was doing, and I told him fine, though I confessed to being a little nervous, hoping to put him more at ease. I soon discovered, however, that the source of his anxiety was, at least for the moment, his parents.

"They had better behave themselves," he asserted, his voice taking on a strange, breathless quality I hadn't heard before. I was surprised for a moment, mostly because the John I had come to know through our previous phone calls, and, mostly, through his letters, had seemed so calm and self-confident, so sure of himself. And if he was sure of anything other than himself, it was the integrity and trustworthiness of his adoptive parents, whom he referred to as "my whole heart and life." His concern about their prospective behavior at the visit seemed strange and out of character, particularly as he continued talking about it, his vehemence verging on a rant. When I got off the phone and asked Cindy about it, she said, "John's just like that. He likes to be in control. You'll see."

I would soon find out just how much of an understatement that was.

We drove over to the Broad River Correctional Institution in our separate cars. Cindy was joined by her roommate, a big-boned blond named Michelle, who wore a black Lynyrd Skynyrd shirt with a skull on it. The skull would soon cause us difficulties when we attempted to enter the prison.

One of South Carolina's maximum-security prisons for male offenders, BRCI provides a stark contrast to Camille Griffin Graham, where Sarah Nickel is incarcerated, less than a mile away. The entire complex is surrounded by a high chain-link fence reinforced with coils of razor wire woven through in layer on layer to create an impenetrable barrier. Everyone who enters the prison must pass through a gatehouse/control room complex whose areas are subdivided by heavy, electronically secured metal doors. The dormitories and other buildings are some distance away, at the perimeter of the compound. Some of the newer buildings—dormitories by their appearance—are two stories high with tall narrow windows that reminded me of arrow slits built into the walls of medieval castles. They are constructed of cinder blocks and have corrugated metal roofs, painted green.

For security reasons visiting hours at the men's prison were restricted to Saturday and Sunday afternoons only, beginning at 12:30, and there were very strict rules about what visitors could bring and wear into the prison. No sleeveless shirts, shirts that expose midriffs or cleavage, miniskirts, excessively tight clothing such as spandex leggings or tops, or any other clothing deemed "inappropriate" might be worn, including shirts with skulls. Michelle had to turn her t-shirt inside out to hide the skull. Additional restricted items included jewelry, with the following exceptions:

one religious medallion on a necklace or chain, one wristwatch, one pair of earrings, and a medical alert bracelet.

Visitors were permitted to bring their driver's license for identification, up to $15 in cash (none of which might be given to an inmate but was for use only at vending machines during the visit), a small clear plastic wallet or change purse, one set of keys, an epinephrine injector with a doctor's notarized, written authorization, and sippy cups for toddlers, although these were also required to be clear plastic.

In the parking lot, Cindy and I were joined by Tom and Nancy. Tall and slim with wheat-colored hair and ruddy cheeks, Tom wore khaki trousers and a plaid madras shirt. Nancy was petite and wore her curly, white-blond hair in a bob. The classic lines of her clothing exhibited what my mother would call "style," and a sleeveless blouse looked good on her, even though she was in her fifties. She was pretty in a surprisingly girlish way. True to John's prediction that she would be more nervous about talking to me, Nancy hung back, hesitating, while Tom came forward, smiling grimly, extending his hand with the air of a salesman determined to make the best of a bad situation. As we stood in line waiting, though, things loosened up a bit. Tom was nervously talkative—simultaneously friendly, inquisitive about what I was writing, curious about my take on Sarah, and worried over what I was going to say about John. I tried to respond to all his questions at once by explaining that I started writing this book to answer my own questions: to find out what happened and why. Once I find out, I said, I just want to tell that story.

Once we discovered that Nancy's sleeveless blouse wouldn't pass muster with the lieutenant, we had to go back outside and wait for her to run to Family Dollar to buy a t-shirt. The long line of visitors waiting to be checked in inched past us. Most of the visitors were black, reflecting the racial composition of the prison population. Many of them were also wearing suits and dresses and, I surmised, had come directly from church services. Nearly everyone was subdued and polite.

As we stood with sweat dripping off our faces, broiling in heat that must have topped one hundred degrees at least, Tom told me he was a former vice president of marketing at L'Oreal, which is where he worked when they lived in Darien, Connecticut. He would ride the train into NYC every day and traveled to Paris a lot on business. During that part of John's life, Tom wasn't around as much as he would like to have been, and that may be why, I suppose, he and Nancy now found themselves asking themselves what any parent would be asking: "What could we have done? How did we fail John?" Tom literally voiced these questions.

When he had turned fifty-one, Tom decided to make a major change in his life. He told me he wanted more job security and independence, as well as more time to spend with his kids. (John has a younger brother, also adopted.) This was why they moved to Hilton Head in 1998, and bought the business they now owned, Hilton Head Rentals and Golf, which specializes in vacation home and villa rentals. It was weird, Tom said, to be fifty-one and starting over, saying, essentially, "OK, now what do I want to be when I grow up?" He paused in his story because Nancy had returned with her t-shirt, a plain white Hanes. We moved to the head of the line, inside the air-conditioned building, where our sweat instantly congealed. Behind us the heat rose in waves from the black asphalt pavement. The prison, for a moment, had become our refuge.

At security check-in, we had to show our driver's licenses, walk through a metal detector twice, after which we were allowed, in groups of three, to enter a sally port, a long walkway facing a glassed-in area where several officers stood and scrutinized us as we passed, holding up our IDs as we walked by. We then stood to wait at another radio-controlled door, which, when it opened, admitted us onto a covered breezeway recently planted with petunias and spiky purple heart. This led to yet another locked door, where we waited for the camera mounted above the door to register our arrival. Finally we were admitted to a hallway where a guard directed us to the visitation room. We were assigned to tables 32 and 33. Two inmates pulled the tables together for us, and we sat down to wait for John.

The room was quite large, the size of a small gym, and I found myself wondering if that was its usual function. While we were waiting I noticed that the color scheme there was different from CGGCI, where they favor forest green for the trim and chairs, and the whitest white for the walls. The walls at Broad River were also white, while the trim was gleaming brown (Crayola brown). Two of the walls displayed murals painted by inmates. One of the scenes imparted a peaceful, rural ambience: a sailboat docked at a boathouse beside a lake. On another wall two sunbursts flung antic rays of color into the room. The chairs we were given to sit in were maroon molded plastic, like the cheap patio chairs you can find at Home Depot or Lowe's, rather than the sturdier metal-legged ones they have at CGGCI. Immediately I realized that these chairs would be less lethal when thrown or otherwise used as a weapon. The floors at BRCI were covered with ceramic tile in a color between gray and taupe, rather like the color of dirt in this region of South Carolina.

When John came in, the first thing I noticed about him was his size. Although he is six feet tall, two inches shorter than his father, he has an imposing physical presence. He had told me he works out with weights every day, and his heavily tattooed arms were three times the girth of mine. His head was shaved, and his deep-set eyes seemed to bore into mine when they were not restlessly scanning the visitation room or locking onto the faces of his other visitors. He had a moustache that was coming in gray, and his face was thinner, had more definition than it did in his photographs, so that he was more attractive, physically, in person, than in his photos. The tattoos covering his arms included a beautiful woman with swirling hair, several hideous clowns, the names of his parents and his brother, and, on his hands, a Templar emblem signifying the five elements (earth, air, fire, water, and spirit), surmounting a symbol of eternity. He had gotten all these tattoos while incarcerated—either at Beaufort County Detention Center, or at BRCI. This is one of the ways that inmates entertain themselves, as well as a minor way of bucking the system, since tattooing is against prison regulations. It's only minor, however, as long as the inmate doesn't contract hepatitis, or worse, from a contaminated sharp. Both hepatitis and AIDS are rampant in South Carolina prisons, and dirty needles and unprotected sex are the two ways they are transmitted from one inmate to another. John wore the same color and style of SCDC uniform that Sarah had worn— pale khaki with the black SCDC letters across the back and the stripe down the leg, plus a t-shirt underneath.

After hugs and greetings, Cindy and Michelle were dispatched to the vending machines to purchase sandwiches, chips, and drinks. The rest of us sat down and began talking about music because it was a comfortable topic and everybody was nervous, especially John. Music is John's great love, and it is his dream to own a music store when he gets out of prison. For Father's Day, he had given Cindy instructions on burning, for his dad, a CD of songs recorded by the Doors between 1962 and 1971, and now he wanted to know how his dad liked it, and of course Tom loved it, even though, he now confessed, he had listened to the Beach Boys all the way to Columbia. Father and son exchanged wry glances about their different tastes in music (though Tom does really like the Doors), and John proceeded to tell me a story about how his dad once accompanied him to a Marilyn Manson concert when they were still living in Connecticut.

"Marilyn Manson?" I asked, unable to conceal my surprise, wondering if he wore his golf khakis and madras shirt.

"Yes," Tom began, a blush showing through his pale complexion, "I had been working such long hours, you know, and I was really feeling like I was getting out of touch with John. I had always liked music myself, and I realized, hey, John likes music, this is something we have in common, so maybe if I go to a concert with him it will help us reconnect. I felt like I was becoming an old fogey, and I didn't want to be that, so I asked him to get me a ticket and . . ."

John interrupted, "And you should have seen him." John gave his dad a sidelong glance, smirking, before he continued. "He was pretty uncomfortable at first."

"Well, yes, I was uncomfortable," Tom confessed. "I had no idea what I was getting into."

"But by the end of it, he was getting into it just like everybody else, had his hand in the air, making the sign, pumping it up." John raised his own hand, making a gesture commonly seen at heavy metal and rock concerts that generically means, "Rock on!"

Tom lifted his hand, pinkie and forefinger raised, his thumb holding the other two bent to his palm, mimicking his son, smiling fondly at the memory. But then John recalled the sign's darker meaning, and its association with the occult. "Hail Satan," John said, teasing, extending the joke, then added, "Yeah, but you didn't know."

His father grinned sheepishly, lowered his hands back into his lap.

By now Cindy and Michelle had returned, their arms overflowing with food. There were two steak hoagies, one chicken-fried steak sandwich, three bags of chips, three bags of M&M cookies, and a soda for each one of us. All the food was put into a mound in the middle of the tables. Conversation stalled for a moment, and I took the opportunity to ask John about his daily routine. Sarah had told me that life is much harsher for the men. John's answers contradicted her information.

According to John the atmosphere at BRCI was, generally, very laid back. There were two men to a room, each of which had a sink and a toilet. Rather than being woken up by a blinding light shining in their faces at 5:30 A.M., the men simply had their doors unlocked. They could go to breakfast or not. They could report for work, or not. They could sleep in all day if they so desired. John said he sleeps until lunch, then works out in the gym, socializes on the yard, has dinner, and plays Dungeons and Dragons until it's time to get locked in for the night. In his cell he reads or listens to music, or writes letters into the wee hours of the morning. Because he had earned the privilege by six months' worth of good behavior, and his parents supplied him with the money, John's identification badge had a tag on it that said "Hobbycraft," which indicated that he was permitted to purchase arts and crafts supplies. He used these supplies to create homemade greeting cards. The back of each one bore the legend, "Just for you." This was another way that he passed the time.

Cindy was eager to ask me about Sarah, and why I thought she had lied about her involvement in the plan to rob her mother.

This was a hard question for me to answer, because I didn't, at that point in time, know for sure if she had lied or not. The only people who really knew were Sarah and John, and maybe Kevin, and they all three had told different stories. I responded, "If Sarah is lying, I think she has told herself the same story for such a long time now that she believes it is the truth. I can tell you this. I don't believe she intended for her mother to be killed that day."

Tom and Nancy nodded in agreement. Nobody at that table wanted to believe that Nell Davis was meant to die that day.

After a while the conversation drifted toward Tom and Nancy again, and when I began asking Tom more questions about his career change, and what inspired him to choose Hilton Head, an odd thing happened. John started leaning across the table and inserting his head into my line of vision. On his face was an odd grimace. Since John obviously wanted my attention, I began asking the questions I had come there to ask—questions about the case, so that I could see his expression when he answered, something that wasn't possible when we talked on the phone or when he answered my questions in his letters.

When he and Kevin Bergin had testified at Sarah's trial, one essential difference in the story that they told the court concerned what they intended to do when they went to the Davis home at 31 Bellinger Bluff on the afternoon of October 20, 1999. John had said the plan was to disable Nell Davis and rob the household safe. Kevin had said that, from the very beginning, from the time that he even planned to come down to South Carolina, the main purpose was to commit a murder. I had already asked John about this on the phone and in a letter, and he had given me the same answers he gave in his statement and in court. So on this day, when I could see his reaction, I asked John a slightly different question: "Why did Kevin came to South Carolina to meet you, instead of meeting you in Detroit? Or just staying put until you all got wherever you were going?"

"Kevin didn't want to go back to rehab," John told me, clasping his hands together and planting them on the table in front of him. "I told him I had a ride. We were going to head out together."

The bit about not wanting to go back to rehab seemed an odd reason to travel all the way to South Carolina before heading back north, until I remembered that neither Kevin nor John had known how to drive. In one of our previous conversations, John had told me that Kevin had taken the train to South Carolina.

"And why did you want to leave town?" I asked, repeating a question he had probably only answered about a hundred times.

"I wanted to leave because I owed people money."

This was something new. In his statement to police and in court he had just said he was planning to leave, run away, something that was never questioned. Why didn't police ask him why he was running? Do they just take it for granted that kids have no reason for such behavior? That there is no *good* reason, perhaps? Or, in this case, was the crime that followed so horrendous that it didn't *matter* why Sarah, John, and Kevin originally chose to run away?

"Sarah wanted to leave for the same reason."

Sarah owed people money? This, too, was news to me. I tried it out with the rest of John's version of events, and it worked, it made some sense. If John and Sarah had owed people money, that would explain why they wanted to leave town together. But this was the first time it had come up, and that made it less convincing. The other story, the old one, about John wanting to leave town because of his "serious" court date, didn't explain why Sarah would want to go too, unless she didn't want to go to court to testify against John. John's version of Kevin's motive was somewhat more convincing. Kevin was eighteen years old, but from everything else I have learned about him, he was still almost entirely dependent on his parents to support him. Therefore, if they had insisted that he go back to rehab, he probably didn't have much choice. John offered a way out—a ride out. All Kevin had to do was help with a robbery to secure some funds and guns, and the necessary ride.

Now that we were discussing Kevin, Nancy contributed to the conversation, having witnessed the incident at the Depot where Kevin flipped out and attacked his father, back in 1997. "I'd never seen anything like it," she said, shaking her head, her blond curls bobbing. "It took three or four policemen to pull him off, and Kevin's not very big. He practically levitated in the police car, his arms and legs were completely stiff and shaking."

While Nancy continued to describe for me her impressions of Kevin's attack on his father, I noticed that Cindy had leaned across the table to whisper something to John. A moment later the two of them, with Michelle, excused themselves to make another trip to the vending machines. The mound of food in the middle of the table had been slowly diminishing, as John polished off the sandwiches while the rest of us nibbled on cookies and chips. When the three of them returned, I sensed immediately that something was wrong. Everyone was quiet for a moment, and then, as if they knew what was coming, Nancy and Tom exchanged glances, then cast their eyes down at their laps. At a table nearby, a set of dominoes crashed loudly onto the ceramic tiles. Michelle, who until this point had contributed absolutely nothing to the general conversation, leaned in to launch her attack.

"Are you going to write about the trial in your book?" she asked.

"Yes, of course," I answered.

"Then tell me something, since you so obviously have already taken Sarah's side, why should these nice people sit here talking to you and answering your questions?"

I didn't respond for a minute, because I was stunned. I did not think I had obviously been taking sides. I was just honestly trying to find out what happened. Perhaps my having been in touch with Sarah for a longer period of time and my sense of having gotten to know her better had created some bias in her favor, but the evidence, at least so far, didn't add up to my forming an opinion of either her guilt or her innocence, though I did have the sense, already, that she had not been treated entirely fairly by the justice system. What I said was, "I'm not taking sides. If it seems that way, maybe it's because I've been talking to Sarah for longer than I've been talking to John. I feel like I know her better. Anyway, I don't see what I could have said here today that would make you think I was taking her side against John."

Michelle shook her head dismissively. "It's not necessarily what you say. Your body language says it all. When you talk about Sarah, you're relaxed and open, but when you talk to John, or when John talks to you, you cross your arms and lean away in a defensive posture. It's obvious."

Maybe what she was saying about my body language was true, but it was not because I had made up my mind about anything. It had more to do with my feeling of being intimidated by John's physical and psychic presence, particularly after the incident where he had started grimacing to interrupt my conversation with his parents.

Now John joined what was rapidly descending into a verbal fracas, attacking Sarah. He slammed his hand on the table, called her "the biggest liar."

"She's got three different faces for three different people, Rosalyn. She pretends to you that she hasn't got anybody but you to care about her, but she's got all these different people visiting her and putting money in her account. She's just playing you off one another."

He asked me if she had told me about a nickname she had at Hilton Head High. "Fish," he said, smirking and licking his lips. "They called her that because she gave so many different guys head."

I glanced over at his parents, who had averted their faces. John continued his tirade.

"I stood by her, even through that, and she spit in my face! I was her best friend, and she betrayed me!" As he concluded he shoved his chair back from the table, as if he was going to get up, but didn't. Where, after all, was there for him to go? Sitting across the table from him, feeling as if I had been assaulted by his rage, I noticed the tears in his father's eyes, and my heart cracked. I knew I would eventually recover from the fear that rose in me, but his father's tears, the sense of helplessness and loss that he must have suffered, would stay with me forever.

■ ■ ■

The visit ended quietly after the emotional fireworks. John had a hard time saying good-bye to Cindy and especially to Tom and Nancy. Cindy and Michelle kept their distance from me as we returned to the parking lot, but Tom and Nancy lingered to talk. Tom frankly expressed great concern about the effect my book could have on John's future, and specifically on the next stage of the appeals process, his PCR (postconviction relief) hearing, where a new attorney would argue that John's original attorney, Scott Lee, was ineffective counsel. The PCR would be tough, mostly because John, having been fully advised of his rights, had chosen to plead guilty to both murder and armed robbery. Looking at the case from his current perspective, though, Tom said he didn't know why they let John agree to do that.

What made accepting the plea bargain seem like a good idea at the time was the hand-of-one, hand-of-all law. This is the idea, mentioned previously, that if one member of a group that sets out to commit a crime commits a murder, then everyone in the group is guilty of that murder. Presently, though, the law, and John's sentence, seemed to them equally absurd, considering that the only person who, they believe, actually assaulted Nell was Kevin Bergin, and Kevin had made a full confession.

"I just don't know what we are going to do if John's PCR isn't successful," Tom said. He looked off into the distance, where all he could see was the razor-wire fence and prison compound slated to be his eldest son's home for the next twenty-five years. "And Nancy and I are concerned that your book may have a negative impact, even if you don't mean for it to. It's like," he began, then paused, looking at his wife, as if for inspiration. "It's like when a realtor shows a house and they don't want the owners to be there because they may say something that seems entirely innocuous to them, but it may impress the buyers differently. Like, 'This living room is almost too big. We just don't know what do to with all this space.'"

"I think I know what you mean," I said. I didn't know what else to say, because he was right.

"I mean, if the PCR isn't successful, that's it," he says, and I can see a hint of tears again. "We won't have any hope. John won't have any hope. By the time he gets out, we'll be gone."

■ ■ ■

Later, after the feeling of having been assaulted had begun to wear off, I tried to objectively consider John's analysis of Sarah's character and reminded myself that if what John has always said about Sarah's involvement is true, he has every right to be angry. The comment he had made about Sarah having three different faces for three different people is very similar to what her stepfather, Mike Davis, told me about her, and I know that it is to some degree true. In my early visits to CGGCI, she had sometimes displayed quite different moods (though generally never more than one per visit) and even personalities. Sometimes she had tended to be quiet and matter-of-fact in her answers to my questions, and she seemed emotionally vulnerable, yet also reserved. As we got to know each other better, she began to display occasionally a "badass" personality, showing off her status among the other inmates and guards, speaking in a cocky manner, and telling me about her love affairs and other social dramas that went on between visits. As our relationship progressed, however, and she began preparing for her own PCR with her new attorney, Gary Coggin, her demeanor had become more serious. The conversation at our visits had focused primarily on her case and her lawyer's preparation.

One topic Sarah and I have always discussed, from the day I met her until now, is how she occupies her time in prison. She has always had a job. Since I have known her, it was landscaping. More recently she had requested, and received approval for, a transfer to the library. Sarah has also, since I have known her, participated in a program called Operation Behind Bars. For OBB she makes presentations to juvenile offenders who have been remanded to a reception and evaluation center, and who are taking a "tour" of the women's prison. By telling her story to young offenders, kids who have been doing the same kinds of "stupid shit that I used to do," Sarah says she hopes to keep them from ending up where she is now. She also, for several years, participated regularly in something called "praise dancing," which is modern dance moves set to Christian music, and, later, when a ballet instructor volunteered to teach classes, she once again took up ballet, something she had loved as a child. She has taught herself sign language and has participated in a retraining program for retired greyhounds, preparing the dogs for adoptive homes. She has participated in nearly every dramatic production that has been staged since she arrived at the prison, and pursued every single educational opportunity that has been offered. All these topics are things we discuss when we meet, when we talk on the phone, and when she writes me letters.

In order to verify what Sarah had told me about her activities, I spoke with Stanley Leakes, an associate warden at CGGCI who, I was told, knows Sarah well and has followed her progress since her admission to the prison in 2001. Leakes informed me that "Sarah Nickel is one of our biggest success stories," adding, "You should have seen her when she came in here, compared to now. We are so proud of this young lady, and all she has accomplished."

And so, yes, I think I have seen different faces of Sarah, but they have evolved gradually, and what I have observed is a process of maturing over the four years that I had known her when I met John Ridgway. And yes, I am sure she did, and does, show different "faces" to different people in different circumstances, just as almost everyone does. Does anyone, for instance, speak to their children in public the same way they speak to them at home? Does anyone show their boss the same "face" they show their spouse? Certainly John showed me one face in his letters and an entirely different one when I visited him in prison. However, I would not want to judge him any more harshly than I have Sarah.

This is what I have learned about John: He loves his parents, expressing his feelings about them quite openly in his letters to me. "They're real good people. I reflect not one-millionth of the good they are and represent. Their love and support and determination for me started long before my arrest, I assure you." He also thinks "the whole fucking world" of his birth mother, Cindy, and feels, "very, very fortunate" to have such a family. Even Sarah, interestingly, he wishes well, at least in his letters, expressing over and over the hope that her PCR would go well. He still said this, even after the debacle of our visit, when we exchanged another set of letters.

John's other great love is music, and when he gets out, he has told me, he doesn't want much—just a little house in Connecticut, a wife, some kids, and his own music store. His favorite band, at least when he and I were corresponding, was the death metal band Opeth. He really wanted me to give them a listen, so I finally did and found that I could only tolerate about fifteen seconds of Mikael Akerfeldt's growls and metal guitar before I felt a migraine coming on. But later, when I finally worked up the courage to listen to their CD *Damnation,* I was stunned by the haunting beauty of songs like "In My Time of Need" and "Hope Leaves." The intelligence John displayed in his wide-ranging ability to discuss many different topics in politics, religion, and philosophy, however, made me want to delve deeper into the mystery of his fascination with death metal, so I asked him why he liked the band so much. He wrote back, "Well, I am big into extreme music. I like music that's unorthodox, that pushes the boundaries, but I like talent, not chaos. Bands like Watain, Dissection, At the Gates, Nihilist, early Mayhem, Autopsy, Funebrarum, etc. are bands that are also extreme but amazing. Yet I also love psychodelia, the sounds you find in Pink Floyd, the Doors, Camel, Yes, Grateful Dead, Porcupine Tree, Frank Zappa, etc. Opeth has perfectly blended these two genres and created their own, that started with their second LP—*Morningrise.* You hear it most clearly in *Ghost Reveries,* their newest masterpiece." As for the band's preoccupation with the theme of death, John says, "To me death itself, not the cause, is as natural as birth and, like change, inevitable. So why not be comfortable with it, you know? I know that's all kind of Buddhist, which I gladly admit, but Opeth's lyrics are also about isolation, love, determination, perseverance, and overcoming all odds. I can relate to a lot of it, feel the music."

Sitting alone with my notes, years after the flurry of letters that preceded our one and only visit (though John invited me to come again, I did not take him up on his offer), I look at what I have just written with a new understanding. *Isolation, love, determination, perseverance, overcoming all odds.* Certainly these are characteristics and feelings that potently come across in John's letters. Other emotions I hear and find in Opeth's lyrics, anger and despair—well, I think I have seen evidence of them as well.

In a letter responding to my request to go over certain details of the crime, he writes, "Kevin stabbed her after Sarah and I and he were in the car and he got back out after she was in the compost box! She [Sarah] heard nothing, there was no bloody knife. And I believe Mrs. Davis was already dead by then unfortunately, which I hate to write. That kills me every time I think about it. I feel sick. Genuinely sick, which is why I rarely do details. To this day I can't watch really gory flicks, I get sick because of what I witnessed. Hook me to a polygraph, I promise you. This *never* ever should have happened, Rosalyn, I hate that it did."

Two years later, at John Ridgway's PCR hearing, I would hear Scott Lee, the lawyer who originally represented him, take the stand for no other purpose that I could discern than to tell the judge what a wonderful young man he had found John to be back in the days when they had met regularly at the Beaufort County Detention Center to discuss John's case and, ultimately, to negotiate his plea bargain. Lee's exact words were, "I found him to be a very delightful, respectful young man who had gotten himself into a horrible situation." He also said, "I think John Ridgway by a long shot was the least culpable of the three." Lee further informed the court that he had, on Ridgway's behalf, written Solicitor Murdaugh a letter asking for mercy, "essentially a mitigation letter," he added, noting that this was the only time in his thirty-year career that he had ever done something of that nature. And Lee was Ridgway's court-appointed attorney, paid under the terms of the Indigent Defense Fund.

Ridgway's new lawyer was John Blume, the crème de la crème of PCR attorneys in South Carolina; most of his work is with death penalty cases. Blume carried himself like a celebrity, like nearly all expensive lawyers. His brief encompassed several arguments, including one about John being on Zoloft when he entered his plea, but the main one had to do with there being a substantive defect in the guilty plea. When I heard Blume say this, I initially thought he was questioning the hand-of-one law, but that was wrong. It had something to do with a procedural flaw in the way the guilty plea was presented to the court. The judge, the Honorable Michael Nettles, appeared perplexed by counsel's arguments and kept coming back to the question of whether or not John was, at each stage of the process, advised of his rights and of the nature of the plea he was entering. The answer, each time, was yes. What it all boiled down to, despite the technicalities of procedure, is the hand-of-one, hand-of-all precedent, which, Scott Lee told the court, is the linchpin of why he advised Ridgway to plead guilty. So no matter how many times Mr. Blume kept coming back to his argument about there being a flaw in the factual basis of the plea, the judge kept repeating some variation of the following: "I don't think there's much question of the facts in the case."

Eventually he said he would go and take a look at the law, and that he'd be in touch with those concerned about his decision. It didn't look good for John.

Before the courtroom was adjourned, Mr. Blume made a personal request on behalf of his client, asking that John be allowed to speak with and hug his parents, whom he had not seen for six months because of a loss of visitation privileges. From Sarah, who gets news of John through the prison grapevine, I had heard the reason for this deprivation. John had been in solitary, in "the Hole," for six months, having been caught with his illegal cell phone. Sarah said that his birthmother, Cindy, had been permanently barred from his visitation list for trying to smuggle another cell phone in to him. The judge asked the guards who accompanied Ridgway if they had a problem with allowing John a moment with his parents and then pretended not to hear them when they said yes. Or perhaps he misinterpreted their "yes" as assent. Anyway he allowed the visit.

John was pale, bloated with extra weight, and he moved even more heavily than the shackles binding his arms and legs would seem to have required, like someone underwater. He and his parents embraced briefly with Cindy on the periphery, with only the briefest exchange of words. Tom and Nancy appeared older, grayer. Tom's shoulders stooped slightly, or perhaps he was just leaning forward to make sure he heard every single word that the judge said.

No, the stoop remained, even when he stood to leave the courtroom. He led the way, followed by Nancy, and then Cindy, who, about two feet shorter than Tom, took two steps for every one of his. They moved slowly, and I couldn't take my eyes off them and their stricken faces because it was like watching a small funeral procession. I wondered if they were thinking what I was thinking, if their attention, like mine, had been snagged right away, with Judge Nettles's opening remarks to John's lawyer: "I've reviewed the transcript. Clearly your client testified in the trial. What remedy does your client envision? Clearly he would be back to square one in the process. Is your client aware of this?"

Square one means that if John's guilty plea were to be rendered invalid, he would have to begin the process all over again; that is, he would still be charged with murder and armed robbery, and once again have to make a decision about whether to enter a plea or go to trial. In all PCR cases where applicants are granted relief in the form of a new trial, the judge's decision is immediately appealed by the state's attorney general. The South Carolina Supreme Court, which hears such appeals, overturns the judges' rulings in approximately 80 percent of the cases. If you talk to a bunch of defense attorneys about this situation, they will tell you it reflects the sad state of affairs in civil rights in South Carolina. If you talk to a bunch of people on the other side of the fence—people in the solicitors' offices, in the attorney general's office—they will tell you that a lot of the people who get reversals on a PCR get them because of a technicality, and that guilty people shouldn't get off that way.

I am not sure, however, that either of these situations applied to John Ridgway, and I imagine the young man's unusual situation explains why Scott Lee went out of his way to help John Ridgway, though I doubted it would do much good.

When I spoke to Tom and Nancy in the hallway outside courtroom number 2, the large courtroom where Sarah's original trial was held, we all had trouble finding the words we wanted to say. I still wanted Nell to be alive. The Ridgways still wanted their son back. Finally Tom said, "Don't you just feel like this was the perfect storm of unfortunate events? That if you took away one element of the equation, none of this would have happened?"

What element, I wonder, is he thinking of.

If John hadn't been set to go to court the next day?

If Nell had had to run errands after school and not been home?

If Kevin had missed the train to South Carolina?

If Mike Davis had come home early?

If Sarah had told her mother there were two guys with knives and a baseball bat in the backyard?

If Nell had said, "See about the rabbit yourself?"

If Kevin had overdosed on crack, Dramamine, huffing gas, or any combination of the various drugs he was taking at any time prior to October 20?

If the cab that brought John and Kevin to Bellinger Bluff had had an accident?

But mostly if John and Kevin hadn't gathered two knives and a baseball bat, and taken them to 31 Bellinger Bluff, where Kevin used them, and his bare hands, to bludgeon, choke, and stab Nell to make sure that she was dead, dead, dead. It is the last of these that really gives the lie to Tom's poetic characterization. "The perfect storm of unfortunate events" implies a lack of human agency, a kind of accidental quality, and planning a robbery involving weapons is no accident. If John is telling the truth, events certainly unwound in a way that was unexpected and unfortunate.

Watching Tom, Nancy, and Cindy slowly walk away, the chorus of Opeth's "In My Time of Need" went round and round my mind in an endless loop:

> *At times, the dark's fading slowly*
> *But it never sustains*
> *Would someone watch over me*
> *In my time of need*
> *Summer is miles and miles away*
> *And no one would ask me to stay*
> *And I, should contemplate this change*
> *To ease the pain*
> *And I, should step out of the rain*
> *Turn away*
> *And I, should contemplate this change*
> *To ease the pain*
> *And I, should step out of the rain*
> *Turn away.*

22

The Church of Satan

I've been looking at photos of Nell this morning, wedding pictures and Halloween pictures, mostly. One of them was taken in her parents' dining room. I know because I can see part of their piano behind her. Her hair is long, and she wears a light-brown velvet blazer with a white turtleneck underneath. The photo must have come at the end of a roll because it's half black. I see Nell smiling and I imagine the darkness encroaching. I think about a film I once saw called *Shooting the Past.* A character named Oswald, the curator of a photography museum, speaks of the photographs of happy people who are "one photograph away from disaster, from something that will change them forever." I wonder who took the last photograph of Nell alive, and whether she looks happy. I have one of her with her son Willie, taken not too long before the tragedy. Her face is drawn and haggard, her expression resigned, almost as if she senses what is coming.

■ ■ ■

Because John said that *The Satanic Bible,* by Anton Szandor LaVey, had an important influence on his and Kevin's thinking at the time of the murder, I have read the book, which professes to be the first authentic codification of true satanic beliefs and rituals. In the book's preface, LaVey announces that "with very few exceptions, every tract and paper, every 'secret' grimoire, all the 'great works' on the subject of magic, are nothing more than sanctimonious fraud—guilt-ridden ramblings and esoteric gibberish by chroniclers of magical lore unable or unwilling to present an objective view of the subject" (LaVey 21). Within the pages of his own book, by contrast, "you will find truth—and fantasy" because both are necessary to comprehend "Satanic thought from a truly Satanic point of view" (22).

Following the preface and a brief prologue, LaVey provides the reader with "Nine Satanic Statements," which are elaborated in later chapters, and

which form a kind of diabolic counterpart to the Ten Commandments of
Judeo-Christian tradition. These statements consist of the following:

1. Satan represents indulgence instead of abstinence!
2. Satan represents vital existence instead of spiritual pipe dreams!
3. Satan represents undefiled wisdom instead of hypocritical self-deceit!
4. Satan represents kindness to those who deserve it instead of love
   wasted on ingrates!
5. Satan represents vengeance instead of turning the other cheek!
6. Satan represents responsibility to the responsible instead of concern
   for psychic vampires!
7. Satan represents man as just another animal, sometimes better, more
   often worse than those that walk on all-fours, who, because of his
   "divine spiritual and intellectual development," has become the most
   vicious animal of all!
8. Satan represents all of the so-called sins, as they all lead to physical,
   mental, or emotional gratification!
9. Satan has been the best friend the Church has ever had, as He has kept
   it in business all these years! (LaVey 25)

Some scholars who have studied LaVey's work suggest (as LaVey himself
has indicated) that his satanic statements are to some degree based on the
philosophy, called "objectivism," of the early twentieth-century writer Ayn
Rand. In books like *Atlas Shrugged,* Rand rejected the ethics of self-sacrifice
and renunciation, while she celebrated the power of the individual mind,
defending the superiority of reason and science against all forms of irrationalism. LaVey seems to have embraced Rand's rejection of self-sacrifice
and renunciation, but his book's frequent references to the so-called dark
powers of the universe that remain misunderstood (but will, he assures us,
one day be discovered by science), and his belief that one can bring about
the death of an individual by performing a ritual that summons this power,
reek of irrationalism. Hence Rand's system of beliefs is called a "philosophy," while LaVey's is a self-avowed "religion."

Essentially LaVey's Satanism boils down to the idea that the individual
should celebrate his individuality, indulge his own appetites and desires (be
they carnal or otherwise), repay any wrongs done to him with a vengeance,
and above all stop worrying about suffering in any type of fictional after-
life. *The Satanic Bible* describes two fundamental types of magic   ritual or
ceremonial, and nonritual or manipulative. The latter involves finding the

best way to use your mind and body to manipulate people and thus get what you want from them. Basically it's making the best of your good attributes. For instance, if you are an attractive young woman, you use your sexuality to manipulate men into giving you what you want, whether it be goods, services, a job, or simply their attention. If you are less attractive, or perhaps just older, you might want to use "sentiment" to work your will on people whom you are able to attract. In this case you would manipulate your target by providing him or her with a sumptuous meal, entertaining stories, or appealing to his or her sense of pleasure in other ways. The third type of appeal is termed "wonder," which may be used by a man or woman with unusual personal magnetism (that is, charisma), or perhaps a strange or sinister (or even "diabolic") appearance. According to LaVey such a person uses his or her appearance, or the strength of his or her personality, to inspire awe and, again, persuade people to work his or her will (110–13).

One of the reasons John wanted me to read LaVey's book is because it would, he claimed, dispel any notion I might have that Nell's murder involved a satanic ritual. Reading the chapter entitled "On the Choice of a Human Sacrifice," however, I can't help wondering if he remembers the book correctly. There are occasions, according to LaVey, when human sacrifice is appropriate. "The only time a Satanist would perform a human sacrifice," LaVey writes, "would be if it were to serve a two-fold purpose, that being to release the magician's wrath in the throwing of a curse, and more important, to dispose of a totally obnoxious and deserving individual" (88). Several paragraphs later LaVey pronounces that "When a person, by his reprehensible behavior, practically cries out to be destroyed, it is truly your moral obligation to indulge them their wish" (89–90). Maybe John is not aware that, during Sarah's trial, Kevin talked about how he felt bad, "Not because of the woman we killed but because of the kids." Regarding that woman, he added, "I mean she's a beast." Although other portions of *The Satanic Bible* suggest that the annihilation of your enemy is to be carried out symbolically, through a hex or cursing ritual, I can't help wondering whether these passages, by promoting the idea that it is "your moral obligation" to destroy certain types of people, helped to shape not only the beliefs but also the actions of Kevin Bergin and John Ridgway as they planned and then executed the events that culminated in Nell's murder.

Indeed, after having met John Ridgway, I find myself wondering if he still employs the second type of "magic" outlined in LaVey's book, the non-ritual, or manipulative, kind. The day I visited him in prison, I observed the impact of his physical presence from the moment he entered the visitation room. Sitting among a group composed of his adoptive parents, his birth mother, and his birth mother's roommate, I saw John deftly control the conversation, noting how everyone at the table deferred to him, agreeing to buy certain types of music for the collection that Cindy was building for him during his incarceration, and even agreeing to arrange their lives in certain ways to please him. Shortly after John had joined us in the visitation room, I had learned that Michelle wore the Lynyrd Skynyrd shirt with the skull on it at his insistence, even though John knew it would cause trouble when she tried to enter the prison. During the visit, when John sensed the conversation slipping away from his control, he had behaved outlandishly, grimacing and using his body to disrupt the exchange of information between his father and myself. When I refused to commit to believing John's version of events that happened on the day of Nell's murder, he became enraged. Why? Again I believe it had to do with the issue of being in control. In his letters and phone calls, John had been almost overly friendly and cooperative toward me. This willingness to cooperate, in fact, is what had originally impressed Detective JoJo Woodward, making him perceive John as such a valuable witness. It had also impressed Scott Lee, the lawyer who would later go to court and testify that he had found John to be the "least culpable of the three young people involved" in the crime, a young man so "delightful" that he would write a "letter of mitigation" to the solicitor, asking for special consideration when it came to his sentencing. But when John sat across from me that day at BRCI and wasn't able to get me to say I believed his version of "the truth" about Nell's murder, he found himself in an uncomfortable position, unable to assert control. If he is telling the truth, naturally he would feel both angry and frustrated, but giving way to an emotional outburst reveals either a lack of self-control in someone whose behavior seems otherwise very self-conscious and controlled, or an attempt at intimidation. Sitting where I sat, it felt like the latter.

Of greater relevance, though, is the question of whether he exerted this type of control over Sarah in the days leading up to, and, more important, on the day of, her mother's murder. Sarah claimed that he did, and that she felt herself controlled and manipulated by John. In a letter dated October 27, 2005, well before I had any contact with John, she wrote, "I liken John to a modern day Svengali, only there was one thing he could never make me do—he could never make me love him in a romantic sense. I loved him as a friend and I cared about him but I was not attracted to him in any way.

He had a lot of control over my mind and that's very hard for me to admit. He exploited my weaknesses, he used me, and in his own twisted way he loved me." Here she states that the letters he has written to her since the start of their incarceration "chill me [to] the bone" and goes on to say, "I've never been as scared of someone as I am of John Ridgway. I wasn't even this afraid of Mike. For a girl always looking for love when I was younger, it sure is funny that now a man tells me he loves me and I'm petrified." In another letter, this one dated November 11 of the same year, she says, "John's letters seem to try and make me think he's changed for the better, but I'm not stupid. He's a master manipulator and I'm sure he's only gotten better at it since our incarceration."

But then in May 2006, after I had begun talking to John and when I told Sarah that I was planning to visit him, she began writing to him, initially using his birth mother as a conduit. I remember her saying that she wanted to do this, and asking me if I thought this was OK. Since my own impression of John had been favorable, I told her I didn't see why not. I admit that it struck me as strange, considering what she had said about him in her letters to me, but I naturally wanted to see what would come of it.

Sarah's first letter to John is mostly about her life in prison, the different kinds of activities she has been involved with, such as Operation Behind Bars, and the soap opera of her love life. This letter closes with Sarah saying she's really glad that she and John have gotten back in touch because "we used to be best friends." She adds, "I didn't know if ya wanted to mend those fences or not, but now that I know we've got a lot of work to do!" This is followed by the curious promise that "if they call me to testify in October I'll say 4 words only: 'I plead the 5th'. What are they gonna do, lock me up?"

There is always the possibility that Sarah was writing to John, trying to patch things up, because she knew that I was going to visit him and she was worried about what he was going to tell me. Knowing that, in the words of her own attorney, you gotta give something to get something, she offered John the only thing she thought she had to give him, the assurance that, should she be called to the stand to testify in a way that would incriminate him at her PCR, she would refuse to do so. When she finally did go to court, however, one of the arguments Gary Coggin, her PCR attorney, presented was that her original attorney had failed her by omitting to argue that she was coerced. And who was she coerced by? John Ridgway and Kevin Bergin. Who, he argued, did most of the coercing? John Ridgway.

In contrast, however, to her empty promise about pleading the fifth stands the content of some of her other letters to John, which exhibit a remarkable ring of authenticity, a voice that is strong and true.

This is an excerpt from a letter dated July 8, 2007:

Yes, life is crazy—I wish we could sit face to face & just talk. I bet we could talk as if we haven't been separated for 8 yrs. You were my best friend—the only person who truly accepted & understood me. You respected my intelligence— not too many people did that. I wish ya would have let me deeper into you— would you mind? It's not too late. I always felt like we connected on a level that no one else understood, like we were in our own little world. Did you ever feel that way? I never truly fit in w/ anyone except you. It sucks that we got so strung out & did so much stupid shit. But the past is the past & we've both grown up & changed a lot. Most everyone we went to high school w/ wouldn't even recognize me. I'm glad you're happy w/ Rae—what's she like? I'm glad you'll always be here for me & I'll always be here for you. We've been through too much to have it any other way, ya know? And why do you say I probably couldn't handle being married to you? Explain please!

After reading these letters that Sarah had sent to John I realized what I had already begun to suspect: that Sarah *had* to have been lying about John telling her to either do certain things, or he would kill her and her siblings. If she had been afraid that he would do that, there's just no way, I believe, that she would be writing him these types of letters now.

This was one of those moments when I have discovered something new about the case that requires me to step back and reassess everything else. What I have come to understand, each time I am forced to repeat this action, is that it involves not only a reexamination of the facts, but, to a greater and greater degree, a reevaluation of my own involvement, a harsher judgment of my own bias. Sometimes I feel as if I am engaged in a wrestling match, not with some external antagonist, but with another part of myself, engaged in some kind of eternal dialectic struggle that is doomed to progress from one idiosyncratic "version" of the truth to another. Perhaps this is because, when you have human beings and human emotions involved, there simply *is* no clean and pure truth of the kind that I had, when I started this journey, hoped to find. But I wasn't giving up yet.

23

The Judge Wore Leather

One blustery afternoon in March 2006, I felt I finally knew enough about the case to interview Judge Luke Brown, who had presided at Sarah's trial. Sitting in my car, in a parking lot across the street from the Beaufort County Sheriff's Department Hilton Head Substation, I called him, explained who I was, and why I wished to speak with him. He immediately agreed to see me, much more readily than many of the people I'd approached. "Come on down the house," he said in a voice that boomed through the tiny speaker in my cell phone, and, following his directions, I drove directly to Ridgeland, before he had time to think twice about what he had agreed to.

Upon arriving at Judge Brown's Ridgeland residence, the first thing I noticed was that it stood about one block (down the street and around the corner) from Mike Davis's Main Street Pharmacy. Covered in white siding, its shutters and door trimmed in glossy black, the house seemed to have begun life as a modest bungalow with a wide front porch and brick columns that were now painted white to match the siding. At some later date rooms had been added to each side until, in its current state, the house nearly filled a small city block. Two glossy black rockers and a wooden swing, suspended by chains, fit comfortably on the porch.

The judge greeted me at the door, wearing a cranberry flannel shirt and soft blue jeans. At eighty-six years of age, he was stout and white haired, ruddy complexioned, and a good deal more imposing in person than in photos of him wearing his black robes. For some reason, perhaps because of the booming, sonorous tones of his voice and the way that he walked with his chest thrust out, he reminded me of Foghorn Leghorn, Warner Brothers' gigantic cartoon rooster who was hilariously plagued by a tiny chicken hawk determined to have him for dinner. Perhaps because I had skipped lunch, I had a disturbing image of myself as that peewee chicken hawk, on a similarly futile quest.

We crossed the formal living room and made our way into what appeared to be an addition to the main house, a room of crowded bookshelves and a TV set. He directed me to have a seat on the sofa while he took a chair beside it. A young granddaughter came in looking for a particular movie among the boxes of videocassettes lining one of the bookshelves. With her he was indulgent and proud; with me he was affably garrulous, assuring me that he would answer my questions to the "best of my memory," boasting that he knew the law inside out, having worked as a lawyer for SLED (South Carolina Law Enforcement Division) for thirty years and been a judge for about twenty before he retired. He said he remembered the Nickel case, that it was a terrible, terrible crime, and told me that I was not the first person to come to see him. Sarah's cousin, he said, or maybe it was her aunt—somebody from Savannah—had come to see him a while ago asking if there wasn't something he could do on Sarah's behalf, to help her appeal. He wanted me to understand that, just as he had told the other lady, it was now out of his hands. I told him I knew that, and explained, again, my relationship with Nell: that she was my childhood friend, that I just wanted to understand what happened to her, including *how* and *why*. The fact that intrigued me the most, at the moment, was the proximity of Mike Davis's business to Judge Brown's home. Ridgeland is a small town (its population was then estimated at around twenty-seven hundred), and it seemed likely, especially considering that Mike's was once the only pharmacy in town, that the two men would have met, perhaps been acquaintances.

"Living out here, in this small community, you must have heard a lot about the case before you ever knew you were going to be presiding," I ventured. He gave me a puzzled look, then seemed to turn inward, searching his memory. "I don't listen to the local news," he said, and then, after a moment, he made the startling revelation that what he "knew about the case then," he "learned from Mike Davis."

"When I'd go to pick up my medicine, Mike would have questions about the case. He'd tell me what was going on, and he had questions about what to expect." He slapped his hands on his knees, his spine straight as an arrow.

"Were you and Mike friends?" I asked, fascinated by what I was hearing.

He considered again, but more briefly this time. "I'm not sure I knew Mike personally before all this." He paused, then continued, more sure of himself. "I'm inclined to believe I knew him. We talked about hunting and fishing."

I didn't even have to bring up the question of whether Judge Brown thought he should have recused himself from the case, based on his acquaintance with Mike Davis. He brought it up, saying, "Nobody asked me to," then adding, "I reckon they could have, but they didn't."

I thought back to my conversations with several local attorneys who had voiced the opinion that Brent Kiker had spoken to Brown in chambers about removing himself from the case, but was rebuffed for doing so. It didn't really matter, though, what went on in Judge Brown's chambers because Kiker had the chance to make the request in public, and didn't.

I began to understand what was driving Judge Brown's candidness. He honestly believed that everything he had done with respect to the case of *State of South Carolina vs. Sarah Nickel* was above board and beyond reproach. That's why he didn't mind telling me anything and everything I wanted to know; he had nothing to hide. When I asked him his impression of Sarah as a witness, he described her as "sharp" and "intelligent," adding, "I didn't believe her story, though. Why didn't she run away from those boys at the gas station?" he asked, echoing Mike Davis. "They were both out of the car. Why didn't she take off? Why did she take her mother's jewelry?"

I agreed that those things, especially the jewelry, did make Sarah look culpable. "What about Ridgway and Bergin?" I asked. "What were your impressions of them on the witness stand?"

"I believed they were telling the truth, that the whole plan had been her idea."

Interestingly that is not what they said in court. That is what Sarah's lawyer predicted that they would say in his opening remarks. But they didn't. They, Bergin and Ridgway, actually said it was a plan that the three of them had hatched together, after Sarah had told John about a safe in her parents' bedroom that supposedly contained money and guns.

I asked Judge Brown what he thought about Brent Kiker.

"She had herself a good little lawyer. That young man did a fine job. Sarah was lucky to get such a lawyer."

I pondered the implications of "little."

When I asked the judge if he could share with me what kinds of things he considered when determining Sarah's sentence, since he had given her the maximum for armed robbery, he boldly said, "I listened to the trial and I determined that that jury made a terrible mistake. I would have convicted her of murder. I felt she'd gotten off so light I'd give her the whole thirty years."

Not as surprised by this response as I might have been earlier in our conversation, I still took a moment to absorb the shock I felt at hearing this man breezily confess to taking away an individual's right to be impartially judged by a *jury* and sentenced accordingly. I asked him if things might have gone differently for Sarah had she admitted to being involved in the crime.

"If she had told the truth from the beginning," he answered, "the solicitor could have made a deal with her to get a stiffer penalty for those boys. Whoever makes the deal first has the advantage. I could see her getting Man 1 [first-degree manslaughter] if she'd cooperated instead of going to trial."

So, essentially, Sarah had gotten thirty years in prison for lying.

The only question I asked that Judge Brown didn't respond to with a direct and ready answer was the one about whether his daughter had dated Mike Davis in the year following Nell's murder, before the case went to trial. Instead he began by holding up one hand and counting on his fingers, naming each daughter and briefly outlining her relationship status during the year in question. After accounting for the others, he said, "The only one it could have been was Pam. I don't think she was dating Mike, but I'll find out and let you know." For a fleeting moment, I believed him.

A few minutes later, after I had excused myself to go to the bathroom in another part of the house, I heard Judge Brown's voice booming out in a room separated from where I was by a second door, another way in. He was speaking to a daughter named Stephanie, one of those he had counted off and dismissed as a candidate for dating Mike.

"Stephanie, do you know if Pam dated Mike Davis?" he asked her.

I held my urine, waiting for her answer, hoping that she would answer loudly enough for me to hear her response. There was a pause, long enough for me to be afraid that she may have decided to ignore him. Then, "Where is the lady?" I heard Stephanie ask, her voice barely above a whisper.

When he thundered, so close to the door I nearly fell off the toilet seat, "In the bathroom," she changed the subject. Perhaps realizing, for the first time, that he may have said too much, he let it go. I could hear his footsteps stumping out of the room. I met him back in the living room, where we talked for a few more minutes about how he planned to spend the next few years of his retirement.

"Several years ago, after I tried everywhere and couldn't get medical clearance to get my pilot's license renewed, I decided to buy a motorcycle," he tells me. "It wasn't big enough, so I gave it to my daughter and got another, a touring BMW. I thought I would ride it across the country but decided that the Cadillac was more comfortable, so that's probably what I'll do." He reminisced some more about the joys of riding his motorcycle, but he did not invite me to sit down; rather he steered me toward the front door, saying he was expecting somebody to come by with some papers, and expressing the hope that he was able to lay some of my questions to rest.

When I said good-bye to Judge Brown, he watched me through the screen door for a few seconds, wearing the same quizzical expression he had sported at the beginning of our interview, when he was trying to recall when and how he had become acquainted with Mike Davis.

I took an untried route back to Bluffton—choosing a road that veered off the map of Jasper County, but resurfaced on a second map, the one for Beaufort County. The road twisted and turned unexpectedly (at one unmarked intersection I had to guess, right or left) and took me past Thomas Heyward Academy, the private school Sarah attended after her mother and Mike married.

It was a long drive, and I found my thoughts about the interview twisting and turning like the road. My dominant feeling, however, was amazement. I was flabbergasted by the judge's open admission of impropriety. Although he obviously didn't see it as such, his conversations with Mike Davis during the period leading up to the trial constituted a definite conflict of interest. Anyone with the slightest degree of savvy in the realm of human relations knows how difficult it is to be impartial toward someone you have come to know and like. Having talked to Mike about the crime, having learned, from Mike, about the tumultuous relationship Sarah had with her mother, having listened while Mike explained the basis of his conviction that Sarah was guilty, that she had participated in the crime that resulted in Nell's death, having received from Mike the medicine that kept his blood pressure under control, how could Judge Brown believe in his own impartiality, in his ability to set aside his relationship to Mike when hearing the case against Sarah?

No, Judge Brown didn't tell me the specifics he and Mike Davis had discussed, but I figured it was safe to bet that Mike at least expressed to the judge the opinions he had expressed to me, someone whom, until Sarah's PCR, he had never met in person. This idea was bolstered by the judge's admission that one of the things that convinced him of Sarah's guilt was her failure to run away from the boys when they stopped for gas.

The next day I had the opportunity to speak to Dudley Ruffalo and his wife, Ferebee, two attorneys who consulted on Sarah's case when Brent Kiker was preparing to go to trial. Dudley was immensely tall and carried himself with a stately walk reminiscent of an eighteenth-century country gentleman. Even his clothes had a hint of the dandy in them. Ferebee, former Rice Queen in the Savannah Saint Patrick's Day parade, had thick, straight blond hair that curved in just below her chin and moved constantly when she talked. Her sequined pink sweater, which would look cheap on most women, only enhanced her aura of high-class elegance. When I voiced my outrage over what I had learned from Brown, Ferebee attempted to calm me by presenting another side of the judge. She told me he's really a good old guy. "Good old boy" my mind substituted, unwilling to hear anything that would alter my perception. But gradually I succumbed. I *did* want the *whole* story.

Brown had already told me that, in his final years as a judge on the fourteenth circuit in South Carolina, he most enjoyed going to sessions in Walterboro because he could ride his Harley down the long, flat roads, feeling the wind rush against his face, pretending that things really hadn't changed all that much.

"I remember him riding up to the courthouse with his little cooler strapped on the back, containing his lunch," Ferebee recalled. "He'd unstrap the cooler and come sauntering in, wearing a black leather jacket, with the cooler in one hand and his helmet under the other arm, disappear into chambers, and reemerge in his black robe with his hair all combed back."

By some offenders, especially first-timers, he was primarily remembered for the *leniency* of his sentencing, resulting in the aforementioned nickname of "Lukewarm Brown." Ferebee recalled a case involving a young man who had killed his father, a passenger in the car he was driving, in a drunk driving accident. She had negotiated the charge down to involuntary manslaughter with a commuted sentence. When the young man made his required appearance in court for the formal entry of his plea, Judge Brown, as part of the required procedure, asked him if anyone had threatened or coerced him into making his plea of guilty.

He replied, "Well, your honor, Ms. Ferebee did say she would beat me with a stick if I didn't take the deal."

Brown reportedly responded, "I'd beat you with a stick myself. It's a good deal, son. You killed your daddy."

This story surprised me, led me back onto the twisting, turning path of thought I'd traveled during my return drive from Ridgeland to Bluffton, but made me want to choose a different direction when I reach the crossroads. Again I had to ask myself, if Brown was ordinarily so lenient with first-time offenders, what made him treat Sarah Nickel so differently, when she had been convicted only of armed robbery? If he had told me the truth about the reasons driving his decision (and he certainly didn't seem to be trying to hide anything), then Sarah's severe sentence was the result of his sincere belief that she was lying. Whether or not she lied, however, the fact remains that no evidence or testimony provided by the state suggested that Sarah had killed her mother. And, so far, there was really no way for me to know, for certain, whether she planned for her mother to be killed or not. Yes, she took her mother's jewelry, and no, she didn't run away from the boys at the first apparent opportunity. But she did run, and the only witness who claimed that Sarah wanted her mother killed was Kevin Bergin, who had beaten Nell senseless with a baseball bat, who had stabbed her nine or possibly ten times, who had been the least cooperative when initially making his statement to police, and who suffered from a smorgasbord of severe mental illnesses. According to John Ridgway, the witness whom detectives investigating the case deemed the most reliable, the trio had talked about killing Nell as a possibility, but the plan they ultimately decided on was to disable Nell, force her to give them the combination to the household safe, and then leave with whatever loot they had managed to extract from it. Maybe that is serious enough for a thirty-year sentence. I don't know; I'm not a judge. It is certainly a more calculated crime than a drunk-driving accident that results in a death.

Most interesting, perhaps, is that when I try putting myself in the judge's shoes, imagining that I had learned the details of the case from Mike Davis beforehand, and then sat on the bench listening to all the testimony and evidence, I cannot say that I would have been any more lenient. On the other hand, getting to know Sarah, hearing the story from her perspective, has created in my mind, my heart, my spirit, a kind of ballast, a counterweight, perhaps, which is something I have to account for, along with all the other information I have gathered, when I reach my own personal verdict, the judgment I will have to live with for the rest of my life.

∎ ∎ ∎

Muddy Creek Road, where Sarah and John Ridgway used to hang out, belongs to a part of Hilton Head Island that most people never see. It's the seamy side of the "millionaire's playground," the underbelly, the ghetto that has yet to be gentrified by speculation and development. To get there you take William Hilton Parkway leading out of Bluffton toward Hilton Head, and then, at the last turnoff before the Cross Island Expressway, you turn right onto Spanish Wells Road, traveling parallel to the expressway for a couple of miles before you see the sign on the left-hand side.

About half a mile long, Muddy Creek Road, when I visited it in 2006, was flanked by busted-up mobile homes sitting atop concrete blocks interspersed with houses that looked cobbled together. A few appeared to be sided with plywood painted muddy brown; others were constructed out of concrete block. One had a strange-looking oil furnace sitting to one side with a huge stovepipe that presumably, in cold weather, fed heat into the house. Yards were sandy without evidence of any conscious landscaping; some were littered with auto parts. Three tarpaulin-covered lumps stood guard outside one particularly rundown-looking trailer—car or truck engines, I guessed, because of their shape and size and the inky blots of motor oil staining the sand. There was one large structure with plywood walls that appeared to have two very large rooms with an outside stairway leading to an upper level—a chop shop, perhaps? It didn't seem to be a business, for there was no visible sign of activity at 3:30 on a Thursday afternoon. As I drove along the road, I saw only three people. One, a middle-aged woman in curlers wearing a pink housecoat, stood in a doorway, hands propped on the doorjamb. Two black teenagers passed me, both male, one on a motorcycle, the other riding an ATV. They shouted to each other words made unintelligible by the drone of their motors.

When I wrote to John Ridgway, telling him I went down to Muddy Creek Road to check the place out, he wrote back, painting his own portrait of the place as it was when he and Sarah used to "hang" there. Along with "The Gardens, The Oaks, and Gum Tree Road and Blazing Star," Muddy Creek Road figured among the "major crack spots on the Island. . . . You can pull up to any kid from 10 to 40 and buy crack or coke or weed. You can find female prostitutes the same ages. You can get guns there too. And anyone that isn't a cop, and can prove it, is cool there. It's the exact opposite, contradiction manifest, of the majority of what is Hilton Head Island. I used to love it there, Sarah was comfortable with me at least." He elaborated further that "twenty bucks would get you high and you'd work from there. Girls can 'trick' for more dope, or do anything sexual a guy, or guys wish, and guys can get rid of whatever stolen goods they wish. I want no part of that bullshit now, but at 15, 16, 17 it was great for me. Total defiance, a good place to vent and forget I guess."

Reading his letter I thought back to my experience of the place, wondering if I could have hailed one of the young men I had seen, asked him where I might score some crack, or if I had come back at dusk or in the evening, would I have seen more evidence of the kind of atmosphere evoked by John's description. In the afternoon sunlight, light that seemed too harsh and revealing for curbside drug deals and prostitution, the place seemed as wan and hopeless as any poverty-stricken neighborhood, a place where dreams die as soon as they are born, where the feeling of freedom and release is, as John's own experience proves, a fleeting illusion.

24

Madmen, Freaks, and Evil People

"Madmen," "freaks," "evil people," "weirdos"—these were all terms Brent Kiker used during Sarah's trial to characterize John Ridgway and Kevin Bergin, who were often referred to as an item, as if they were a single entity. I had already, sincerely, told John Ridgway that I didn't believe that either he, Kevin, or Sarah Nickel were freaks or monsters, that I believe people do evil things, but that there are no purely evil people. I don't know, of course, if that is true. Maybe there are evil people—people who have no soul, who have not one iota of goodness within them, perhaps people like Jeffrey Dahmer and Charles Manson. If so I have been fortunate never to have met one, and I hope that I never do.

Because there was so little physical evidence of Sarah Nickel's involvement in her mother's murder, the State of South Carolina, represented by Randolph Murdaugh, was heavily dependent on the testimony provided by John Ridgway and Kevin Bergin to make its case. Ridgway was the first to take the stand, and the story that he told was very similar, though not identical, to the story that he had told in his statement to the police, when he was interviewed just hours after the crime occurred. At that time he had said that he and Sarah were planning to run away, and that he had spoken to her on the phone on the evening of October 19, the day before the murder, and that "basically what happened was today, we decided we were going to go to Sarah's mother's house, at Sarah's request, and Kevin was going to, well at that time it was undecided, going to knock her out with some object." The idea was that when Nell came outside, "Kevin could knock her out with the bat in order for us to get the code to a safe" that was inside the house.

At Sarah's trial he provided more detail about the plan, or rather plans, because, according to John, there were "a bunch of different" ones. Some of them involved "killing her whole family, some involved killing Ms. Davis. Some involved killing Mr. Davis." When he and Bergin reached the Davis house, Sarah came outside, as they had planned the night before, and told them she was going to get her mom to come out behind the shed by telling her that something was wrong with a pet rabbit whose cage was located there. Then Sarah "said something about the bitch is gonna die" and went back into the house.

Under further questioning Ridgway added that Kevin was supposed to hit Ms. Davis a "single time," with the bat. When she was incapacitated from that blow, they would try to get the code to the safe from Ms. Davis, which would enable them to secure "thousands of dollars and guns and possibly jewelry." John said that they believed this to be the contents of the safe because Sarah had told them. When asked to provide more detail about the plan, John reiterated that a lot of different versions were discussed, some of them involving the killing of various members of the family. There was also one plan "to kill nobody and tie everybody up." The "basic overall [plan] was to get the money and the guns. It turned out at first, basically to do whatever had to be done to do it. Then it got to a point where, well, eventually no one needs to die." And that, John concluded, is the plan they settled on.

When Brent Kiker cross-examined John Ridgway, he went over the details of the crime again, presumably to see if Ridgway would contradict something he had said previously, under direct examination. Such an error on Ridgway's part would provide an opening, a tiny tear in the fabric of his testimony, which, exploited by a skillful attorney, could reduce the entire garment to shreds. Ridgway doggedly stuck to his original story.

The majority of Kiker's cross-examination, however, chose to focus on something entirely different from Randy Murdaugh: on the role of Satanism or witchcraft, and any associated rituals, in the crime.

Ridgway had already admitted, when questioned by the solicitor, that he was into witchcraft and Wicca but protested that it "didn't have to do with killing people or anything." After establishing that Ridgway and Bergin had, previous to the day of the murder, engaged in a ritual of purification, Kiker got Ridgway to admit that he and Kevin owned the many books and paraphernalia having to do with the occult that were contained in a bag found in Nell's Tahoe. Kiker was most interested, as soon became obvious, in a book called *The Necromantic Ritual Book,* which belonged to Kevin Bergin. Ridgway denied knowing anything about the book, however, aside from its title. When Kiker continued to pressure him, asking, "Do you know if certain ceremonies contained in some of these books involve rituals with corpses?" Ridgway finally gave him something to work with, answering, "I've heard there are such things but mostly those are just necrophiliacs that have serious problems."

Kiker did not take the opportunity to define necrophilia, which *Webster's New World Dictionary* defines as "an abnormal fascination with death and the dead; esp. an erotic attraction to corpses." Rather than clarifying the issue for the jury, he rephrased John's statement as a question: "Necrophiliacs that have serious problems would buy books like this?" When John agreed, Kiker continued, "Kevin has a serious problem, doesn't he, John?"

This "problem" of Kevin Bergin's was exactly what the defense wanted the jury to be thinking about, as would become blatantly apparent in Kiker's cross-examination of the next witness.

■ ■ ■

The state chose to have Kevin Bergin testify after John Ridgway, no doubt, because he was the more sensational of the two witnesses, the "hatchet man," as Gene Hood had referred to him. As if to warn jurors of illusions created by the prosecution to mislead them, Brent Kiker had cautioned the jury that Kevin Bergin would appear "clean cut," with his goatee shaved off.

This was perhaps an oversimplification. Yes, the goatee was gone. Yes, his head had been shaved. But it went much further than that. If you look at photos of Kevin Bergin around the time of his arrest, you will see a gaunt, eerily attractive young man whose heavily lidded eyes, slanted downward at the corners, give him a sensual, sleepy appearance. He has high cheek-bones, or maybe they just seem high because his cheeks are hollow. His jaw curves delicately forward in an almost feminine line, but his chin is firmly masculine, slightly asymmetrical. If you watch the videotape of his police interview held on October 21, 1999, you will see a pale, haggard young man with a spark of something disturbing in his brown eyes. But it is a spark. It is alive, moving with energy. There's someone there, thinking, feeling.

The Kevin Bergin who took the stand on January 17, 2001, to testify for the State of South Carolina would not have been recognizable, physically, as the same individual, and this was not just due to the haircut. Although he had not put on a tremendous amount of weight in jail, his face was bloated, without any angular definition aside from the widow's peak that crowns his forehead. His chin, once prominent, had receded into the moonfaced roundness of his cheeks. His eyes, which had nearly disappeared beneath his puffy eyelids, were absolutely empty.

After establishing who he is and what he has pled guilty to, Solicitor Murdaugh asked him when he had come down to South Carolina and for what purpose. Bergin responded, "Purpose to commit a murder," and with those words he launched his own version of what had happened on the day that Nell died.

Bergin's testimony agreed with Ridgway's in many respects but added convincing little details, describing how Sarah had hugged John when she first came out and how she then had started jumping up and down with excitement. What is perhaps most notable, he repeated John's statement that, just before Sarah went back to get her mother, she had said, "The bitch is gonna die," something he had also mentioned in his original interview, just a few hours after the murder.

Much of Kevin's testimony at the trial agrees with other information he gave police at that initial interview, but, significantly, he waffles when he claims that Sarah told him to kill her mother, on the single occasion that he spoke directly to her. At first he only recalls that she told him "she didn't want the kids harmed."

Later the solicitor returned to the question of what Sarah said to him on the phone, asking him to repeat it. Bergin affirmed that he had one conversation with Sarah on the phone, and that she said, "she didn't want the kids harmed. And the one brief meeting," he started to say, but Murdaugh interrupted him.

"Wait a minute, now. Why would she have said that, Don't want the kids harmed?"

Bergin answered, "'Cause we were talking about what exactly we were gonna do. We didn't know . . ." The solicitor interrupted again.

"Okay. Tell me—Tell me what you told Sarah and what she told you then."

Bergin answered, "I didn't—I don't remember what I told her. All I remember is that we're—we were just—we were handing the phone back and forth between me and John. John was talking to her and then hand it to me for a couple of minutes, then he's talk [*sic*] to her again. And I remember they were talking about originally she wanted us to kill both parents. So, you know, we didn't know whether we should kill both parents. But she specified she wanted both parents killed but she said she didn't want the kids harmed. That's what she was telling me on the phone. She was saying I don't want the kids harmed. You know, and John was saying she had said that, too. So that's all I remember talking to her."

When asked how long that was before the actual murder, Kevin responded, "A couple days."

What seems key to me is that John had another conversation with Sarah the day before the murder, and it is in this conversation, John repeatedly claimed when he spoke to me on the phone, that they decided "no one needs to die."

During his testimony, when he talked about the actual murder, Kevin somewhat corroborated John's claim, and Sarah's words that were allegedly spoken to Mary Nelson immediately after the murder, when he explained that he "wasn't trying to hit her [Nell] that many times but I think I was like real nervous and pumped up trying to like, you know, psych myself out. You know what I'm saying? So I could be able to do this by myself. Trying to manipulate myself in a state of mind where I could do something like this." He admits it was a mistake to hit her so many times before they could get the combination to the safe and states that the only reason he stabbed her was "to make sure she was dead."

Knowing that Brent Kiker would ask Kevin what he was doing while John and Sarah were in the house, getting Sarah's stuff, Murdaugh addressed the issue. Bergin responds, "I kept strangling her and she started—I don't know whether it was raining or not but there were these bugs all over [her]. They're just flying everywhere. It was like they could smell the evil or something. Just bugs. Just covered in bugs. Must have been attracted to the smell of blood or something. And I was just sitting there covered in blood, bugs all over me and I was just trying—I was like Jesus Christ, I just want to get this over with, you know. I was like—it was just sickening. I just had felt like—I just felt sorrow because of the point of taking a human life and I just felt it was just stupid, what we were doing. But I just wanted to get it over with, you know. Now she's already hurt, we might as well just kill her. So I just kept strangling her."

When Brent Kiker took over to cross-examine the witness, the first thing he did was to point out the inconsistencies between the version of events that Kevin was delivering in court and the story he told police in the hours after he was arrested. But when Kiker asked Kevin to agree with this characterization of his testimony, Bergin refused, then qualified his refusal saying he just didn't give police as much detail before. But Kiker persisted, pointing out ways the story had changed in substance. For instance, when Bergin first spoke to police, he said he had never talked to Sarah before seeing her at her home. Now Bergin said, "At the time I talked to police I didn't want to implicate anybody but myself. Because, see, I don't implicate friends on matters. I don't implicate other people. That is looked at as being a rat."

"I see," Kiker responded, allowing a moment for the implications of what Bergin had just said to sink in. We could see that it hadn't, not really, when Bergin continued:

"As they did to me."

Kiker tried to ask another question, but Bergin interrupted. The issue of having been ratted out was obviously a sore spot. "But I was more loyal than they were to me."

Presumably Kevin was thinking of the night they were arrested, and the way that he was, in his mind, betrayed first by Sarah, when she abandoned the vehicle that neither he nor John could operate, and then by John, who immediately told detectives everything that had happened.

For the rest of his cross-examination of Kevin Bergin, Brent Kiker focused on Bergin's alleged Satanism and how it related to rituals described in *The Necromantic Ritual Book,* one of many books on the supernatural and the occult that were found in a bag stowed in the rear of Nell's Chevy Tahoe, a bag that both Kevin and John admitted belonged to them.

25

The Necromantic Ritual Book

Written and privately printed by Leilah Wendell at her own Westgate Press in New Orleans, *The Necromantic Ritual Book* strikes me as a wacky, idiosyncratic, New Agey metaphysical manual aimed at instructing "initiates" in the means of uniting their spirit with something that Wendell refers to as the "death energy," embodied in the personage of the Angel of Death, Azrael.

Although a casual reader might take Wendell's book to be frivolous or silly, she is quite serious about her topic, and her Azrael, at least, is grounded in Christian, Hebrew, and Islamic theology, where he is the archangel of death, conceived as a being with four faces and four thousand wings, his whole body consisting of eyes and tongues, their number corresponding to the number of people inhabiting the earth. His task is to constantly record and erase in a large book the names of human beings as they are born and die.

Wendell attempts to personify Azrael, attributing to him human feelings such as the desire for understanding, reverence, and love. Through offering him these things, she believes that those who come to share consciousness with him come to understand his world and feelings. Perhaps most intriguing, given Kevin Bergin's evident craving for anything that would provide him with intense feeling, is her promise to those who carry out these rituals: that the experience will be a profound emotional interaction. It is one that not only will stay with the practitioner during this lifetime, but will carry over into the next (Wendell 1). She also talks about the power of faith and the respect that must be shown to the "catalyst," her word for corpse, when such a thing is required by one of the rituals she describes (Wendell 2–3).

Words about the power of faith and love, and the importance of respect, were hardly what I expected to encounter in a book about rituals involving death and interactions with dead bodies, but this is heavily emphasized throughout the book. I was further intrigued when, as I continued to read, I was cautioned against the tendency of many people to think that the practice she describes as "Necromantic" is the same as "Necromancy" (Wendell 3). According to Wendell that belief is absolutely false. Although, she says, in earlier times such rituals were ghoulish and brutal, causing necromancy to be considered a "black art," it no longer should be considered as such.

She is right about necromancy's reputation as sinister; wrong, though, about its history, at least to some extent. In much earlier times, in the Greek and Roman civilizations for instance, necromantic ritual, defined as the summoning of the spirits of the dead, was viewed as a legitimate way to seek knowledge, though the dead were not always as informative as one might wish. The oldest surviving mention of necromancy appears in the narrative of Odysseus's voyage to Hades, where he evokes spirits by means of rites he has learned from the witch Circe. Necromancy gradually came to be associated with sin and evil through the influence of Christianity. In Deuteronomy, one of the books of the Old Testament of the Bible, Moses explicitly warns the Israelites against the practice of divination by means of the dead, which he viewed as a pagan abomination. Later Christian writers argued the impossibility of bringing someone back from the dead, stating that so-called spirits were actually disguised demons, adding another level of danger to the practice of spirit summoning. In the Middle Ages the Roman Catholic Church officially condemned the practice, and necromancers were prosecuted alongside witches.

The employment of dead bodies or entrails in necromantic ritual is also an ancient, if not widespread practice. The Roman writer Lucan mentions a ritual that involved pouring warm blood directly into the veins of a corpse as if to restore it to life, and Cicero writes that a man named Vatinius, in attempting to evoke the spirits of the dead, offered up the entrails of children. Saint Gregory Nazianzen, bishop of Constantinople in the fourth century, mentions that boys and virgins were sacrificed for the purpose of conjuring the dead and divination.

The modern Catholic Church does not conduct witch hunts or persecute witches, and it takes a decidedly more ambiguous position toward the idea of spirits. According to *New Advent*, the Catholic encyclopedia, the church accepts that, with God's permission, the souls of the dead may appear to the living, and even speak of things that are yet unknown to the living; necromancy, however, which is defined as the art of summoning spirits, is considered to involve evil spirits, and to produce dangerous results. So, in other words, if spirits come to you without being summoned, all is well and good; otherwise let them rest in peace, or you may get more than you bargained for.

Historically, necromantic rituals have been referred to as dark or "black" magic, but Wendell defines them as neither black nor white. They are, rather, rituals of twilight, the time of day when light and darkness meet. Light and dark are simply two sides of the truth, and if one is missing, there is no balance in the universe (Wendell 4).

The first time I read this, I immediately jumped up out of my chair and ran to get Kevin Bergin's psychiatric report, flipping to the section headed "Conclusion Regarding Criminal Responsibility." Here the team that examined Bergin noted his statement that "he had committed the murder because he needed to release sin into the world and that the spirits were commanding him to commit a killing and make it look like a murder. The purpose was to release sin into the world because without evil there can be no good."

During a later interview, Bergin admitted to fabricating these specific delusions in an effort to achieve an insanity defense; however, when one looks at the big picture of his behavior, at the large collection of books about the occult and the fact that he and John were practicing other rituals in the days leading up to the murder, it seems reasonable to assume that the material in this book influenced his thinking, including the way he thought about death, and particularly the notion that he could restore some kind of cosmic equilibrium to the universe by killing someone, as if the appearance of a murder, of a deed perceived as "evil," would highlight or even create, by its counterbalancing effect, something "good."

In Wendell's theology necromantic rites do sometimes involve intimate contact with dead bodies, which serve as the "catalyst" for the initiate to connect with what she calls the "death energy," and, in doing so, with the Angel of Death, Azrael (Wendell 1). Several rituals are described in great detail, so that, obviously, someone who wished to perform them would be able to do so. One of these is the High Necromantic Ritual. This is what Brent Kiker was referring to when he told me that he thought Kevin Bergin had gone to the Davis home to commit a murder in order to perform such a ritual. Whether or not that was Bergin's intention, the fact is that he had a bag, entered into evidence at the trial, that contained most or perhaps all (it isn't entirely clear) of the ingredients specified by Wendell for conducting this rite. These included a mirror, jasmine incense, goat's milk, a vial labeled (but never tested) "magician's blood," Tarot cards, and an athame, a ritual knife commonly used in Wiccan (and satanic) rituals (Wendell 12). There is also Wendell's suggestion that the ritual be performed next to a body of water, specifically a stagnant or slow-moving body of water, so that its flow is undisturbed (Wendell 11). The Bellinger Bluff property where Nell Davis was murdered lies adjacent to Hazzard Creek, a slow-moving tributary of the tidal Chechessee River.

At Sarah's trial Brent Kiker put a tremendous amount of effort into trying to prove that Kevin Bergin had gone to the Davis home in order to commit a murder that would enable him to perform this ritual, while Kevin Bergin consistently denied that any such thing had taken place. Without Bergin's admission of guilt, Kiker had to rely on the evidence, so the question is, does the evidence suggest that this ritual was actually performed? For one thing items in the "bag of tricks" (as Kiker referred to the books and paraphernalia John and Kevin brought to the scene) were not blood spattered or otherwise indicative of the notion that they had been used that day; thus the physical evidence supports Bergin and Ridgway's testimony that the murder had nothing to do with such a ritual. Still it is certainly suggestive that the young men were transporting a small library of books associated with the occult and a variety of ritual implements, which, aside from two suitcases full of clothing, a bag of toiletries, and some music CDs, were their *only* possessions. These items, and whatever guns and money they extracted from the safe in the Davis household, were all they intended to take with them to begin their new lives in Detroit. And in fact later, when Kevin Bergin finally decided to break his silence and communicate with me, I would discover that it was not *The Necromantic Ritual Book* that exerted the most influence on their behavior that day, but *The Satanic Bible,* by Anton LaVey, the book that John had steered me toward when I asked him what, if any, role Satanism had played in events leading up to Nell's murder.

26

"How he'd like to kill someone"

Sarah Nickel was not required to testify at her own trial, and Brent Kiker, like any good defense attorney, advised her against it for the simple reason that, "Once you get up on the stand, you have to let the solicitor have his turn. It's a can of worms." He knew this, and by the time Murdagh got through with Sarah, she knew it too, but pronouncing the very same words that John Ridgway would say when he agreed to speak with me about the murder seven years later, she proclaimed, "Of course I will. I've got nothing to hide."

Jurors for *State of South Carolina vs. Sarah Nickel* had already seen their share of courtroom drama, from Randy Murdaugh's brandishing of Nell's bloody t-shirt, to the pathologist's detailed catalogue of Nell Davis's wounds, to Kevin Bergin's description of the flies that buzzed around her bloody corpse, as if they could "smell the evil." When Sarah, a petite blond whose face bore a haunting resemblance to her mother's, took the stand, they collectively held their breath. Her lawyer didn't beat around the bush.

"Sarah, did you kill your mother?"

"No, sir, I did not."

"Did you help kill your mother?"

"No, sir, I did not."

"Did you plan the murder of your mother?"

"No, sir, I did not."

"Have you met Kevin Bergin—had you ever met Kevin Bergin in your life prior to October 20, 1999?"

"No, sir."

Unlike her codefendants Sarah had been a constant presence throughout the trial, sitting at the table between Brent Kiker, who questioned the witnesses, and his partner Anne Douds, who helped Sarah understand the proceedings and assisted Brent's efforts to keep the case organized and moving forward. So Sarah's appearance wouldn't have been a surprise. What was startling, even unsettling to the jury, was her voice. It was low, husky, a smoker's voice, entirely lacking the lilting cadence of preadolescent innocence that some women's voices never lose. Sarah's sounded like she'd never had it.

Kiker's next set of questions concerned a note and a series of events relating to the previous runaway attempt on October 7, 1999. On that day Sarah had left home and gone to John Ridgway's house because, she testified, her mom was talking about sending her back to rehab. She changed her mind, however, and returned home on October 8 because, she claims, "John was even heavier into drugs than he had been in the past. And while he was high on those drugs he said a lot of stuff that scared me." When asked to elaborate, she continued, "He was talking about how he'd like to kill someone and telling me about how bad a burning body smelled. Just things like that."

On the twenty-first of October, Kiker recalled, Nickel was supposed to be in court, and he asks her to describe for the court what was to be her role in that proceeding.

"I was—I believe I was supposed to testify against John Ridgway."

"And was he on trial?"

"Yes, he was."

"And was it a criminal trial?"

"Yes, it was."

"And did John care if you testified against him?"

"He was very, very hostile about me testifying against him."

"And when you say hostile, what do you mean?"

"He told me that if I testified against him that he knew people who could take care of me."

These "people," Nickel claimed, were "any number of people that he had bought drugs from." She did not elaborate further but, when asked if she perceived this as a real threat, answered in the affirmative. "Yes, sir. I thought he was serious about that."

Nickel also described having another conversation, via telephone, about the trial and John's expectations regarding its outcome. "I asked him about the incident of him cutting another student," she said, adding, "at the school he went to."

"And did John indicate whether he was going— planning on attending his trial the next day?" Kiker prompted.

"No, sir. He told me that since he had cut that student he—he thought it would make him look bad in court and he wanted to leave."

This cutting incident had taken place at Beaufort-Jasper Academy for Career Excellence on October 12. According to the victim the incident followed his repeated refusal to let Ridgway copy his class work. Ridgway announced that he would cut him on the count of three and then carried out his threat. He was arrested and charged with assault and battery of a high and aggravated nature, and possession of a weapon on campus.

When Kiker inquired if Ridgway had asked her to come with him, she answered, "Yes, sir, he did."

"And what did you say?"

"I believe I said something like okay, whatever."

But when asked if there was any kind of plan, if Ridgway had described "in any way how this leaving the area would be accomplished," Nickel answered in the negative. When asked whether she had packed any bags for her trip after getting off the phone, she admitted that she had. Did she pack her bag because she was afraid? Ambivalent? Or was Ridgway telling the truth about her involvement, that she was in on the plan from the beginning, planning to be part of the robbery from the beginning? Either way that packed suitcase was an inescapable fact that she had to admit to, regardless of what she would say about her involvement in the rest of the so-called plan.

Because the suitcase suggested that Sarah colluded in the plan, Kiker asked what she had done at school on the days just prior to her mother's murder. "Did you tell all your friends, you know, good-bye forever, I'm hitting the road?"

Well, of course she didn't. That would have been stupid, and if there's one thing nobody involved in this case will assert, it's that Sarah Nickel is stupid.

What did she do at school the day of her mother's murder?

"I attended all my classes," she said. "I talked to my friends there. Just a normal school day."

As if to underscore the day's normality, Kiker urged her to recall a conversation with Mistee McClain, who had already testified for the defense, regarding some plans for the upcoming weekend, which were to go to a movie or attend a football game.

All that was left, now, was the trip home after Nell picked her up from school: Haley and Willie were already in the car. They went straight home.

Sarah put away her school stuff. She went to talk to Haley about what she did in school that day. She asked Haley if she had any homework she needed help with. She had a short conversation with her brother but can't remember the topic. She went into the kitchen to get a glass of water and stood at the kitchen window looking out at the backyard that faces the marsh. She saw John Ridgway peeking around the corner of the shed.

"What did he look like?"

"He had something on his head. I later found out it was a hairnet and pantyhose. But it wasn't covering his face at the time. He had on a dark green shirt and khaki color pants."

"And what did you do next?"

Interestingly Nickel's answer states not what she did, but how she felt. "I was extremely shocked to see him at my house."

"Why were you shocked to see him?"

"My mother didn't like him. She did not allow me to speak with him. And he knew this. He knew his name was not allowed in our house and he knew he wasn't allowed to call our house, and I was surprised to see him there."

When Sarah admitted to going outside to meet John, Kiker asked, "Why did you do that?"

"I wanted to know why he was at my house. I wanted to know what he wanted."

"Did you think he may hurt you?"

"No, sir, nothing I saw about him at the time made me believe that he would hurt anyone."

But when she got outside, what she saw then made her think differently. Coming around the corner of the shed, she saw another person holding a baseball bat "choked up like he was about to swing it."

"Did he say anything? To you?"

"He said, Let's do it. Let's kill the bitch."

Kiker repeats these words, which are, essentially, a paraphrase of what Kevin and John had claimed, when they were on the witness stand, that Sarah said just before she left them to go inside and get her mother.

"So what did you do?"

"I was just extremely scared and John turned to Kevin and said Kevin, shut up. John turned to me and said Look, we're not here to hurt anybody, we just want to leave. He said go inside the house, unplug the phones and don't do anything stupid. And I said I don't know what you're talking about. I said how can I do that, I don't want to do that, no. And he said you have to, just don't fuck up."

Next she claimed that they told her she had to go inside and get her mom, and that if she didn't, they would kill her two younger siblings.

Sarah testified that she did what they asked, believing that by doing so, she would protect her siblings and that Ridgway and Bergin would "just go away," an idea that seems naive in the extreme. Kiker led her through the next series of events, her returning to the house and getting her mother, telling Nell that she needed to come outside because something appeared to be wrong with a pet rabbit whose pen was located behind the garage.

Up to this point, Sarah's testimony regarding what happened at Bellinger Bluff is very similar to John Ridgway's. Nearly every movement is the same, and even much of the language is the same, with one major difference: Did Kevin say, "Let's kill the bitch"? Or did Sarah say, "The bitch is gonna die!" Leave that out, and it is conceivable that both John and Sarah believe they are telling the truth. John could, in a drug-induced haze, have *mistakenly* believed that Sarah was part of a plan to rob her family, and even have misinterpreted her reluctance on the day of the robbery as minor hesitation about being a party to the event, rather than a genuine desire to have no part in it. This cannot be true, of course, if she did, as both he and Kevin Bergin had claimed, jump up and down excitedly, saying, "The bitch is gonna die!"

It is worth noting, though, that this statement is missing from John's first account to police, even though Sergeant Woodward had Ridgway three times go over the scene in which it was supposedly uttered, specifically asking what Sarah had said at that moment, just before she went in the house to get her mother, because Sarah's words were such an important part of the case against her. According to John's original statement, Sarah's last words to him before her mother came out, which Woodward had him repeat three times, were, "Here she comes."

After giving the jury a moment to absorb what his client has said so far, Kiker asked her a question that he knew must be rattling around inside the jurors' brains: "Sarah, when you went inside, why didn't you lock the door?"

This was a tough question. She must have known the jury had been wanting to ask her this one since the trial began.

"I don't know. I was scared. I didn't know what they were capable of. They had told me they weren't gonna hurt anybody if I did what they told me to do. And if I didn't do anything stupid. And I thought that not doing what they said was stupid."

Later, when I asked Sarah why she didn't tell her mother to call 9-1-1 right then, especially since she knew her mother had a gun in the house, she said she didn't know. She said she was scared and wasn't thinking clearly, and that all she could think about was how the house had "all those windows all over the front and the back."

It's true; 31 Bellinger Bluff has so many windows that if you stand in certain spots you can see all the way through, from one side to the other, even though it's a reasonably large house, 2,828 square feet of living space in the main house. I consider her fear, and what she said about how "that house is out in the sticks and who knows how long it would have taken the police to get there." Maybe it's because I was once alone in a house with a prowler outside, trying to break in, and a police dispatcher on the phone, trying to talk sense into me until a cruiser could get there, but when she puts me in the picture like this, I am slightly less skeptical of her panic. It still makes my skin crawl when I recall the police taking me outside, once they had searched the grounds, to see where the unknown person had opened the doors to our storage room and the crawl space under our house, searching for a way in.

"And did your mother come out?" Kiker asks.

We all know that she did, and that the two of them walked across the driveway, over to the shed, and that "as soon as Mom came around the corner she—Kevin hit her on the side of the head with a baseball bat. He hit her over and over and over again. It seemed like he'd have stopped hitting her." As for her response to the action that was unfolding: "I didn't know what to do. I was scared. I think I went into shock. I was just frozen. I couldn't move."

As Sarah's testimony continues, she tells the same story, though in slightly more detail, that she had related in her statement when she was arrested. There is some additional dialogue, "Kevin said this," "John said that," but there is little that adds to the story, other than making it appear that Sarah was, like her mother, an innocent victim. There is, however, one significant new detail. When Sarah and John had come back after getting Sarah's clothes and her mother's purse and jewelry, they had gone outside where, Sarah testified, after stabbing her mother, Kevin Bergin had tried to hand her the bloody knife.

When prompted to tell what happened next, Sarah described how she followed instructions to go inside and get some bags "for them to put their bloody clothes in." After John and Kevin had changed clothes, and the clothes were in a plastic bag, Sarah reported, "that's when John handed me the keys and walked me over to the car and said start it up. And so I put the key in the ignition and started it."

Sarah must have known that she was approaching yet another moment when the jury members would feel that she faced a crossroads, and wonder why she chose the direction that she did. She stumbled over her words. "I—I—looked at him and I said take it and go. I said just leave. And he said I can't drive, neither can Kevin, you have to take us. And so they got in the car. I got in the car and I started to drive off. I was shaking all over and I could barely keep my foot on the gas pedal." Again, claiming that she was following John's instructions, she started heading toward I-95, though a need for gas forced them to make a quick stop.

"And so what—what were you doing at the gas station? Why didn't you jump out of the car and run away?" Kiker asked, raising an issue that stung the memory of her stepfather, Solicitor Murdaugh, and Judge Brown enough for all three of them to ask me the same question five years later.

"I thought that they would catch me. I didn't know what they would do. My father lived nearby and that's when I made the decision to run to his house and I knew that he would protect us from them."

It's fascinating to me that Sarah's failure to run away at the gas station is the thing that bothers her stepfather (which, I would wager, is why it bothered the solicitor and the judge) the most, other than the murder itself, and it makes me wonder at what I have come to consider Mike Davis's failure of imagination, or even logic. What additional criminality did Sarah display by not running away from the boys at a gas station, where she reasonably might not have felt that she could have found someone to protect her? (Aren't gas station attendants getting assaulted and robbed all the time?) What criminal benefit did she gain by trying to escape from them in a way that seemed to her to be safer? Randy Murdaugh had a theory about this, but he wouldn't mention it until his summation, when it is too late for either Sarah or her attorney to respond.

After taking the jury through a description of her "shortcut," saying how John was "trying to console me in his own little way by telling me that they never meant to kill her, that they just wanted to knock her out," she described turning onto Knowles Island Road. She drove on past her daddy's mobile home, because his truck wasn't there, and then, very slowly on down to her friend Heather's, where, when she saw Heather's brother James, she "slammed the car into park. And John was like looking at me trying to ask me what I was doing and I told him I was freaking out, I couldn't do it, I—I was freaking out, I didn't know what to do and I jumped out of the car. And just started running. And ran to the front door," telling James, "Get in the house, get in the house, because," she said, "I could hear them coming after me. And I tried to run faster."

Sarah said she made it to the steps, "jerked open the glass door, said help me, they just killed my mom, call the police. And her [Heather's] grandma said go get the shotgun. From my closet. I turn around and go down the hallway toward the bedroom. I look out the window, I looked out the door and Kevin was standing right at the bottom of the stairs and John was behind him a little bit. James was between them and he was just holding his hand like what are you doing in my yard. I went and got the shotgun, handed it to his grandma, handed it to James and he loaded it."

And this is when Bergin and Ridgway, realizing that all was lost, ran back to the car and made a futile attempt to get it moving, followed by an equally futile attempt to hide the evidence of their crime. After throwing one knife, two pairs of latex gloves, one panty hose, various items of clothing, and three shoes into the bushes, they disappeared into the woods.

Having reached the end of the narrative, Sarah's attorney returned to the salient points one more time before surrendering his witness to the solicitor.

"Okay, Sarah, when those boys showed up at your house did you—did you know that they were gonna rob your mom?"

"No, sir."

"Did you try and help your mom in any way?"

"I couldn't. I was too scared. I didn't know what to do."

"Looking back on it do you feel like there's things you could've done differently?"

"Yes, sir. I know I could lock the door and call the police but I wasn't thinking; I didn't know what was gonna happen. They told me they weren't gonna hurt anybody and I believed them. And now my mom is gone and I'm never going to see her again."

This last bit is of course true, but it belabored the obvious and feels like a play for sympathy, like a scene from a melodrama, especially when Kiker says, "All right. I have nothing further."

Solicitor Murdaugh's first questions zeroed in on Sarah's allegation that she was threatened by Ridgway with bodily harm if she followed through with her intention to testify against him on the following Friday. Sarah confirmed that she was indeed afraid both of Ridgway, that he, himself, was capable of harming her, and of his "drug dealer friends," whom she now refuses to name, saying, "For my own safety." Murdaugh soon changed tack and began asking Sarah about her relationship with Nell. Sarah admitted that it was a "rocky relationship" but denied ever making threats to harm her, or more specifically, to kill her. Murdaugh was especially interested in testimony given by Lisa Pulice, Sarah's guidance counselor at Hilton Head High, who claimed that Sarah had threatened, in her presence, to kill not only her mother, but her best friend, Amy Heath, and the guidance counselor. Sarah, like her friend Amy who had already testified for the defense, insisted that the threat did not represent a real intention.

It wasn't really all that important, though, whether or not Sarah agreed with Lisa Pulice on what was intended that day at Hilton Head High, because when Sarah decided to take the stand and tell her own story, she opened wide the door that would allow the admission into court of one of the most damning pieces of evidence the prosecution possessed, the one piece of evidence that that judge had, in his single motion in favor of the defense, kept out of the jury's hands until this moment: her diary.

After listening to Sarah deny nearly every assertion that Lisa Pulice had made regarding her behavior, and especially after he had had to listen to the testimony of the two men whom he considered her coconspirators, Randy Murdaugh, who had thus far treated the defendant in a fairly gentle manner, owing to her gender and age, must have felt as if he had a lump of something hot and hard sitting in his chest, right on top of his heart. Now this lump was full nearly to bursting, as if the evil of this case had infected him with its poison. What he was about to do was lance that boil, let that poison spew. He may have hated doing it, but he had to; otherwise he could not heal; Mike Davis could not heal; the community they belonged to could not heal.

The first cut was quick and to the point.

"Miss Nickel, have you ever made any threat that you were gone kill your mother?"

"I did not say I'm going to kill you. I believe I was mad and I said—I don't remember what I said but if you mean did I threaten her and mean it, no, sir."

"That wasn't my question. I said did you ever use words that would indicate that you wanted to kill your mother."

After getting Sarah to admit that she had used words to this effect, and that she and her mother had not had a particularly good relationship, he proceeded to introduce the diary. He first asked Sarah if she ever wrote about killing her mother, and, once the judge had overruled Brent Kiker's objection, read from a notebook with, of all things, a kitten on the front. "I ask you, Miss Nickel, if you ever wrote 'Haley just called me and asked me when I was coming home. She was about to cry when she asked me. It broke my heart to see her hurt. I hung up the phone and cried so hard. I love her and Willie to death and I would never let anyone hurt them but I know I'll end up hurting them both when I kill mom. She deserves to rot in the fiery pits of hell. I'll take her there myself'. Did you write that?"

"If that is my diary that was taken from my room, then yes, I wrote that."

"Did you also write, Miss Nickel, 'I'm never going to Mom's house again. She's an unbearable bitch and I was about to slap the living shit out of her. She's so fucking selfish, I could just kill her. God, I hate her ass so much. Got to go catch up on my beauty sleep.'"

The line about catching up on her beauty sleep seems somehow parallel to the image of a killer eating a hamburger after popping a cap in someone.

"Did you say that?" Murdaugh prompted, "Did you write that?" I have heard, from those who were present, that this is when his voice lost its patient, cajoling quality. He was hard as nails, dry as dust, accusatory as a pointing finger.

"If that's my diary, then, yes, sir, I wrote that."

"Okay, then, I'll ask you to look at it and tell me whether or not this is your diary and whether that is what you wrote." Murdaugh passed the diary over to her. She examined the writing, then handed it back.

"You did hate your mother, didn't you?" Murdaugh asked flatly, and not very loudly, though the courtroom was so still his words seemed to ring through the silence, at least according to one person present.

"No, I did not."

"Well, why did you write in there that she's a selfish bitch?"

"At the time I—" but he didn't let her finish. His anger was showing clearly now, and he could feel another wall of emotion behind him, coming from the jury box. According to Juror Number 13, they were angry, too. He could thank his lucky stars that Nickel decided to take the stand. If she hadn't, with only Ridgway and Bergin making themselves look like bumbling cutthroats at best, like Satanists at worst, she might have gotten off scot-free. So he interrupted her, demanding, "Was she a selfish bitch?" not the worst thing a girl can call her mother, but fairly close to it.

Kiker saw what was happening and tried to come to his client's aid, saying, "Your Honor," but Sarah proceeded to answer, saying, simply—

"No." She had foregone the formality, or the hypocrisy, of the "sir."

Her lawyer continued, as if she still needed rescuing, "—she needs— she can answer—right to answer her question," but she obviously was already doing that.

"No," she repeated.

And the judge, despite the fact that she had already answered the question, decided to take the opportunity to treat this lying, bloody-minded teenager as patronizingly as possible. Speaking to her as if she was a little girl wearing a pinafore, he said, "When he asks you these questions, you can answer yes or no or I don't know and then, if you like, you can explain them, so." Then, to Murdaugh, he said slyly, "Repeat your question," and Murdaugh reined himself in accordingly.

"Why did you call her a selfish bitch?"

"Those were my feelings at the time."

"And those feelings lasted for some two years, didn't they?"

"No, sir, they didn't."

"Excuse me?" Murdaugh asked, to make sure the jury heard Sarah's answer to this question.

"Me and my mother were working on our relationship," Sarah said, her voice so low it was almost a whisper.

"You were working on your relationship?" Murdaugh's voice was a balloon filled with incredulity.

"Yes, sir."

"And your relationship was such that ya'll had become a loving family?" The balloon swelled dangerously.

"No, sir. We were working on it." Nickel seemed dazed, but her eyes were dry. Murdaugh shuffled papers on the table.

"Going back to what I asked you a moment ago, you were afraid of John Ridgway?

"Yes, sir."

"Because he had threatened to do you bodily harm if you came to the hearing the next day, did he not?"

"Yes, sir."

"What was the hearing about?"

"Trouble that he had gotten into. I believe it was in '98."

When asked, "Who was in that trouble with him?" she had to answer, "I was."

This was another door that, by taking the stand and testifying, she had opened and by doing so had invited the prosecution to come inside and have her for dinner. Until she raised the issue herself, her previous runaway incident involving John back in the fall of 1998, which is almost a mirror image of this one, had been mentioned only indirectly, when Ridgway testified, because it helped explain why he wanted to get out of town.

With each question that he asked, Murdaugh must have felt as if he were closing a loophole that Sarah might slip through. Not only had they run away together, but they had stolen a car—this time from her stepmother, Tracy. And where did they go? To Darien, Connecticut. Perhaps the jury didn't remember that Kevin lived in Darien. Because the charges were dropped, they would never know that both money and a handgun were stolen from Sarah's father, Joe. The major difference, of course, between the two events is that one resulted in a death. Otherwise John and Sarah would simply have found themselves back in Midlands Reception and Evaluation, for a longer stay this time, after which both of them would likely have been sent to rehab.

Initially Sarah held up well under Randy Murdaugh's relentless, rapid-fire questions, answering without hesitation, and her answers were usually in the form of an uncomplicated affirmation or denial, yes or no, followed by "sir." Like any good prosecutor, he tried to get her confused by little inconsistencies in her own story, perhaps hoping that if he could find one loose thread, and pull it hard enough, the whole fabric would unravel. For instance, in recounting Sarah's version of the way events unfolded, Murdaugh said, "As I understand John Ridgway, you walked out to see what John Ridgway was doing behind your shed?"

"Yes, sir."

"And you are deathly afraid of John Ridgway because he had threatened to do you bodily harm if you testified tomorrow?"

"Yes, sir."

"And yet you walked out of that house to the shed that he was hiding behind? Is that correct?"

"Yes, sir."

"And you went around and talked to him?"

"Yes, sir."

"And the reason that you did that, you told the jury, is because you didn't see anything about him that would be a danger?"

"No, sir, he did not look to harm at the time."

"Even though he had a pantyhose up on his head."

He then took her through the other actions that pointed to her involvement: her unplugging the upstairs telephone, her bringing her mother outside "even though there's a crazed-looking fellow with a baseball bat standing around." But Sarah stuck to her story, saying, "He said he wasn't going to hurt anyone and I believed him." Murdaugh was able to turn this one around on her, though, when he immediately asked, "But you also believed him when he told you he was gone hurt you, didn't you?"

"Yes sir," she answered, "and I also believed it at the time he told me he was going to kill me if I testified against him."

Murdaugh moved on to another set of questions, ones having to do with the safe in her parents' bedroom, and why John Ridgway thought there was $20,000 stashed there, which was why he and Kevin Bergin wanted to see if they could get into it after Nell was unconscious. Sarah admitted that she heard the boys trying to get the combination from her mother, and that she knew John thought there was money in the safe.

"How in God's name would he know that there's a safe in that house if you hadn't told him?" the solicitor demanded.

And this time Sarah was rattled. But she answered the question readily enough. "He asked me where they kept their guns. And I told him in a locked safe. That I did not know the combination to."

"Why would he have thought there was money in there?" and then "Why would he have thought there was jewelry in there?"

To both questions, Sarah responded, lamely, "I don't know, sir."

Once again Murdaugh abruptly changed tack, as if he was leaving the jury to draw their own conclusions. If they could connect the dots, more power to them. If not, that is what his summation would be for.

Next he asked the defendant what would seem to be an entirely irrelevant question, "Were you wearing shoes when you went to Heather Nelson's house?"

Rather than producing the shoes, he held up a photograph, allowing Sarah to confirm that these were indeed her shoes and that they were indeed removed from her feet and lodged up under the front seat, as they appear in the photograph, which was now circulated among the jury members. Murdaugh waited a moment, until they had all had the chance to see it, before he asked his final question, because it was the climax of his performance, and he wanted everyone's attention. "Let me ask you a question. One thing that—that sort of amazed me in your testimony a moment ago and I want to let you explain it to me." He referred to Kevin Bergin's attempt to give Sarah the bloody knife after he had stabbed her mother: "You said that after you heard the thumping out there you walked back around and Kevin had blood all over him. And had a knife in his hand and tried to give you the knife?"

"Yes, sir," Sarah answered uncertainly.

"Now, if you were not a part of this whole thing why in the name of God would a man give you the knife that he just killed your mother with?"

"I don't know."

"Doesn't make sense, does it?"

"I don't know why he wanted to give it to me."

Having pointed out all the inconsistencies in Sarah's behavior and having concluded with an image that would linger in at least one juror's mind, Mr. Murdaugh said, "I have no further questions."

Brent Kiker's redirect helped Sarah a little by establishing a context for her diary entries, to the extent of showing that she wrote in her diary every day, and therefore the two entries about her mother were, metaphorically speaking, two isolated shoals in a sea of prose that addressed a myriad of other topics. This gave Sarah the opportunity to tell the jury that she had been living with her dad when she wrote the entries, but that she had had bitter arguments with her mother around the time they were written, which predated the murder by about a year. It also seems worth noting, although Kiker did not point this out, that Sarah wrote explicitly violent entries about her mother only when she was living with Joe. During redirect Kiker also asked Sarah for more detailed information about her conversations with John regarding her parents' safe. It had come up, she said, because the Davis home had been broken into and her stepfather's guns were stolen. After the burglary her parents had gotten an alarm and a safe to store the guns in.

While Kiker's performance on redirect was not as powerful as Randy Murdaugh's, it did help Sarah. Most notably it acted as a kind of release valve for the tension that had built up in the courtroom as Murdaugh had, through the testimony he elicited, created the portrait of a young woman who was a clever liar, perhaps clever enough to let someone else kill her mother for her and take the full blame. Murdaugh didn't use labels like "monster" or "freak," because he didn't need to; as far as he was concerned, Sarah's deeds, stripped of whatever weak excuses or explanations she might offer, spoke for themselves. Still, when Brent Kiker talked to her as if she was an ordinary person, and elicited explanations for her behavior, and allowed her to provide a context that softens the impact of those vicious diary entries, Sarah Nickel slowly transformed back into a human being, and that may have been what saved her from being convicted of her mother's murder.

27

The Beginning of the End

On the afternoon of January 18, 2001, Randy Murdaugh ended the witness phase of the trial of Sarah Grace Nickel on a note of anticlimax. He called his final rebuttal witness, Stephen D. Campbell, an employee of Hilton Head Medical Center, where Nell Davis, the murder victim, had also been employed. Mistee McClain, a previous witness for the defense, had claimed that she saw Sarah with her mother at an awards banquet at the hospital on October 15, and that not only were they getting along, but the two girls, at that time, had made plans to get together the following weekend, which would have been the weekend after Davis was murdered. When Campbell took the stand, Murdaugh simply asked him to state his name and occupation and asked him if he had been acquainted with the victim. Campbell answered in the affirmative. Murdaugh recalled the date on which McClain's testimony had placed the awards banquet. He asked Campbell, "Is that when the awards banquet was?"

"No, sir," Campbell responded.

"When was it?"

"Twenty-fifth of September, 1999."

"Did you go to it?"

"Yes, sir."

And that was all.

Judge Luke Brown dismissed the jury telling them that when they returned the following day they would hear summations by the attorneys. He reminded them once again not to discuss the case with anyone else, or to allow anyone to discuss it in their presence. He reminded them not to read any newspapers, listen to any radio, or watch TV.

With the courtroom cleared, it was time for Sarah's attorney to go through his motions, which action might as well have been given the slang interpretation of the phrase, because that is all it amounted to: going through the motions. He renewed his motion for a directed verdict based on his original challenge that the state's indictment was flawed, since there was no evidence that Sarah had been violent toward her mother in any way. He had to have known, even as he urged the judge to consider this motion, that the hand-of-one rule would, as it had before, be used to justify the charges of both murder and armed robbery. Kiker also objected, again, to the introduction of previously suppressed information, that is, Sarah's journal, although at this point it was pro forma. The damage was done when the jury heard Sarah's words read out in court:

"I love her and Willie to death and I would never let anyone hurt them but I know I'll end up hurting them both when I kill mom. She deserves to rot in the fiery pits of hell. I'll take her there myself."

Sarah's only hope now lay with the court of appeals, and that, really, was why Kiker was speaking now—to get his objections into the record.

Two other motions Kiker made were to have the jury presented with other options besides just "murder" and "armed robbery" that could fit the testimony they were given, depending on which parts of which testimony they chose to believe. This is how he explained it to the judge: "The jury's entitled to believe, you know, little bit of one testimony and a little bit of others and I think they can conclude, they're entitled to conclude that Sarah Nickel desired to run away, which would not constitute a felony, that in the course of her running away that it was—an unlawful killing took place without malice, express malice on her part . . ."

His goal was to persuade the judge to include involuntary manslaughter as a possible charge—an option for the jury should they not feel comfortable with convicting her of murder. Rather surprisingly the judge left the decision up to Solicitor Murdaugh, who responded, "I can think of nothing that's come out in this testimony that would cover a—would require a charge of involuntary manslaughter."

Judge Brown, as usual, let the solicitor have his way. "I deny that motion."

On the following morning, January 19, Kiker tried once more to have the judge modify the charge to the jury, this time making a motion that the "lesser included offense" of larceny (that is, simple theft) be mentioned along with those of armed robbery and murder, again with the intention of presenting the jury with more options to choose from.

By this time, though, the judge had run out of patience. He said, "She's either guilty of it or she's not guilty of it. Now, she says I didn't take anything. So I deny your motion."

But Mr. Kiker didn't give up so easily. He said, "Well, her testimony, your honor, is that they forced her to take items out of the house."

"Yeah, she's saying I didn't take them," Judge Brown responded.

"The evidence produced by the prosecution is that she willfully took items out of the house."

"Yes."

"Jury's entitled to believe anything they want out of the sum of the testimony and if there are facts in the record that would constitute the crime of larceny, then I'm entitled to a lesser included offense charge. . . . I believe that there is evidence in the record which would support it and the jury is entitled to find it if they so choose."

The judge said, "I deny that motion."

And with that, the trial moved at last into its final phase.

■ ■ ■

Sarah Nickel, dressed in a navy blazer and a white blouse, could feel her heart racing as the jurors entered and seated themselves. Most of them avoided meeting her eyes, which she knew was not a good sign, but she fought that knowledge, praying for a miracle, praying for her mother's intercession on her behalf, for anything that would save her. Judge Brown began his folksy welcome speech to the jury, reminding them of how they were to behave, who would speak first and why, what they should do and not do during the course of the day's events, how they should tell the forelady if they need a break.

Speaking for the defense, Mr. Kiker addressed the jury first. In the course of his summation, he would tell the jury that this is the most important case that he has ever been involved with, and the weight of that conviction has to have sat heavily on his young shoulders. I wouldn't know exactly how heavily until I saw him at Sarah's PCR hearing, in April 2008.

"Ladies and gentleman, this is the last opportunity that I will have to speak on behalf of Sarah Nickel." His tone was as grave and formal as a minister's. He might have been speaking at a funeral. And for all he knew, it was a funeral. His client could get a life sentence if she was convicted of murder, and a life sentence, for a seventeen-year-old, is a kind of death.

"Sarah Nickel did not murder her mother. Sarah Nickel did not plan to murder her mother. Sarah Nickel did not help these killers that you met in the courtroom this week. She did not help them murder her mother." Kiker proceeded to tell the jury what the case was not about in the attempt, probably vain, to undo some of the damage that had been done by the state's laborious presentation of the gory details of Nell's death. "One of the things this case is not about," he said, "is who killed Nell Davis. We all know who killed Nell Davis. Sarah's mother was killed by Kevin Bergin and John Ridgway. Kevin Bergin was the one who beat her over the head with the baseball bat. And you heard about the brutality of the murder and I won't go into it again now." He wouldn't go into it again because the important question was whether or not Sarah was "in on it, too. Did she—did she call up these boys and tell them to come and kill her mother? Did she call them up, did she induce them to commit this crime? Or did they do it on their own for some other reason?"

After humorously pointing out the many advantages that the state had had over him in presenting its case—all the resources of the Beaufort and Jasper County Sheriff's Departments and SLED, the South Carolina Law Enforcement Division, in addition to "a solicitor that's been doing this longer than I've been alive," Kiker added. "And so what the law does to kind of make it a little more fair, they say the state has to prove the crime beyond a reasonable doubt."

When he defined reasonable doubt he was very specific and deliberate: "What that means in your deliberations is they have to prove to you to such an extent that when you go back to that jury room all twelve of you sit around the table and you talk about the case and you weigh the evidence and you say, I can say with a firm conviction, with a virtual certainty that Sarah Nickel was the one who planned and assisted in the murder, in murdering her mother."

As the judge's charge had made clear, and as Kiker reminded them once more, Sarah's mere presence at the crime—even the fact that she didn't assist her mother, didn't try to keep the boys from hurting her—wasn't enough. Sarah had to have taken an active part in the plan, at the very least, in order for the rule of "hand of one" to apply. As Kiker reminded the jury, "Nobody's saying that Sarah Nickel had this knife in her hand and plunged it into her mother's chest. Nobody's saying she had this bat in her hand and beat her mother over the head with it. And nobody's saying that Sarah Nickel put her mother in that box."

Kiker did have a lot going for him. One or both of the state's chief witnesses were clearly liars. In Kevin Bergin's original statement to police, which Brent Kiker had gone over in his cross-examination of Bergin, he had initially claimed that it was Sarah who had beaten her mother, with a board or a bat (he wasn't sure which). He had also stated that he had never met or spoken to Sarah Nickel before the day of the murder, when he saw her at her house on Bellinger Bluff, but later testified that they had spoken once one the phone. Although Bergin did, in his original interview, confess to the murder, had there not been overwhelming evidence of his guilt, it seems doubtful that he would have. Up to, and even on the very the day he entered his plea, I would later learn, Bergin had second thoughts and considered going to trial where he would have certainly pled "not guilty"; otherwise there would have been no point in going to trial. On Monday, January 8, eight days before Sarah's trial was scheduled to begin, he appeared in court with his attorney, Gene Hood, to formally enter the plea that had been negotiated with Murdaugh's office. The process did not go smoothly. Bergin balked and walked out, returning only after his father and Hood had, undoubtedly, explained the hopelessness of facing a jury. By this time the police had far more than John and Sarah's testimony to substantiate Kevin's guilt; they had forensic evidence gathered from the bat and the knife, and from the clothes Kevin was wearing, as well as the gloves that, in his mind, would have shielded him from detection. In his summation Kiker was quick to remind the jury of the inconsistencies in Kevin's story, and to point to other evidence of his willingness to lie.

Most troubling of all, perhaps, was the fact that Kevin and John disagreed on the reason for going to the Davis home. In one of the most dramatic moments of Sarah Nickel's trial, he had gone there, Bergin said, "For this purpose.... Purpose to commit a murder." Ridgway, on the other hand, both in his statement to police, in conversations with me, and on the witness stand, claimed that the plan had been to disable and rob Mrs. Davis, but not to murder her. Interestingly Bergin's original statement to police had made the same claim: "The whole plan was to leave from her place, to . . . not to hurt anybody, to take off." The question was, if he was lying now, why was he lying? To please the solicitor? After all, as Kiker kept reminding the jury, Bergin wouldn't be sentenced until after Nickel's trial was over, and if Murdaugh chose—if the outcome of Nickel's trial were unsatisfactory—he could force Bergin to stand trial after all.

And then of course there was the *Necromantic Ritual Book* that had sat in a bag in the shed adjacent to the spot where Nell was murdered. Kiker reviewed some salient features of the rituals he had gone over in painstaking detail during Bergin's trial, reminding the jury how Kevin had spoken about the book as if its contents were no big deal, as if a book about rituals with dead bodies were something that anyone might be interested in reading. Kiker furthermore recalled the pathologist's characterization of the stabbing as "overkill" and informed jurors that the "culmination of this whole book [*The Necromantic Ritual Book*] is to—to plunge a knife into the heart of the already dead corpse. And that's to keep you from being haunted. By the corpse."

Unfortunately for Sarah this was the first time Kiker had mentioned this particular passage from the book. If it did possess the importance he assigned it, he certainly bungled the focus of his previous presentation and perhaps confused the jury. What shouldn't have been confusing, though, was the fact that, initially, John Ridgway and Kevin Bergin had told entirely different stories to police, and that, initially, they had run away into the woods while Sarah had escaped from them and called for help at what she said was the first safe opportunity. Further evidence that the boys had lied had come from members of the Nelson family, Mary and James, who testified for the state. They both claimed that Kevin Bergin, "the skinny one," had chased Sarah all the way to the door of their mobile home where Grandma Mary had confronted him with the barrel of a shotgun. Both Bergin and Ridgway denied going anyway near the residence and said they turned around when they realized that Sarah was calling the police. The question is, if they had been nowhere near the residence, how would they have known Sarah was calling the police?

There was an additional point on which Bergin's testimony differed from Ridgway's that Kiker failed to mention, which was Bergin's claim that John had taken over the task of "choking" Mrs. Davis when Bergin got tired. John claimed that he was "checking" her to see if she still had a pulse.

What the jury had to have been wondering, at this point, if they hadn't wondered before, was why the state would want to cut a deal with Kevin Bergin, the man who brutally murdered Nell Davis, in order to get Sarah Nickel. It's a tough question, and Brent Kiker couldn't give the answer he would like to have given: that this trial was at least in part fueled by Mike Davis's personal conviction that Sarah was involved, and Mike Davis's personal relationship with the judge, which Kiker suspected but could not prove. So he said what he could say, what he hoped would make sense, enough sense for the nine women and three men of the jury to believe that although Sarah was present, and although she made some stupid decisions, such as agreeing to leave town with John when he called her the day before the murder, such as going and getting her mother out of the house rather than warning her of the boys' presence, that she was not part of a plan to take her mother's life.

And if it weren't for those entries in her diary, I believe that he would have succeeded. In fact I wonder if the case would have ever gone to trial. Kiker knew how damaging those entries were, and so he had to frame them, put them into some kind of perspective for the jury. He described the police going into Sarah's closet, finding a box that had all her poetry and diaries, which she'd been keeping since fourth grade. These diaries were where she wrote everything, including the words about wanting to kill her mom. She also wrote about her boyfriends and "everything else you could imagine." So police went through these writings of Sarah's that covered a period of six or seven years, the same way, he asked the jury to imagine, they would go through the computer files of a suspected arsonist. And what they found, in all that mass of material, were two entries, the latest one dated a year prior to the murder, and nothing since. Surely for someone like Sarah, who wrote down everything that was important to her, there would be something, some clue that she was planning something big against her mother. There was a note to Nicole Cocola, but that only alluded to running away; there wasn't the slightest hint of violence, or some kind of big surprise that would impress everyone after Sarah was gone which, given Sarah's low sense of self-esteem, one would have expected.

But the police had John and Kevin's stories—even though they didn't exactly match up—on the one hand, and Sarah's diary entries—even though the most recent one was more than a year old—on the other, in addition to which they had Mike Davis, and his absolute conviction that Sarah had everything to do with what had happened to his wife. What the jury also had—though Kiker didn't want to remind them of this—was the knowledge that John and Sarah had been friends for more than a year, and that one of their previous runaway attempts, in November 1998, was, minus the violence, nearly a carbon copy of this one.

Kiker knew that his last, best chance to clear his client was to tell a story—her story—of what happened on the day Nell Davis died. It is the story that that he had chosen, for the most part, to believe, because he believed that Sarah did not plan to kill her mother, and if he could persuade the jury of his own faith in Sarah, perhaps they would vote to acquit.

His narrative was straightforward, emphasizing features of Sarah's testimony that, he believed, attested to its truthfulness: her attendance at school on the day of the murder, her alleged plans with Mistee McClain for the weekend following, the state's lack of physical evidence linking her to the crime, the state's lack of phone or computer records showing prior contact with Kevin Bergin, the fact that she had to pack a bag after the boys arrived, and most important, the fact that she ran away from them—despite the full tank of gas and the successful getaway—she ran away, to the Nelsons' mobile home, clearly terrified, pursued by the two boys who turned back only when they either saw Mary Nelson standing at the door with a shotgun leveled at their heads, or when they heard her yelling, "Get the shotgun!" which the jury had heard when they listened to the 9-1-1 tape.

One of the most uncomfortable moments of Brent Kiker's summation came when he had to deal with the testimony of Mike Davis. Davis had told the jury that approximately a month prior to the murder, Sarah and her mother had had an argument that left Sarah "just trembling and shaking and just totally out of control." When Davis had gone upstairs after the fight to check on his stepdaughter, he found her, he said, "in this shaking rage," something he'd never witnessed before, and she had said to him, "I just want to kill her." Then, he said, approximately ten days before the murder, he and Sarah had been in the kitchen together, when he had told her to do something, he couldn't recall exactly what. In response, he said, she "sort of worked a little smirk," then picked up a kitchen knife and "kind of holds it at me, sort of smiles at me a little bit with it and I said, Sarah, that's just what you probably need to do but if you ever pull a knife on me you'd better pull one that's made out of candy because I'll make you eat it." And at that time, according to Davis, she had said, "If you mess with me

I'll have Kevin take care of you." Davis claimed that once everything else happened and he heard these names, John Ridgway and Kevin Bergin, it all came together and the name did mean something.

The problem was that he didn't tell police. Davis claimed to have told Randy Murdaugh, but Randy Murdaugh isn't who would have been conducting the investigation at the point when Mike Davis put two and two together, unless it was months after the crime occurred. The interviewing of witnesses, the gathering of evidence to present to a grand jury, which would determine whether or not the case would go to court, would have been handled by the Beaufort and Jasper County Sheriff's Departments. Until that had happened, Randy Murdaugh wouldn't even be in the picture. So Kiker had called Sam Roser, the officer who interviewed Mike Davis following the murder, as a witness for the defense, asking him if Davis mentioned the incident with the knife. No, Roser answered, he had not. And neither, Kiker pointed out, did the state produce any other officer who was able to say that Davis had given the information to him rather than Roser. "They didn't do it because he didn't report it and he didn't report it because it's not true."

Brent Kiker closed his summation once again admonishing the jury to believe that "what Sarah Nickel got on that stand and told you was the truth. That is what happened the day of her mother's murder."

When I read those words, I had to pause and wonder if perhaps his argument might have succeeded just a little bit more if he had stuck to the idea, which he had presented previously, that the jurors were well within their rights to believe some portion of one person's testimony, some portion of another's, and perhaps a third portion of yet another's. Because once Randolph Murdaugh got through with them, there wasn't a juror in that courtroom who was going to believe that Sarah Nickel was telling the truth, the whole truth, and nothing but the truth.

28

Short but Not Sweet

In the printed transcript of *State of South Carolina vs. Sarah Nickel,* Brent Kiker's summation to the jury takes up thirty-six double-spaced pages. Spoken in court it lasted just about an hour. After a ten minute recess, given at the request of the jurors, Randy Murdaugh rose to take his turn. His speech was less than one-third the length of Mr. Kiker's, but it would seem shorter still because he did not hesitate or backtrack or repeat himself. He warmed the jury up with a dose of his usual down-home humor.

"Madam Foreman and ladies and gentleman of the jury, feel like I need to get my walker to come up here and talk to y'all, I'm so much older than that other lawyer over there. And I am old and I'm tired and I'm worn out and I know y'all are. And I promise you I'll be brief."

Once again the jury got to hear the definitions of murder and armed robbery and how, under one interpretation of the hand-of-one rule, someone who is an accomplice to the planning of an armed robbery that results in a murder is guilty of that murder, even if they had no part in the actual killing. That, Randy Murdaugh knew, was the linchpin that held his case together. If the jury didn't understand it, or agree with it, the state didn't have a case, and everybody might as well go home.

When he began speaking about the case, Mr. Murdaugh told the jury that they were going to have to decide what the truth was, and used an analogy from the kitchen to describe the process he wanted them to go through, saying, "None of y'all are old enough to remember an old flour sifter. You used to have to put the flour in this sifter and go through it because that left some of the chaff in it and all that. You had to get right down to the flour. Well, that's what y'all have got to do. Y'all have got to take the evidence from that witness stand and these physical items and you've got to sift through them and get to the truth." He told them to use their common sense, as well, to recall "times when you sit and listen to somebody and you know they're telling you the truth. You just had that feeling." On the other hand "you listen to somebody and you say, well, that can't be true; that's not true."

And then there was talk about reasonable doubt. Reasonable doubt he also explained with an analogy: "I like to liken it with if there was a window behind y'all, and if there were shades over that window, and if the sunlight was streaming in there, if it was real bright, all of a sudden it darkened up and you heard thunder outside, what you would think was thunder, and you heard water splash up against the window and then you saw some-body walk in that door with an umbrella, shaking water off an umbrella, you don't know that it's raining outside but it's a pretty dern indication, isn't it?" Reasonable certainty is actually the concept he was illustrating, but the example did much to convey what he was after. And it allowed him to circle back to his previous theme of common sense. If you had good common sense, you would know that it was raining. In judging this case, he wanted jurors to "use good common sense to determine what the truth is." He paused just long enough for there to be some drama, some suspense about what was coming next. He gathered himself, rose to his full height, showed how far indeed he was from needing a walker or cane or any kind of support to face a jury. "Now, the one underlying thing that I have seen in this thing is that nobody is telling the truth. Except Sarah Nickel. And if y'all believe that, then y'all turn her loose, find her not guilty."

Bait and switch. Either/or. These are the tactics I teach my writing stu-dents to look out for when they are analyzing other writers' arguments, looking for ways that they are being manipulated. Even though he had, only moments before, constructed a foundation of reason and "common sense" for jurors to build their deliberations on, he had just obliterated that foun-dation with an emotional bombshell. And Brent Kiker, with his determined insistence that Sarah Nickel was telling "*the truth*," practically handed him the ignition.

"Y'all turn her loose," he said, and then paused long enough for the jury to mull that over. When they had, he continued, giving them another op-tion, the one that he hoped they would take, the other half of the either/ or proposition with which they had been presented: the one that involved using "common sense."

"But let's look at the evidence. We know that on that night that Kevin Bergin beat, stabbed and strangled Nell Davis, we know that he killed her. We know that they came there with some sort of a plan. What defense counsel would have you to think is that the two of them came there, that Sarah knew nothing about it.

"But let's look at what we heard from this witness stand about that. We heard Sarah Nickel tell y'all that yes, John Ridgway was going to trial tomorrow. And he didn't want to go to trial. So he called me up and he knew I was gone testify against him because we stole my stepmother's car. Went to Connecticut. And he said if you testify—I don't remember what she said but the gist of it was that if you testify against me I'm gone hurt you. Remember that? So she's scared of him.

"We know that the next day, for some unknown reason, they showed up at Sarah's house. We know that they show up right after she—right before she comes back home from school. We know that they cannot drive a vehicle. And it's pretty obvious because, lord knows, they would've left out of there that night from the Nelsons' house. They cannot drive a vehicle.

"We know, by everybody's account, that they were behind the shed. We know that Sarah, her brother and sister and mother went into that house. We know that Sarah says—whether it be true or not, that's for your determination—that she looked out the window toward the marsh, from the kitchen I believe she said. And that she saw John Ridgway looking around the corner of the shed. And it was nothing unusual about him to make her scared, and yet on the day before he had threatened her if she went and testified."

Until now Murdaugh's voice, though characteristically sonorous, had been measured, controlled, almost conversational. But with that last sentence, a note of incredulity had crept in. "Nothing unusual about him to make her scared." Hmmm. Something to think about there: she's not scared, yet on the day before, she had been threatened.

Murdaugh continued, "And that he had a stocking cap with a hairnet under it. Now, bless God, Mr.—Madame Foreman and ladies and gentlemen of the jury, from the distance that was, how would you see a hairnet on the head without a—with a pantyhose over it—but how could she know unless she was in on the plan that there was a hairnet?

"That doesn't make her guilty. Sure. But it gives you an insight into what's happened."

Murdaugh proceeded to recall Sarah's claim that when she walked out to talk to John Ridgway, she saw Kevin Bergin for the first time. "And I think her testimony was that Bergin had the bat and said let's kill the bitch. John Ridgway says go get your Momma. She said I don't want to do that.

They said do it. Might have to hurt you." Knowing he was coming to the punch line, Murdaugh's eyes zoomed in for contact. He said, "Well, let me tell you something. Y'all remember listening to the 9-1-1 tape?"

Some of them nodded. Surely all of them remembered, but he had to make sure. "She says I didn't know Kevin Bergin; I knew John Ridgway. But I never had seen Kevin Bergin before. That's what Sarah Nickel says. But listen to the 9-1-1 tape. When they ask her what happened, they said, who did it, she said John Ridgway and Kevin Bergin. Well, I assume that when she came over there she sees a man holding a bat that she doesn't know that says Let's kill the bitch. John Ridgway says, 'Excuse me, Sarah, this is Kevin Bergin. I'd like to introduce you to Kevin Bergin. Would you mind going and getting your mother and bring her back out here?'" How would she know Kevin Bergin? If it happened the way she said it happened? She had to have known, she had to have been a part of the plan and she was a part of the plan."

By shifting the story's point of view, the vantage point from which the scene was observed, Randy Murdaugh highlighted the inconsistencies in Sarah Nickel's story. And as the story reshaped itself to accommodate this new perspective, an alternative "truth" emerged. Murdaugh was wise enough to know that he didn't really have to bear the "burden of proof"; he just had to cast doubt on Sarah's honesty, on her veracity, on her probity, call it what you will. Because if she would lie in a situation like this, if she would lie about something as serious as her mother's murder, even if she didn't actually kill her mother, she probably was in on the plan. And that's just common sense.

In his summation Murdaugh also capitalized on the fact that Sarah had packed two suitcases. "If," he reasoned, "according to Sarah's story they were kidnapping her and making her do this, why would they have bothered to make her pack a bag because what they would've done is gotten down the road and killed her just like they finished killing her mother. You pack bags when you're going along for the ride." Perhaps remembering that without Sarah, "down the road" would have been very finite, with neither of them knowing how to drive, he recalled officer Bobby Tuten, who had described the bags as having been neatly packed, and asked the jury to take a look at the amount of clothes in each bag, a clear indication that Sarah had joined the two as a willing partner, rather than a hostage.

Brent Kiker had warned the jury that Randy Murdaugh would use his "fire and brimstone" voice when it came his turn to speak. He had also warned them that the solicitor would reintroduce the murder weapons and the brutality of the crime. Partly to prove Kiker wrong, which was part of the game, and partly because he didn't need to, Murdaugh hadn't reintroduced any of the weapons or gone into any explicit detail about Nell Davis's murder. But when he came to the part where he had to speak about the jewelry Sarah had been wearing when she was arrested, Nell's diamond earrings. Murdaugh offered the jury the two different interpretations of this fact. "Heather Nelson says she made the statement, that they made me—the earrings, they made me take them out. I assumed that that meant out of her ears. She said it meant out of the room. But she says that John Ridgway looked at those earrings and said these must be valuable. Put them on. If it was not a part of the plan and if Ridgway is gone steal them, why would he give them to Sarah?"

The incident of the earrings provided a natural segue to the next outrageous incident that pointed to Sarah's guilt. "They say they're out there and that Bergin has stabbed Nell Davis. And she comes up and he tries to give her the knife. God bless, do you do that if you've just killed somebody? Do you try to give a complete stranger on the opposite side the knife?"

What does your common sense say? the jury must have been thinking. He wouldn't even have to say it.

Of Sarah's escape from the boys, Murdaugh's only response was to ask why she didn't attempt it sooner, at the Texaco station for instance. Kevin Bergin was in the shop buying chips and sodas. John Ridgway was outside the car pumping gas. She was inside the car, sitting behind the wheel. That's what she said, in her testimony. Why didn't she just drive away, then?

Finally he held up a piece of physical evidence. And it wasn't the bat, or the knife, or the bloody t-shirt Nell Davis was wearing the day she died. It's the shoes Sarah Nickel was *not* wearing when she was arrested. Saying, "Little things sometimes tell you where the truth lies," he held up a pair of Saucony running shoes. "These were her shoes. And I show you State's exhibit number thirteen. And they are off of her feet, underneath the front seat where she was driving. If she was trying to get away, again, is it reasonable that you'd take your shoes off or do you leave your shoes on 'cause you know you gone run at the first chance you get?"

If you were in it "for the long haul," as Randy Murdaugh would have the jury believe, why would you run away at all? That was something he could not account for, but he didn't have to, because somewhere in her story, Sarah Nickel had lied.

So he returned to one lie—or at least he felt sure that it was—that had to be the most upsetting to jurors, the denial that she knew Kevin Bergin.

"One of the most telling things is that she said I do not know Kevin. And she said that several times. And yet her stepfather got up and says that as little as eight days before this—think it was and I might be wrong about the time but a short period of time before—she was in the kitchen and we had a fuss. She took a knife out. I told her it better be a candy knife 'cause I'm gone stick it down your throat if you ever do it again. She said I'll have Kevin take care of you."

What strikes me now, and it seems odd that it never has before, is that Murdaugh would exaggerate the threatened violence of Mike Davis. On the witness stand, Davis had recalled, and made it sound like he spoke in a joking, friendly manner during the original exchange, "Sarah, that's just what you probably need to do but if you ever pull a knife on me you'd better pull one that's made out of candy because I'll make you eat it." The pure volume of words, the admission that he understands her position—"that's just what you probably need to do"—softens the literal meaning, lessens whatever aggression might be implied by the words themselves. The difference, I think, speaks to Randy Murdaugh's anger, a contagious anger, one that will, if it hasn't already, infect the jury with a sickness that has but one cure: two guilty verdicts, one for armed robbery, the other for murder.

"Counsel'll tell you that Mike Davis is lying about that. Just as everyone on the State's side has lied. According to counsel and according to Sarah."

The final blast with which Randy Murdaugh hit the jury features just the kind of brutality Brent Kiker had been afraid of. After reminding the jury of Sarah's "numerous threats against her mother," he brought in Sarah's diaries, the only other pieces of physical evidence that he would touch during his summation.

"We also know that this is not of a recent vintage. Because we know that she wrote," and here he holds up the notebook with a flourish, squinting at the sloppy, girlish scrawl, 'Haley just called me and asked me where I—when I was coming home. She was about to cry when she asked me. It broke my heart to see her like that. I hung up the phone and cried so hard. I love her and Willie to death and would never let anyone hurt them.'"

Here he paused, looking over the tops of his glasses at the jury. "Remember Kevin says that Sarah didn't want us to hurt Willie and the little girl." He returned to the journal entry, "'But I know I'll end up hurting them both when I kill mom. She deserves to rot in the fiery pits of hell.

I'll take her there myself.'" Another pause, to let that sink in. He shuffled through his papers, found the next entry, held it up.

"And then later she wrote, 'I never—I'm never going to mom's house again. She's an unbearable bitch and I was about to slap the living shit out of her. She's so fucking selfish, I could just kill her. God, I hate her so much'"

"We know," he said, "that this was a vicious, brutal, a nasty murder. We know that Sarah Nickel hated her mother. We know that she stressed that hatred on numerous occasions. We know that thirteen days before this she had tried to run away because her mother was gone try to put her in rehab. We know that John Ridgway's momma brought her back to her. That, ladies and gentleman, is the theme of this entire thing. But for Sarah Nickel, but for Sarah Nickel this would not have happened.

"How would John Ridgway and Kevin Bergin know where to come? Why would they come?" Murdaugh asked, and he requested that the jury consider whether Ridgway and Bergin would not have done something simpler, such as rob a Jiffy Mart, or some place in Hilton Head, rather than taking a cab all the way out to Bellinger Bluff Road, "probably forty miles," he added. It's really about half that, but the point is, why would they be so stupid as to go to this out-of-the-way place that they have no way of getting away from because they can't drive a car? It doesn't make sense. *Use your common sense,* again, is the unspoken refrain.

He mentioned one more thing before he wrapped it up, and that was the idea that there's just no way John Ridgway could have known where the safe was in that house, much less that it contained anything of value, unless he had been told by Sarah, both of which point to a conspiracy between all these people. "Directly and unequivocally," he concluded, the testimony points to Sarah being a part of the plan. The only thing that was really open to debate is what the plan was. Was it to kill? Or was it to rob? It doesn't really matter. "Because they murdered Nell Davis. They beat her in the head and they stabbed her. And if she went there to assist them in a robbery of her parents, then she is guilty of murder. If they went there with the intent to kill her, which you could conceivably believe from reading all this, this hate in her heart, then she is guilty of murder." He paused, just for a beat. "And she is guilty of murder."

He had told these jurors in the beginning, and of course they knew, that they would have to reach a verdict. What they perhaps didn't know, but what he told them now, is that verdict is derived from the Latin word *veredicto,* which means to speak the truth. "Whatever your verdict be, let it speak the truth. Mike Davis, Julie, the mother of Nell Davis, these people will be waiting to hear what your verdict is." He added one final flourish—"We will be waiting to hear what your verdict is and waiting for you to return justice in this case"—before taking a seat.

It was a Friday, late morning, and no doubt members of the jury were looking forward to the weekend. It would be an understatement to say that it had been a long week. For some of them, it would have been one of the most stressful weeks of their lives. Several of them would be dead within the next five years, including jury forewoman Terri Angelillo.

Having received their charge from the judge, the jurors were dismissed for lunch and began their deliberations at 12:45 P.M. Four hours later they returned to the courtroom requesting to hear audiotape of Sarah Nickel's testimony. That took about an hour. They returned to the jury room to resume deliberations at 5:53. At 7:45 P.M. a note from forewoman Terri Angelillo asked that Judge Brown again read them the law regarding reasonable doubt and murder. At 8:45 the jury of nine women and three men came back to the courtroom with a note stating that they were dead-locked.

Judge Brown responded to this news like a parent responding to a child who's decided he wants to give up on a project—maybe a summer job, or some other challenging undertaking. He gave them a pep talk. "Well, if you would never be able to reach a verdict I would have to declare what we call a mistrial. And in a mistrial it leaves the case exactly where it is. In this same courtroom. In all probability. With the same lawyers, same witnesses. Twelve other people would try this case. And decide what you can't. . . . Decide."

This is somewhat misleading, actually. If the trial really had resulted in a mistrial, it is unlikely that the case would have gone to court again, primarily because of the expense incurred by the state, and the increasing likelihood, after one mistrial, of having another. The solicitor would have been exceptionally motivated to come up with some kind of deal that would have been acceptable to Mike Davis, as the family of the victim, and to Sarah Nickel, as the defendant.

After the pep talk, Judge Brown reassured the jurors, so they would know he didn't think poorly of their performance thus far, then let them know how unusual it is for a jury in his courtroom to be in their position.

"You would think, well, gosh, there'd be a lot of juries who can't reach a verdict. Now, I was an attorney for thirty years. I've been a judge now twenty years. And I [can] count the number of mistrials that I've been in-volved in on these two hands."

Judge Brown droned on, his manner grandfatherly, his tone paternal, as he urged them to fulfill their duty: "Jurors generally reach verdicts. Sometime they—they have to deliberate longer. Sometime they have to get more law. Sometime they have to deliberate less. Juries almost never just go out and come back in. And so you don't have to be ashamed by the fact that you haven't been able to reach a verdict." They didn't have to be ashamed . . . yet. He didn't have to say it, but the threat was there. If they didn't eventually reach a verdict, they would be shamed, because they would, as he had just told them, have left the case "exactly where it was . . . in this same courtroom," where twelve other jurors would "decide what you can't."

"Now," he began, picking up an idea he had already referred to briefly, "I want to remind you from time to time a juror doesn't have to violate their conscience just to agree with another juror. But our law does say that a juror should listen with an open mind to another juror, willing to be con-vinced, keeping that thing in mind that you don't have to violate your con-science."

What's interesting is that, unlike all the other concepts he had explained in such minute detail, he didn't explain at all what he meant by this idea of violating one's conscience, he just repeated the same idea several times. It seems to me like he's saying you can vote with the majority even if you don't agree with them and, somehow, that won't violate your conscience. If that *is* what he was saying, then I would say he's wrong, at least according to my understanding of what it means to violate my conscience.

Before dismissing them to deliberate further, he asked again if they needed anything (they still hadn't had supper, for which he apologized), including the making of telephone calls, noting that someone had a sick child, saying he hopes the child is all right, perhaps hoping that letting the other jurors know one of them had a sick child would speed up the process, make those who were in the minority listen "with an open mind" to those in the majority, willing to be convinced, since, after all, they wouldn't have to violate their conscience just to agree.

Once the jury had left the courtroom, Brent Kiker objected, character-izing the judge's instructions as coercive, and moved for a mistrial.

Judge Brown denied his motion.

At 11:15 P.M., a little more than two hours later, the court was notified that the jury had reached a decision. They were speedily returned to the courtroom, and in very short order, the verdicts were read. First, for the charge of armed robbery, the jury found the defendant, Sarah Grace Nickel, guilty. Second, for the charge of murder, the jury found her not guilty.

The surprising thing about this verdict was that, under the law that had been explained to the jury so many times, being guilty of armed robbery made Sarah Nickel de facto guilty of murder. Rather than taking that up with the jury at this time, however, the judge simply thanked them for their service, praising them for their attention and for following the system. He even told them, "lot of people might disagree with your verdict but you don't have to apologize to anyone because you followed the system. When you've done that, as I said, you will have lived up to that oath that you gave."

As for Sarah he delayed sentencing for the time being, knowing that there would be arguments from both the solicitor's office and from the defense. Before leaving the courtroom, in fact, Brent Kiker was already getting it into the record that he wanted ten days to file his motions.

29

Sentencing

It was a cold, clear morning in February 2001. Sarah now wore the same type of Creamsicle-orange jumpsuit that John Ridgway and Kevin Bergin had worn when they testified against her, a potent symbol of her change in status since her last courtroom appearance. Her eyes were puffy with crying and lack of sleep. Dark wings fanned out beneath each one, the stain looking like a bruise on her pale cheeks.

She was so nervous that she was shivering, almost continuously. She hoped that if anyone noticed they would hold the weather responsible.

The hearing began with Brent Kiker presenting each of the motions he had filed the previous week, each of which was patiently listened to and then denied by Judge Brown.

After Kiker and the judge had finished with all the motions and all the denials, it was Murdaugh's turn. The solicitor approached the bench saying he did not see the need to review additional facts in the case, but noting that there were several people who wished to address the court prior to Nickel's sentencing. The first was Mike Davis's friend Scott McNair.

McNair brought to the courtroom that day a petition on which he had collected over a hundred names. "They signed their names," he told the court. The petition reads, "We believe Sarah Nickel, upon her release, poses a threat to the citizens of this area; therefore, request the Court to impose the maximum sentence allowed by law."

Julia Crowley, Nell's mother, was the next to speak. She was pale and dry lipped and looked as if her soul had been sucked out of her brown eyes along with whatever tears she had cried over the past year and a half, for the loss of her daughter, her husband, and, she must doubtless feel, her granddaughter. Before she spoke, she took a deep breath, and it was as if she didn't breathe again until she was finished. Yet she was absolutely calm.

"Your Honor, several months before my daughter was murdered, she was in fear of her life, and she was in fear for Mike's life. She was afraid that Sarah was going to stab them in their bed. I would ask you for justice for my daughter, and I would ask you for protection for Mike and for the other people that Nell loved by imposing the maximum sentence."

When she had finished, she moved with dignity back to her seat. Judge Brown said, "Thank you, Ms. Crowley."

Mike Davis was the last to speak. He reminded the court of Sarah's friendship with one of the boys who committed the crime, and of the fact that the two of them had previously committed crimes together. He noted that she did have the opportunity "at least at some point to save her mother's life, to lock the doors and let her mother get her pistol and defend herself." He urged the court to remember that Sarah "wore her mother's jewelry that she had worn previously to the murder" and concluded by saying, "We do know that she wrote several times about her desire to kill her mother or that she wanted her mother dead. This armed robbery where a brutal murder occurs must be the most severe form of an armed robbery possible, so we beg you for the maximum sentence."

Solicitor Murdaugh also spoke, though on this occasion he was thoughtful and subdued, the "fire and brimstone" persona of the trial put aside. He still had a commanding presence, though, and, as usual, he spoke with an authority that made people want to believe him and do what he said. Pointing out that "very seldom in the years" that he has practiced law before Judge Brown has he ever suggested a sentence, he went on to say, "I have always taken the position that that is a matter that—that's up to the judge and the judge alone, and it still is, sir, except in this case. If Your Honor please, I urge the Court to impose a severe sentence, the maximum sentence in this case. My reason for doing that is that I am convinced that the evidence showed that absent Sarah Nickel, this death would have never taken place, sir, and I can go into detail, but I don't think it's necessary, sir. That's all I have to say."

Brent Kiker also spoke during this phase of the sentencing, mainly asking that the judge consider the jury's decision not to find Sarah Nickel guilty of murder. This, he claimed, indicated that they did not wish for her to be punished to be same extent as the young men who received a thirty-year sentence for armed robbery *and* murder. "If Your Honor imposes a thirty year sentence in this case," he argued, "it would be in effect rendering the jury's verdict a nullity, overruling the jury's verdict." He reminded the court of Nickel's age, sixteen when the crime was committed, seventeen now, and asked the court to impose the minimum sentence of ten years, which he felt was suitable to her level of involvement in the crime.

There were four other people who spoke on Sarah's behalf, a Mr. Berry from Hilton Head, psychologist Dr. Randolph Wade, Sarah's cousin Mary Richards, and her aunt Anita Belding. Both Richards and Belding spoke at length of their affection for Sarah, of the time they had spent with her during her childhood, and they begged the court to release her into their care so that they could take her back to Savannah to live with them. Belding outspokenly told the court that Sarah's manic-depressive illness had come from her: "I told her mother when she was that high that that's what was happening to her, because it happened to me, and I was diagnosed with it." One of Belding's frustrations had been to see Sarah misdiagnosed, over and over. "I pleaded with Nell and I pleaded with Mike over and over again, that she was not getting the right medication, and she was not going to the right doctor, and he told me what I wanted to hear, and then did nothing, absolutely nothing, to help Sarah, and I know that to be true, because Nell told me that." As if this were the last chance for Sarah to receive the proper treatment, Belding concluded, "I'm begging you, Your Honor, please, please let this child come with me so I can take care of her."

Sarah did not get to go home with her Aunt Anita, but she did get properly diagnosed and started on lithium, the standard treatment for bipolar disorder, after her transfer to SCDC.

Randolph Wade was an expert witness Brent Kiker had hired to evaluate Sarah as he prepared her case for trial. Wade told the court about his lengthy psychological assessment of Sarah, which involved multiple interviews, interviews with family members, and review of her records from Midlands Reception and Evaluation, where she was also evaluated the summer before the murder. Wade emphasized first of all the lack of "horrible intent" on Sarah's part at the time of the crime, saying, "I think she underappreciated the possibilities of what could happen," noting that her flight from the car served as evidence that this situation was never "intended to be like it went down."

Wade also emphasized the role of mood disturbance and bipolar disorder in her emotional and behavior problems that were exacerbated by the "great deal of chaos and dysfunction in the family process," and specifically in the process of "blending families." Perhaps most important, though, Wade pointed out that Sarah Nickel was not at high risk for violent episodes, that she simply did not have a background for that. Her background was "not going to school, runaway behavior on a couple of occasions, and substance abuse." "This is not a juvenile delinquent with a violent background, and actually prediction factors based upon who she is and what kind of personality she has and what kind of psychiatric problems she has is not a high prediction for violence in the future either." He continued, "I do not see her as being a high risk for recidivism," meaning someone who would break the law again and return to prison. "The State nor myself do not consider her to suffer from antisocial personality disorder"—the polite way of saying "she is not a sociopath." Wade concluded by emphasizing what I have come to learn is one of the most important features of Sarah Nickel's psychological makeup, and one that, if you look hard enough, seems to lie at the core of every bad decision she has ever made. "This is a young lady, a needy young lady who wasn't always clear about what company she should keep, heavily influenced by that neediness, and got herself in a situation that was—turned out horrible, but I have never seen in her, in my work with her the actual horrible intent for it to go down the way it did and result in this kind of vicious crime and unfortunate death of her mother. And she does have guilt and remorse about what has happened and will pay for that loss for the rest of her life."

Judge Brown, interestingly, stated that he agreed with Dr. Wade's psychological assessment and Wade's opinion "that in all probability she didn't intend for this to happen." Brown went on to say, "I never criticize a jury," but this is certainly not true based on what he said to me about Sarah Nickel's jury. Specifically, to me he had said, "I listened to the trial and I determined that that jury made a terrible mistake. I would have convicted her of murder." But at Sarah Nickel's sentencing, he said, "I never criticize a jury. I don't know how they reach a verdict. I wouldn't dare ask them, but the fact that she was convicted of armed robbery indicates, as you well know under the law, that she was involved in a plan, although the plan might not have included the death of her mother. It would be a real miscarriage of justice if the person who conceived this [something that neither of her codefendants had claimed; both of them said the plan was something they had all agreed on together], in my opinion, got less than those who did the physical murder, and as difficult as it is for me to sentence a child to prison, judgment of law and sentence of this Court that you, Sarah Nickel, be confined to the South Carolina Department of Corrections for a period of thirty years."

And that was it. She was given credit for the four hundred and eighty-three days she had already served at Beaufort County Detention. She will be released on April 4, 2025. She will be forty-two years old.

30

Postconviction Suspense

Seven years later, on April 13, 2008, I left Highway 17 at Gardens Corner, a notoriously dangerous intersection, and headed south on 21 toward Beaufort, where I would be attending Sarah Nickel's postconviction relief hearing on the following morning. Actually, I was to be taking a more active role on this occasion. Sarah's lawyer, Gary Coggin, wanted to call me as a witness.

In South Carolina, the air was crisp and cool, spring with the promise of summer, the sky a clean shimmer of metallic blue. The roadside ditches overflowed with red clover and clouds of lavender-blue chicory. Two laughing gulls flew out of nowhere and then soared in the air in front of my car, their paths crossing and recrossing before they flew up and away, vanishing into the distance.

On my way to Hilton Head, where I would be staying, I entered that long stretch of 170 bordered by marsh that passes the Lemon Island Preserve on the left and then, on the other side, after the bridge and the access road that circles and plunges beneath the bridge to the Lemon Island Marina, Bellinger Bluff Road. I slowed down and pulled over. The first change I noticed was the marina, its large plate-glass windows shattered, its derelict dock with boards tilting at crazy angles. I wondered what had happened to Clark Lowther, whether he had died or just moved on to something else. I know that making a living from fishing isn't easy anywhere, anymore.

Turning onto Bellinger Bluff gave me, as usual, a feeling of breathlessness, but as I drove up to number 31, the house was suffused with loveliness in the afternoon sunlight, as if nothing had ever disturbed its peace. It was high tide, so the water was brimming in Hazzard Creek, moving right up into the green Bermuda grass of the well-kept lawn. I drove around to the side until the swimming pool came into view, and it seemed that I could literally see rays of light slanting all the way through the house, from the back to the front, through those long windows that line the front porch. Out in the yard there was an Adirondack-style swing hanging from a tree, and three cars sat in the driveway. Nobody had told me yet, but somehow I could sense that Mike Davis didn't live there anymore.

I soon learned that a lot of things had changed since my last trip to Beaufort County, nearly two years before. Amy Heath Albee had divorced Chris Albee and, the last I heard, was going out with his brother Wayne. The Nelsons had moved. When I drove out to their mobile home to say hello, the mailbox with the ship's silhouette on top was gone, and the dwelling appeared abandoned without the children's playthings, the swing set, the lawn chairs, and other colorful evidence of their occupancy.

Randy Murdaugh was no longer solicitor for the fourteenth circuit. He retired in 2005 to join a law firm founded by his grandfather in Hampton County, bringing an end to one dynasty while helping to continue another. Pete Nardi, who covered the story for the *Island Packet*, had moved to a bigger paper, and so had Vic Bradshaw, the editor who kindly provided me with lodging the first several times I visited the area. Debbie Szpanka, the public information officer who assisted me at the Beaufort County Sheriff's Department, had also moved on, and it was her departure more than anything else that made me realize how important my timing had been when it came to conducting my own investigation of the circumstances surrounding Nell's death.

■ ■ ■

The next morning I sat in courtroom number 1 at the Beaufort County Courthouse. I was ridiculously early, so I had plenty of time to take in my surroundings: the burgundy carpeting, the harsh fluorescent lighting modulated by globed chandeliers, whose knobby surface created an iridescent effect. Portraits of former judges lined the walls, one of them in robes, most of them in suits, one in his rumpled shirtsleeves. Only one of them was a woman. She wore a red jacket and a mischievous half smile.

The only other person who got to court as early as I did was Gary Coggin, Sarah's attorney. Tall enough to be a basketball player, Coggin turns heads wherever he goes, partly because his ruddy cheeks, snowy curls, and the way his eyes crinkle into quarter moons whenever he smiles make him look like Santa Claus out of uniform. Also like Santa Claus, he has a very engaging manner, a positive attitude even in the most desperate cases, and since he handles his share of immigration and DUI cases, many of them are desperate indeed.

Coggin is a civil lawyer, which is not unusual for a post conviction relief effort, because PCRs are designated civil actions. He had taken Sarah's case at a reduced fee, he told me, because he likes Joe, Sarah's father, for whom he once handled a case involving an exploding lawnmower. Joe had been using the mower to cut his grass when it blew up and gave him some nasty injuries. Gary filed a complaint with the manufacturer, who investigated the claim and quickly offered Joe a settlement. Joe initially refused the offer. The company rep then showed Gary some photos they had taken as part of their investigation into the accident. The photos showed the lawnmower blasted into a contorted, melted, blackened mass of metal. Several feet away from the lawnmower, on the grass, sat the cap to the lawnmower's gas tank, in pristine condition. Gary shared the photo with Joe, advising him to take the settlement.

Having spoken at length to Coggin about his preparation for Sarah's PCR, I knew that he had spent more than a year putting the case together, and that he ultimately had decided to focus on seven issues. The purpose of a PCR hearing is, again, not to serve as simply another appeal, but to determine whether or not the defendant received effective representation by counsel—either at her original trial or her appeal. Therefore each of the seven issues that Coggin would raise had to do with something that either Brent Kiker, Sarah's trial lawyer, or Joseph Savitz, her appeals attorney, did or did not do on her behalf. Subpoenas to appear as witnesses at the PCR had been issued to Randolph Murdaugh, the solicitor who prosecuted the case; Pamela Altman, Judge Brown's daughter who was suspected of having had a relationship with Mike Davis; Mike Davis; and Joseph Savitz. Brent Kiker would be appearing voluntarily, as would I. Sarah Nickel would also be taking the stand again to speak on her own behalf. Coggin had originally planned to subpoena Ricky Bozard, the man who called Brent Kiker to report the relationship between Davis and Altman, but later decided that calling the principles would be more appropriate.

As people began to trickle in, I saw some I didn't recognize and wondered if any of the jurors from the original trial might be there. Joe Nickel was the first of Sarah's family to arrive. He entered the courtroom walking stiffly, his white tennis shoes overly bright in their newness. He was, as always, neatly dressed, in olive-green pants with a gray dress shirt and a Native American belt patterned in red, green, black, and yellow. He sat down then got up again and came over to give me an awkward hug. Then he took a pink folding brush out of his pocket to groom his beard, which he wore in a Vandyke style.

Anita, Sarah's beloved Aunt Nini, came dressed in black from head to toe, her daughter Mary sporting a more optimistic green. They didn't appear to recognize me until I reintroduced myself.

Mike Davis had also come into the courtroom and was talking to someone on the other side. I walked across and introduced myself because we had never met face to face. The first thing I noticed was how much more attractive he is in person than in his photos. This has something to do with the flattening effect of photos that is unkind to many people, but it also has to do with the way that he speaks—with great feeling and focus—and the energy or whatever it is that radiates from people and that makes them uniquely who they are. Although Davis was anything but happy about being subpoenaed, he appeared genuinely friendly and conversed openly about what was happening in his life at the moment. He told me he was in the middle of a divorce from his third wife, the one he was just getting married to the first time I contacted him. They were married three years. It didn't work out, he says, mostly because of the children. "We were always in competition." A few months later he would tell me that she didn't like for him to discipline her girls, and that she was jealous of his first two wives. "'Your dead wives' is what she would call them," he confided, saying, "she complained she was so tired of living with my dead wives."

During my courtroom conversation with Mike Davis I learned that neither he nor Julie Crowley, Nell's mother, agreed to the plea bargains Randy Murdaugh worked out with John Ridgway and Kevin Bergin. He told me that the first he had heard of the deal with Bergin was when it was published in the paper the next day, that Randy had told him about a meeting with Bergin and his attorney, but said it was "just a formality," and that it "wasn't important" for Mike to be there.

"But that's against the Victim's Bill of Rights," I told him, incredulous.

"Victims have no rights, Rosalyn," he said softly, and then he continued telling me about how the police left his house a complete wreck, dumped trash everywhere, left orange crime-scene tape everywhere. "And I had to live there. I was supposed to clean it up. After what had just happened to my wife."

Mike Davis also told me that he had finally sold his house on Bellinger Bluff Road, confirming my hunch of the day before. "I sold it to Randolph's son," he said, "John Marvin Murdaugh. He got a pretty good deal." This makes sense, considering the publicity that Nell's murder generated in the community, and the reluctance many people would feel about living in a house where such a brutal slaying had occurred, even if it had not occurred within the walls of the house itself. Later I would find out that the house sold for $628,000 on December 8, 2006, when the downturn in the real estate market was just a whispered threat that many still refused to believe. When I searched for a comparable in September 2008, a few weeks following the Fannie Mae and Freddie Mac bailout, and in the midst of the biggest stock market crisis we've had since the great depression, I found a house on Bellinger Neck Road (which runs adjacent to Bellinger Bluff) that was slightly larger (in square feet), but had one less bedroom and a smaller lot. Like the Davis home, it had an in-the-ground pool, a detached two-car garage, and a dock on Hazzard Creek. The landscaping wasn't nearly as nice, though, and the house itself looked as if it had been designed by a kindergartner. It was listed at $739,000.

That day in the courtroom I asked Mike about Sarah's half sister Haley. Mike said she is a "good girl," and doing very well. She was in the eighth grade at school, very self-motivated and happy. His son Justin had graduated from college and had a career in marine engineering. He was based in Charleston but had worked jobs in Dubai, Saint Lucia, Dominica, and Costa Rica.

By now Judge Michael Nettles had come in. His wiry auburn hair cut in a flattop, he appeared young for a judge. Later, when I looked him up, I would discover that he was born the same year and month that I was: March 1959.

Wearing a gray sweatshirt over a tank top undershirt and prison-issue dungarees, Sarah Nickel entered the courtroom with her lawyer. She had all her hair pulled back away from her face, exposing her gaunt features. She had on make-up, mascara and eyeliner, but her lipstick was light, a subtle shade. She looked like a prisoner and, for just a moment, I realized as she turned around and smiled at her dad, more like her grandmother than her mother.

The first matter Gary Coggin brought to the court concerned ineffectiveness of appellate counsel, and for this he called Joseph Savitz, the man who represented Sarah for her appeal. The appeal Savitz filed with the South Carolina Supreme Court stated, "The judge erred by allowing the state to cross-examine appellant about her diaries, in which she wrote that she hated her mother and wanted to kill her, because they were the product of an unreasonable search prohibited by the Fourth Amendment; moreover, the introduction of appellant's private papers violated her privilege against self-incrimination under the Fifth Amendment as well." When questioned by Gary Coggin, Savitz accurately recalled that he had based his appeal on the court's use of this inflammatory material that was in Sarah's diaries.

The state's sole purpose in using the diaries was to refute the defendant's denial that she had threatened to *kill* her mother. The diaries were aimed at getting a murder conviction, pure and simple.

Sarah Nickel was convicted, however, of armed robbery and *not* murder. Therefore the appeal that Joseph Savitz wrote was, in Coggin's words, "neither germane nor meritorious" to the applicant's conviction for armed robbery.

Interestingly, when I had interviewed Savitz about Sarah's appeal, he had told me he thought thirty years was a pretty good sentence for a *murder conviction*. I had had to remind him that she wasn't convicted of murder. That is what I remembered most about our conversation, and that is what I told the court when I was called as the next witness. When I looked to see how Savitz would respond to my testimony, I was disappointed to find that he had already left the courtroom.

The second argument Coggin presented to the court that day focused on one of the great mysteries of Sarah Nickel's original trial: the question of whether Brent Kiker had asked Judge Luke Brown to recuse himself. He had not done so publicly, "on the record," but there was the rumor that he had spoken to the judge privately, in chambers, where the judge had told him no, chastised him, and sent him back to the courtroom with his tail between his legs. Now he was going to have to put his hand on the Bible and swear to tell the truth, and I and the rest of the world would know at last exactly what happened. Provided, of course, that Kiker respected the oath he took and did indeed tell the truth.

The question of whether or not Kiker had asked the judge to recuse himself was important because, Coggin asserted, Judge Brown showed evidence of bias against the defendant both inside and outside the courtroom. In court he displayed a "stiff and impatient" attitude toward defense counsel throughout the trial, in contrast to his "informal and friendly" demeanor toward Solicitor Murdaugh. Of twenty-five motions made by the defendant during the trail, only one was granted. Of fourteen objections made by defense counsel during the course of the proceedings, only one was sustained. Yet the jury was supposed to believe that the judge was impartial. If they believed that, they would *have* to believe that Brent Kiker was trying to deceive or confuse them, which is exactly what juror number 13 did believe.

Coggin's brief furthermore charged that in the months leading up to the trial, Judge Brown would regularly visit Main Street Pharmacy in Ridgeland, where he discussed the case with Mike Davis, the pharmacist and owner of the business. Coggin also noted the statement Brown had made at Nickel's sentencing, where he told Kiker that he had given her the maximum sentence for armed robbery because "it would be a real miscarriage of justice if the person who conceived this, in my opinion, got less than those who did the physical murder," acting as if—as he had indeed confided to me—Sarah should have been found guilty of the murder, and he was just doing what the jury didn't have the sense to do.

I hadn't seen Kiker come into the courtroom, but he was there when Coggin called his name, readily standing up and walking briskly to the witness box, where he adopted a relaxed posture almost immediately, though I am sure he is more comfortable on the other side, asking rather than answering questions. He wore a dark-gray suit, a white shirt, and a red tie, and his demeanor seemed to fit his formal clothing more than it had when I first met him. I had recently heard that he was addicted to Nicorette gum, even though he had never smoked, and I knew that when this was all over I was going to ask him how on earth that had happened.

When Gary Coggin asked Brent Kiker if he had asked Judge Brown in chambers to recuse himself from the case, Kiker said, simply, "Yes." When Coggin asked him to explain the situation, this is the scenario he described:

"At one point in the trial, I got to my office, had a message on my machine, saying Mike Davis and the judge's daughter were having a romantic relationship. The following morning I informed the judge and Mr. Murdaugh. The judge had Mr. Murdaugh and me in chambers. Randy Murdaugh said, 'I don't need to be here,' and walked out. I said, 'It's a little uncomfortable if this is true and I don't think you should be presiding.' Judge Brown said, 'Let me call my daughter.' She was apparently close by. She arrived. He didn't give her a cue or anything. I proceeded to ask her. I questioned her in chambers. Extensively in chambers. She said, 'Mike Davis is adorable, I would love to date him but it's too soon after his wife's death.' They had had lunch. Did she discuss the case? She said yeah. 'We talk about that all the time. Just general info.' I asked to see Mike Davis. He said he didn't have a relationship with Pamela Altman. Said this is a non-issue. I told the judge, 'I don't believe they have a relationship, but obviously she's talked to you about the case.' He said I'm gone deny your motion. If she talked to me about the case, I didn't pay any attention to it.'"

At this point Matt Friedman, a young, curly-haired attorney who was representing the state, interrupted to ask Kiker if he had asked Judge Brown to put the motion on the record.

Kiker answered, "I did, but I'm gonna have to tell you it's like this is the most uncomfortable thing. He didn't say anything." Kiker paused for a moment, then continued. "I did not put it on the record. I went out and told Sarah Nickel everything that happened. I felt that it wouldn't do her any good because of how it would embarrass Mike Davis and the judge."

Friedman asked, "Is that in your experience how the State treats the court?"

Kiker answered, "In my experience, that is how the judge treats the defense."

So now I knew. The story of the message on the answering machine was true. The story of Brent Kiker getting "woodshedded" was somewhat exaggerated, but true in its essential elements; that is, Brown had refused to recuse himself. Kiker had asked that it be put into the record, but that request never made it to the courtroom. Thus Judge Brown's (unsolicited) statement to me that nobody had asked him to recuse himself was what the Elizabethans would have called an equivocation, a half-truth. It is what Shakespeare's witches used to seduce Macbeth. It is what made Macbeth believe he was above the moral and physical laws governing ordinary mortals. I was beginning to believe that Luke Brown, like Macbeth, considered himself to be above the law. Brown's flaw may stem from an unselfish motive—the desire to keep the community safe, to serve the cause of justice, to help heal the wounds of those who have been victims—rather than Macbeth's selfish one of ambition; nevertheless bias is bias, and the main reason that we have trial by jury in the United States is to guard against this type of bias.

Mike Davis was called as the next witness. Pamela Altman had decided to ignore her subpoena, believing, perhaps, that her daddy's influence would protect her from being held in contempt and charged. (Evidently it did.)

Davis's answers were, in contrast to Kiker's, brief and to the point.

Did Judge Brown come into the pharmacy?

"Yes."

For prescriptions?

"Yes."

Did he discuss the case with Judge Brown?

"No."

Did he have a personal relationship with Pamela Altman?

"No."

Did he date Pamela Altman?

"No."

Did he go out to lunch with her?

"Not one-on-one."

Did she ever come to his house after the murder?

This time he paused, then said, "Not that I recall."

Coggin asked him to think very carefully before answering, then asked him the question again. This time Davis said, "So many people did, I'm not sure."

Coggin waited a moment, shuffled through some papers, then asked him to think very carefully about his answer to the next question. "Was she at your house when a deputy from Beaufort County came by to collect a computer?"

Davis answered, again, "Not that I recall," but his voice had faded, lacked altogether the conviction that made his first volley of answers so persuasive.

I shifted uncomfortably in my seat, knowing full well where this last question had come from. I was the person to whom the Beaufort County detective (not deputy) confided—"Off the record," he vehemently made me promise—that he had seen one of Judge Brown's daughters at Davis's house when he had gone there to collect the computer. That was why I suspected there was some substance to the rumor Ricky Bozard had started, and why I had shared that information with Sarah's PCR attorney, though, as promised, I did not reveal the detective's name. I have often wondered how Davis would have testified if the officer had been willing to go on the record and appear in court. Equally important, perhaps, is this question: Why wasn't the officer in question willing to come forward? Who or what was he afraid of?

Judge Nettles listened attentively to both witnesses during this phase of the hearing, but he did not ask many questions and seemed almost embarrassed by the scenario that unfolded in Brent Kiker's description of events that had taken place in Judge Brown's chambers. Overall his demeanor suggested that he, like Friedman, was skeptical of Kiker's reasons for not putting his motion on the record, especially considering that he had gone out of his way to get everything else into the record.

When I had met Gary Coggin back in 2005, he had told me that he planned to present the court with about eight arguments. His strategy, he had said, was to show such overwhelming evidence of misconduct in the handling of Sarah's case that any reasonable judge would have to rule in Nickel's favor at her PCR hearing. Watching the way Judge Nettles operated, I would surmise that the number of arguments probably had little bearing on his decision, but I believe Coggin was correct in assuming that, if he could reveal a pervasive atmosphere of misconduct it would help his client.

Two other arguments focused on the issue of "coercion or duress," noting Nickel's insistence throughout her testimony that John Ridgway had used threats and intimidation to cause her to act in a certain way. At issue once again was the question of whether Nickel's attorney had failed either to present a defense of duress, or to offer this as a charge to the jury. Brent Kiker took the stand again, this time to respond to the question of why he had not raised the issue of duress. He answered, "To me, this was always a murder case," and he explained that duress had come to light only when Miss Nickel testified, something he had not known she was going to do up until shortly before she decided to do it, so he didn't really have much time to consider the issue. "If she would have benefited from it [raising the issue of duress], it would have been my fault for not raising it," he concluded.

After Matt Friedman had his turn for questions, Kiker returned to the role of spectator for the remainder of the hearing. The sharp-nosed, auburn-haired judge whose hyperattentive listening style seemed to create a kind of magnetic focus in the courtroom became, though it seemed hardly possible, even more attentive to one of Coggin's arguments: that the court's failure to charge the jury with the "lesser included offense" of larceny—the taking away of the goods of another without consent—was reversible error. Now, in addition to his intense focus, he became animated, leaning forward to say, "very good, very good," in response to what Coggin was saying.

The failure to include larceny in the charge to the jury was not something that Brent Kiker could be held accountable for. As Sarah Nickel's original trial had wound to its conclusion, Kiker had repeatedly asked Judge Brown to include larceny among the charges that jurors might choose from. In Kiker's view, if Sarah had been telling the truth—and her version of events was supported by the physical evidence—it was the only offense she could, without reasonable doubt, be found guilty of. Yes, she had taken her mother's earrings and watch. But she had not threatened Nell with a weapon, or killed her, or dumped her body in a compost bin. Nobody, not even the boys who testified against her, had said that.

When Judge Nettles recessed the court for lunch shortly after noon, he said that he wanted to look further into existing case law relative to this issue. Sarah Nickel was buoyant, trying to contain her optimism as she rose from her seat to exit with the guards who would escort her back to her holding cell at county. As we left the courtroom, I cornered Brent Kiker, and we chatted for a few moments—about the book, and how his career has fared since "the *State vs. Sarah Nickel* fiasco." He told me that it was his last criminal case. First and last.

"Yep," he says, laughing, "It just about killed me."

He didn't say so, but I also knew that it nearly bankrupted his law firm. Reading an affidavit he filed in October 2001 in the attempt to recover part of the expenses he had incurred defending Sarah Nickel, I had learned that Kiker "expended personally" more than one thousand hours preparing and presenting the case. His partner Anne Douds, associate attorney Scott Merrifield, and legal support staff also put in a substantial amount of time. Kiker spent more than $7,000 of his own money, for which he did not request reimbursement from the state, conducting research and preparing for the trial, including conducting a mock trial at a leased facility with paid participants. Why? Because he believed Sarah Nickel did not plan to rob and kill her mother, and he wanted to do the best he could to get her a fair trial. According to the affidavit, his total expenditures on the case, which he computed at a discounted hourly rate, came to $69,640. When I had asked him how much of that had been reimbursed by the state, I expected him to give me a number, and he did. He said, "Zero," because even though a judge had signed an order authorizing the payment of some of his expenses, when he submitted it to the South Carolina Office of Indigent Defense, they simply told him they didn't have "that kind of money," and he let it go at that. It is true that he should have been able to, had he pursued the matter, recoup at least part of his expenses from the Office of Indigent Defense. Lori Frost, who worked as an administrator at the office in 2008, informed me that in 2001 the statutory maximums paid to attorneys in felony cases were as follows: $3,500 for attorney fees, $60 for in-court fees, $40 for out-of-court fees, and $500 for expenses. This may have seemed like a drop in the bucket, or worth less than the time it would have taken to fill out the additional paperwork, but it would have been more than "Zero."

Responding to Brent's remark about the case nearly killing him, I asked, "Was it the stress?"

He just sort of looked at me and rolled his eyes. We started heading for the door.

"Is that how you got addicted to Nicorette gum?"

A blush rose and spread across his cheeks until they were nearly the color of his tie. "Well, Rosalyn, that's a funny story. I have a brother, see, and we used to go out fishing all the time. My brother was using the gum to quit chewing tobacco. So we'd be out there fishing, knocking back a couple of beers, having a good time on the boat, and one time I said, 'Hey, give me one of those,' just to sort of be companionable."

"Did it taste good?"

"I don't know. With the beer, I didn't really notice. Later, I thought it tasted OK. But I did notice that it relaxed me, and I guess that's why I kept on chewing it, and the first thing I knew, I couldn't stop."

"Wow, that's weird," I said.

He gave me a funny look. "OK, yeah. It's weird. I even tried starting smoking one time to get off Nicorette, but I couldn't stand cigarettes." By this time we were out in the parking lot, looking out over the marsh where the spartina grass was bright green with the promise of summer. Behind us stood the fortress of the Beaufort County Courthouse, the sheriff's office, the county detention center, and the public defender's office. Brent said good-bye and went to his car, a cherry-red Mercedes sports coupe. Brent was obviously doing well in his civil law practice. He was already on his cell phone by the time he pulled out of his parking space.

When we got back to courtroom 1 after lunch, the air seemed charged with anticipation. Once the bailiff had called the courtroom to order, Judge Nettles wasted no time informing those present of his opinion. He had decided, based on the research he conducted during the recess, that larceny is indeed a lesser included offense of the crime of armed robbery. That being the case, he said he would take the matter under advisement in order to determine the appropriate redress. He told Gary Coggin that he could expect to hear from him within thirty days. Court was adjourned.

The judge left the courtroom like smoke, like a genie leaving a bottle. One moment he was there; the next he was gone. The rest of us—the ones who had been waiting four years to find out how this was going to turn out, sat like stunned lizards in the sun. All except Gary Coggin, whose job was done. He smiled and gathered his papers, then went over to have a word with Sarah, whose keepers were getting ready to send her back to county, where she would have to spend another night before heading back to Columbia. I waited until her family had had a chance to speak to her, and then I went.

A month later I was sitting in the parking lot of my children's school when I got a call from Gary Coggin about the result of the PCR. The news was even better than he had hoped. Ordinarily, if a PCR is successful, the defendant is granted another trial, based on the idea that the defendant's right to effective counsel was violated. This almost never comes to fruition, however, because the attorney general's office immediately appeals the judge's decision to the state supreme court, and in more than 80 percent of cases, the state wins. What Judge Nettles did was to grant Sarah an additional "belated" appeal, based on the idea that Joe Savitz, her appellate attorney, had failed to provide her with effective counsel. The attorney general's office could also challenge this decision, but they don't have as much to lose, financially, as they do when facing the possibility of another trial. Ultimately they would choose not to.

It still was far from certain whether Sarah Nickel's final appeal would succeed, though it was a good sign, for Sarah, that a circuit court judge had ruled in her favor on the issue of larceny as a lesser included offense. Judge Nettles's ruling stated, unequivocally, "The applicant has shown that the performance of appellate counsel was deficient as measured by the standard of reasonableness under prevailing professional norms and, but for the deficient performance, there is a reasonable probability that the result of the proceeding would have been different."

It was as if, finally, someone in authority had considered the evidence and testimony of the case without having decided, in advance, what the outcome should be. Finally someone was paying attention to the law and the protections it guarantees, even to those who have made bad decisions, even to those who have said things that shock us, even to those who may have hated their mothers.

An Unexpected Letter

About a month before I prepared to send this manuscript off to the publisher in its final form, I wrote to Kevin Bergin, at the Ridgeland division of the South Carolina Department of Corrections, telling him that if he wanted to say anything at all about the murder, or about himself, this was his last chance. Approximately two weeks later I received a fifty-page missive (letter seems too simple a word) in which Bergin basically gave me his life story, including commentary on what was happening in his world around the time he murdered Nell Davis.

I've already spoken about Bergin's early history, based on information gleaned from court records, including his very thorough psychiatric evaluation, which contained a good deal of information about his life. His letter corroborated much of that information, while giving me additional insight into what was going on in the young man's mind at various stages of his life, and particularly during the period when he became friends with John Ridgway.

Kevin Bergin and John Ridgway met when Kevin was around thirteen or fourteen, when John and his family moved to Darien, Connecticut. Echoing John, Kevin writes that they immediately hit it off, being rebellious as hell, as well as sharing a strong attraction to both drugs and alcohol. Disgusted by the corruption, materialism, superficiality, and spiritual bankruptcy of contemporary American society, they began spending time at a housing project called Allen-O'Neil Homes, located in the section of town known as Noroton Heights.

Elsewhere in Noroton Heights, sandwiched between the highway and some train tracks, deep in the heart of what Kevin describes as "a wooded wasteland of old cement tunnels, the foundations of burned out buildings, . . . with old bomb shelters and dirt bike trails and an old construction site/ dump for old cars at the far end of the place" they had their favorite hangout, which they called "the Pitts." In its rundown, burned-out condition, the Pitts seems like the perfect objective correlative for Kevin's alienation from the world, from the "white picket fence American Dream" that, to him, always seemed like the biggest of lies, compared to the reality of the "overly industrialized technological culture that has imposed its edifices on the natural landscape to the extent that there is hardly any landscape left."

By the time John and Kevin met, he writes, they were both complete nihilists, desiring the destruction of civilization, a civilization in which they were made to go to school, to spend their youth slaving away over schoolwork so that when they got older they could go to more school, so that they could graduate and get a job of some kind that would help to perpetuate the "slave system." As rebels against this system, they turned more and more to drugs, alcohol, vandalism, and the mental and physical chaos that resulted from these things. Under the influence of heavy drug and alcohol use, John and Kevin fed off each other's craziness. They dabbled in Satanism and talked about starting a cult family.

When John and his family moved to South Carolina, the two boys stayed in close touch despite the chaos of their individual lives. Although they lived far away from each other, Kevin says that he and John would spend hours on the phone, talking about "all manner of insane things," even doing drugs together while they talked. Kevin was reading a lot of books about the occult, and getting more deeply into the practice of witchcraft. The first rite he ever performed was a work of cursing against the person he held responsible for him having been put into rehab. He says he received news that the person was hospitalized shortly afterward. This led to a strong belief in the efficacy of spells and rituals.

By the time he was eighteen, Kevin was beginning to experience some forms of mental illness, which he describes as "the beginning of madness," because his thoughts seemed to be uncontrollable. He wondered if he might be experiencing some form of OCD, or another kind of mental disturbance. He admits he didn't know it at the time but has since learned that it isn't unusual for people practicing black magic to develop "inner terrors and derangements and obsessions of various types," because of the notion that these practices open you up to spirits that can possess you and eventually drive you completely insane.

This is when he started feeling that there were two opposing forces battling inside him for control over his mind. One, interestingly, was this compassionate person who valued other people, who enjoyed meeting and bonding with people and becoming a true and loyal friend. The other wanted nothing but, as he puts it, "madness & mayhem & death to everything & chaos." Both of these sides, however, shared a contempt for the oppressive world order, and, as he has told me, both sides wanted and needed love and loving relationships with family and friends. This is one of the reasons he desired to form a cult family of people bound together "in unity of soul in a bond of loyalty and love for one another" but that was also "unified in the cause of chaos and darkness."

It was during this period that the idea of killing someone began to emerge, not in a personal sense—there was no particular person he wanted to kill—but in a very impersonal, almost clinical sense. Kevin explains that he was "questioning the very nature & identity of good & evil," that he was "trying to decide whether or not good was good and evil was evil, or good was evil and evil was good." He states that the "strong pull toward the dark side" he felt is what made him believe that he would eventually commit a murder. He admits that what he is about to say is going to sound "screwed up," but he felt that he ultimately had to kill to have that experience, though he qualifies this by claiming that he really wishes it "had just been someone [he] had a beef with and not an innocent person." In killing Nell he "really violated some of [his] own precepts." He notes that he had always hated bullies, and in committing this murder, he had become what he hated.

Throughout the letter Kevin periodically turns to the subject of women, and love, and how this was something that was almost always missing from his young life. For one reason or another, the girls he dated were not the ones he was really interested in, and the ones he felt really drawn to were always somehow out of reach. When he talks about killing Nell, he ties together this source of emotional pain with his general alienation from society: he felt that he was hurting deeply inside and had a need for real love but didn't have it in his life at this point. Therefore it seemed to him "almost ironic that somehow all my hatred, sorrow, loneliness, madness, and pain ends up being taken out on some innocent individual who I honestly think became a scapegoat to represent 'society' personified."

In the weeks leading up to the murder, Kevin says he experienced a variety of portents and omens, such as a dream in which he and John were carrying a dead body, all of which suggested to him that he was not on the right path, that the journey he was on would take him nowhere he wanted to be, but he ignored them all.

When he arrived in South Carolina and hooked up with John, when he might have expected to feel better, especially after he and John had purchased five or six hundred dollars' worth of crack, everything still felt wrong. Even being with John felt wrong. "Anyways," he says, "I had sort of an all around rotten feeling inside the whole week I was down here leading up to the actual day of the crime, and rightly so—there would have been more wrong with me if I didn't feel screwy about the whole thing."

The week before the murder Kevin and John spent at John's house doing various things that included, of all things, cooking (he explains that this occurred because John was taking culinary classes), watching horror movies, and hanging out with different girls whom John invited over. Kevin notes that they never met or hung out with Sarah, although John did talk with her on the phone a few times. This week they also engaged in various acts of witchcraft, including the ritual of purification John had mentioned.

When he comes to speak of the day of the murder, Kevin says he's not going to go over the details of the crime, but he does want to say a few things. One is that "when we committed this crime things were very very wrong for me in a lot of ways and I was suffering deep inner torments." As for the crime itself, he wants me to know that "the basic original gist of it was this chick Sarah that John was friends with had some ongoing beef with her parents—meaning her mom & stepfather—maybe her issue was primarily with her mom, I don't know, but she wanted them both dead. Just them. Not the brother & sister—who she seemed to care about, but her mom and stepdad."

When Kevin was interviewed by police immediately after his arrest, once they had convinced him that John and Sarah were implicating him in the crime, he had said that a primary feature of "the plan" was to kill Sarah's mother. Based on my own research, however, I had begun forming the idea that perhaps "the plan" had taken two or three different forms, each of the three perpetrators, John, Sarah, and Kevin, having a somewhat different idea of what was actually supposed to happen.

At Sarah's trial Kevin admitted that he had only talked to Sarah once over the phone. This conversation took place a few days before the murder, when Kevin was staying at John's house. Sarah was originally talking to John and the phone had then been passed over to Kevin. Kevin had never met Sarah in person, only spoken to her that one time on the phone. Had John spoken to her again afterward? Had Sarah actually said, in that one conversation, that she wanted her parents—both her parents—dead? What Kevin remembered her saying was that she didn't want the children, her brother and sister, hurt. He did not testify, or claim in his letter that she actually said, to him, anything about wanting him to kill her mother. So if not from Sarah, where did Kevin get that idea? It could have come from only one source: John. The only question remaining was, did John get the idea from Sarah? Did she ask him to kill her mother (or both of her parents)? Or did John tell Kevin, without Sarah's knowledge, that the final, go-ahead plan was to kill Mrs. Davis?

When I wrote to Kevin asking if this type of miscommunication, intentional or otherwise, could have been possible, he gave me an emphatic "No!" Although many plans were kicked around, he says, "none of them were a joke. The reason Sarah said she didn't want her brother and sister hurt was because we were plainly talking about murder." Of Sarah's comment to the Nelsons, "They were only supposed to knock her out," he states that this only contradicts her assertion that the two boys supposedly kidnapped her and forced her to go along with them as a hostage. He does say, however, that the statement about how they were only supposed to knock Nell out is true, with the caveat that that wasn't all there was to the plan. Once Nell was incapacitated, they would then try to get the combination for the safe from her, and once they did that, she would be killed. In his words, "Murder was intended from the beginning."

Regarding Sarah's decision to run away and pin the blame on him and John, Kevin believes that she may have done this because she, like her co-conspirators, found the reality of what they had just done too overwhelming. But he insists that, just before it happened, when she met John and Kevin behind the shed to discuss how they were going to lure Nell back there, Sarah was "jumping up and down excitedly and joyously saying 'the bitch is gonna die, the bitch is gonna die.'"

When I write those words, when I read them yet again, I feel some kind of energy stir at the base of my spine and then run up my back into my neck and head. Again I have to wonder: Are these the words of an angry teenage girl who speaks metaphorically, as I once did of a professor: "Dr. Wittig is gonna die when he reads my paper!" or are they the words of an angry teenage girl who believes that her mother is, as Kevin claims, about to be murdered?

A huge part of my reason for writing to Kevin Bergin was my hope that when he wrote back, he would say something that would help me to understand him as a person, as a complex human being, and not just a "monster," as he and John Ridgway were depicted in the press around the time of Nell's murder. Some people, I know, will say that it doesn't matter what he felt, or whether he possessed any of those qualities that we equate with goodness, because what he did was so cruel and evil. Cruel it was, even evil perhaps, but I don't believe that anyone, including Kevin, can be explained that simply. In his letters I found even more than I had hoped for, much of which I have already written about in this chapter, but there is one section in the middle of his first letter that I found particularly interesting. It comes right after he speaks of one psychologist's theory that he may have a form of Asperger's syndrome, an autism spectrum disorder characterized by more than average difficulties in social interaction and nonverbal communication. Commenting on the idea that he may have Asperger's, Kevin writes, "I did not adjust well socially growing up. My mind is like a big gigantic backyard, it's vast. I have always had a very deep mind and soul. I think very deeply and philosophically, but I also feel things on a soul level in a very deep way. It's not necessarily the way other people feel and experience things though." Yet he goes on to say, "I have always felt deep sorrow and longing and even compassion for others. I see people's innocence and their vulnerability and I do desire good things for others, but there is a savagery in me too." He goes on to describe his personality as "complex" in that it encompasses these polar extremes. He explains that the "savage and violent side" of himself originated because of his emotional sensitivity, which caused him to be hurt easily and deeply.

I find this self-portrait fascinating, because it mirrors, again, the duality of his vision of himself and the world that emerges over and over again in his writing; however, it does not answer one question: what, if anything, has he done to exhibit the "polar opposite" of the kind of behavior that resulted in Nell's murder. If he has performed deeds that exhibit kindness and thoughtfulness, I want to know about them. When I wrote to him expressing this desire, he wrote back another of his extensive letters in which he spoke about his interactions with both animals and people. He particularly emphasizes his childhood relationship with a "beloved" golden retriever, recalling that his mother once complained of his showing the dog more affection and kindness than he showed to anyone else. When he speaks about his relationships with people, he mentions his father, who has always been there for him, and to whom he remains very close. When he speaks about the present, he mentions the way that in prison it's really important to look out for one another. "If a guy in a wheelchair needs you to push him to medical, you do it, if someone's having a medical problem, you go get help . . . if someone's having problems, you check up on them." Basically, he says, he tries to "do right by people in general." He describes himself as a "man of my word," saying, "if I tell someone something I do what I say I will. I treat other people with respect." There's one guy, particularly, whom he looks out for, "a solid dude and old timer," someone who doesn't get as much money as Kevin does, so that Kevin makes sure he eats well, especially when he cooks a big meal, cooking being one of the activities inmates are allowed to indulge in, if they can score needed ingredients. This bit in the letter is followed by a recipe, interestingly, involving oysters and sausage, onion and jalapeno peppers, and corn, all sautéed together with butter and, if he has it, soft cheese, then combined with a sauce that includes mustard, ketchup, hot sauce, Sweet'N Low, and a tad of coffee and maybe a little chili powder. Once the sauce is made, all the ingredients are then sautéed together and put over ramen or teriyaki noodles. He goes on to talk about more of the kinds of recipes he has invented, and his delight in cooking is obvious, even before he says, "I can't wait till I'm out and I can really get good ingredients, all kinds of vegetables, good sausage, sauces, plus good oils to cook and sauté in that are healthier than butter or oleo, and a real stove and oven to cook in." Right now he is restricted to hot plates and microwaves.

In his most recent letter to me, Bergin speaks of how he is now allowed to play guitar (both electric and acoustic), which has led him to begin composing music again, something that was an important part of his life before he was locked up. He has also been able to resume creating artwork, albeit with the limited materials he has access to. In a recent letter, he informed me that he has signed up for a music theory class that is soon to be offered at the prison, something that will provide a further outlet and structure for his creative energies.

The more I learn about Kevin Bergin, the more complicated I realize he is. I find him fascinating intellectually (he writes amazing, densely imagistic poetry; his knowledge of world religions is dazzling), but at the same time I remember what he did to Nell, just as, I guess, he has to remember what he did to Nell, though we stand on different sides of that equation. I can't say I feel no kinship with him, however; I know what it is to feel intense dissatisfaction with the obvious corruption and greed of corporate America, and I agree with him that our government has sold out to corporate interests, that human beings who don't want to be a part of that system have a tough time of it, and that that is deplorable. Although I have never felt that I would like to kill someone just to see what that feels like, or for the sake of having that experience, I have felt I would like someone to die, though, like Sarah, those feelings were aimed not at an innocent person who just happened to be in my line of fire, but at someone whom I should have loved, but simply wasn't able to.

32

Putting It All Together

When I began conducting the research for this book, I did so because I wanted to find out the truth about what happened to Nell. I didn't know what I would find. I believed, naively, that finding the truth would bring me peace. Now, at the end, I know that it will not.

For a long time, I believed that Sarah's version of events was at least partially true. I believed that John, Kevin, and Sarah were all lying about some things, and that, in their own minds, they felt justified in doing so. For instance I believed it was probable, given the evidence, that Sarah planned to rob her parents and run away with Bergin and Ridgway, and even discussed the possibility of killing her mother with one or both of them. But I also believed that the idea of actually killing anyone was for Sarah, as John said, a "joke plan," a fantasy that she never believed would be carried out, and that that is why she behaved as she did in the wake of her mother's murder, abandoning the boys at the Nelsons' and running, screaming for help.

John and Kevin both testified that, just before returning to the house to summon her mother, Sarah had said, "The bitch is gonna die." This memorable phrase had first surfaced in Kevin Bergin's statement to police on the night of the murder, after JoJo Woodward had finally managed to break through the wall of Bergin's defenses and gotten him to tell the truth about what had happened at the Davis residence. John, not present for Kevin's testimony, didn't know how their accounts would dovetail, when John testified in court, on this particular detail, fitting together like two halves of a broken mirror whose jagged edges would scrape against my memory for months. During one of our conversations I told John about the phrase and its repetition, asking if he had been coached by his attorney or the solicitor. He told me no, explaining that the phrase had been memorable both because it was the last thing Sarah had said before going into the house, and because when she had left, Kevin had said, "Shit, F, I never met a chick like that."

The "F" was a reference to John's nickname, "Sketchy F," something that had also come out in the trial.

I didn't believe John at first, thinking that he must have been coached (and perhaps he was), but then I had also seen the video of Kevin Bergin's confession and the way that statement—blurted out, after he had "cracked"—had the ring of truth.

In John's opinion, "If anything, it [the comment] made Kevin want to impress Sarah." But in the main, he says, "Kevin just cracked. He had a mask on, a baseball bat in his hand, and no cash. He couldn't have forgot he was there to get that code unless he literally snapped again, or chose to impress Sarah. If you believe nothing else at all and think we were there to kill (which we weren't) at least see we didn't have the code, which means no cash. We weren't going to get far, accomplished no goal. No one was supposed to die." As for Sarah's ·comment? He says, "Maybe Sarah said it in a way like, 'I'll kill you!' when you're mad but don't mean it. With all respect you'd have to ask her, I don't know. I don't think Sarah meant for Kevin to kill Nell, I don't think she truly wanted her dead. I didn't. I think Kevin saying he came down to commit a murder was to help him seem crazy, or he was told to say it by somebody."

Most of all, though, John said he thinks Kevin struck out at Nell because he was under the influence of "heavy, constant drug use," which caused him to just "freak out." This, of course, is what Kevin himself said when, in the wee hours of October 21, 1999, he finally confessed to the murder: "All right. Fuck it. I freaked out all right."

■ ■ ■

The last time John Ridgway wrote to me before this book went to press, it was after learning of my correspondence with Kevin Bergin and some of the questions I had been asking in that correspondence. In one of his letters (he wrote several) he told me that he wanted to make something "crystal clear." He goes on to state that he "never told Kevin to kill Nell. I never told Kevin Sarah said kill Nell. It's 15 years later, I have nothing to lose by telling you the truth. Nothing in court."

Earlier in our correspondence, when I had asked him what he meant by his claim, repeated here, that he has nothing to lose, John said that he has the love and support of his family—his parents Tom and Nancy Ridgway, his brother Jason, and his birth mother, Cindy Frasier—no matter what happens. They visit him frequently and provide him with the financial support and advocacy that make life in prison much more bearable. John has hopes for the future that are buoyed up by this love, but would they still love him as much if they believed that he had indeed participated in the murder of Nell Davis? Kevin Bergin's testimony in court did, after all, say that he and John had taken turns strangling Mrs. Davis. Does John have less (or more) to lose than Kevin?

As for Sarah most of her family has abandoned her. Her father, Joe, and her aunt Nini, are the only people who come to visit her with any degree of regularity, and they sometimes fail to appear when promised. This is partly, Sarah has explained, because of Joe's increasingly ill health. Her brother Willie could have driven him, when he still lived in South Caro-lina, but he was usually busy with other things and now lives out of state. Because Joe's income is limited, owing to his disability, he rarely is able to send money to Sarah's account. Her Aunt Anita, whom Sarah calls Nini, still sends the money that allows Sarah to buy makeup and coffee from the canteen, according to Sara, but Nini goes through phases of refusing to accept Sarah's phone calls. And this is the woman who, at Sarah's sentenc-ing, begged the judge to release Sarah into her custody—to allow her to adopt Sarah, because she loved her and felt "uniquely qualified to take care of her and provide her with her needs." Sarah's half brothers Grady and David never visit. Her cousin Mary, like Anita, takes a sporadic interest in her, and, to be fair, sometimes they talk quite frequently. Around the time of Sarah's postconviction relief hearing, both Anita and Mary had once again begun to show their support, and they made the trip from Savan-nah to be in the courtroom that day. But their interest, like everyone else's in her family, seems short-winded, sporadic, part and parcel, perhaps, of what Joe likes to call "the Nickel curse." Sarah's paternal grandparents are deceased, and her maternal grandmother, Julia Crowley, never wants to see or speak to her again. Her godmother, Ann Handy, feels the same way. Her uncle, Jay Crowley, has not seen her since her mother died. Haley, the half sister who seemed more important, perhaps, than anyone else in her family, was allowed no contact with Sarah throughout her childhood and adolescence. Haley's father, Mike Davis, told me that this would continue until Haley had come of age and could make her own decision, in full pos-session of the facts.

So Sarah is alone. How could she have "so much more" to lose by telling the truth? Well, the answer seems obvious. All the people who hate her or have abandoned her would be justified in having done so.

There is compelling evidence pointing to Sarah's involvement. The diary entries where she writes about killing her mom, her failure to call 9-1-1 when the boys first showed up at her house and allowed her to re-turn inside, her unplugging of the upstairs phone, her failure to warn her mom so that Nell could defend the family with her pistol while waiting for police. These are facts, not someone's interpretation of them. And some features of both Ridgway's and Bergin's testimonies have the ring of truth. Both said, from the moment they were arrested, that Sarah was in on it, and both seemed stunned that she had abandoned the car, with them in it, on Knowles Island Road. Sarah had a history of running away with John

Ridgway, as recently as two weeks before the day that Ridgway showed up at her house with knives and a bat and pantyhose pulled over his face. She also had a history of crack abuse, and crack is a drug that, according to every drug abuse counselor I have spoken with, destroys the conscience of those who use it.

Speaking of conscience, what about her mother's jewelry, the watch and earrings? If Sarah wasn't part of the plan, Randy Murdaugh had argued, why would John let her keep these valuable items? When I sat across from Sarah on one of our many visits, and asked her why she took them, she said it was to keep Ridgway from taking them, which is different from her story in court, but made me think of some of the other odd little things she claimed that Ridgway had done, both at Bellinger Bluff and in the car, after they had left. Was it possible, I wondered, that he was hoping to make Sarah feel better about her mother's death by letting her keep them? That this was another way of soothing her, just as he had tried to soothe her, as he told me, with hugs and with words, telling her, when they hit the road, to think of all the bad things her mother had done and then she would feel better?

So, with all these factors pointing to Sarah's complicity in some kind of plan, why did she run away from Ridgway and Bergin to call the police? Why didn't she just follow through with the plan to head for Detroit? Perhaps, as Sheriff Tanner suggested in the early stages of the investigation, she was just very shrewd and manipulative, shrewd enough to use the boys to kill, and then set them up to take all the blame. Or perhaps she was in on the plan but unable to deal with the reality of her mother's mutilated corpse. There is a third possibility—that, as Ridgway claimed, her mother was not supposed to die, but Kevin just "lost it," similar to the way he had snapped and attacked his dad in September 1997. Ridgway claims that he and Sarah were both "freaked out" and confused about what to do in the aftermath. This would explain why Sarah wanted to run to her daddy, and why, when he wasn't home, she ran to the home of a neighbor and friend, Heather Nelson.

Then there was a second letter, one that I didn't have the opportunity to read for a long time because, although it was a part of the case files, it had disappeared from there before I accessed them. I have often wished I could hear more of Nell's side of the story, hear her talk about what her relationship with Sarah was like in the weeks and months leading up to her murder, and this second letter, which Sarah decided to share with me, allowed me to do just that. The letter isn't dated, but two events that it refers to, Sarah moving back to stay with her dad, and the death of Nell's father, suggest that it was written sometime in the spring of 1999. It begins with a reference to another letter (of which I don't have a copy) that Sarah had written to her Mom, one that led to Nell having "another sleepless night. One of many over the past few years." She complains that Sarah's thoughts are selfish—"Poor me, poor me, what a pitiful life I have had"—and goes on to state that she has given Sarah "the best that I could considering the lack of support I've gotten from Joe." She accuses Sarah of elevating Joe onto "a high pedestal" while she criticizes her mother's "every move," talking to her "in such a hateful and disrespectful manner." The letter is by turns accusatory, declarative, pleading, and admonitory, and sometimes a blend of all three. "If you would just treat the people in your family with a little kindness you would see a great return," Nell writes, and then, "I don't have enough fingers on my hands to count all the times you have told me how much you hate me. Well, sorry but I love you! I always will no matter how rotten your behavior is." Nell complains that Sarah wants to be herself and live her own life without her mom "controlling" it, while asserting that this is not appropriate because Sarah lacks the ability to make good decisions: "I constantly tried to offer you choices to increase your privileges but you just rebelled even more."

Another section of the letter adopts a lecturing tone: "It is so easy just to worry over yourself instead of others. That's where a little dose of Christianity might help. It is really helping me. I have never been happier with my life than I am right now and it has nothing to do with you moving out or anything anybody else has done. I have finally found the Lord and have accepted him as my savior. I put my life in His hands and he has put me at peace. I could never have made it through the death of my dear father without knowing about the greatness of his salvation and the hope of eternal life." I confess that when I read this I began to feel uneasy. Nell as a born-again Christian? I guess I am glad she found something to give her peace and a sense of hope, but these words just sound all wrong. They don't belong to the Nell I knew. And I guess that's part of the point: I didn't know Nell anymore. I lost her long before she died.

After sharing her opinion about the efficacy of Christianity, Nell abruptly changes tack and apologizes for failing to immediately inform Sarah when Nell's father, Jack Crowley, had died. But her apology isn't really an apology; it's the beginning of what will become another assertion about Sarah's self-centeredness: "I'm sorry you took it as cruelty when I didn't immediately tell you of his death. You see Sarah once again it wasn't about 'you' and 'your' feelings. I learned it at 5:00 in the morning and I drove myself to Augusta crying the whole way. No I didn't think then to call my daughter whose last words to me were 'I hate you.' My mother and I had to make many arrangements and I needed to love and support her in her time of grief. I stopped at your father's trailer on my way home to tell you and to invite you to the funeral. I'm sorry that you had read it in the newspaper already. You never even hugged me or told me how sorry you were that I lost my dad. Who is cruel?" And then, as if the anger that led her to write this letter has finally drained away, she breaks off and exclaims, "I miss you and I love you! I know it is hard being a teenager. Remember I was one too!" But in the midst of avowing her love for Sarah, she states, "I will always tell you what to do and I will always try to control your life because I am a mother and that is what <u>caring</u> parents do. My mother still tells me what to do and sometimes I take her advice and sometimes I don't but the difference is that I am an adult and you are not." She tells Sarah she is sorry that Sarah grieves over her parents' divorce but warns her against digging too deeply to find out the reasons behind it. "Be careful because it might make you feel worse," she admonishes.

The next topic she addresses is Sarah's relationship with Mike, and by this point I have the sense that I am going to hear about everything that was wrong, or perceived to be wrong, in this family. Nell says she is "sorry for the poor relationship you and Mike have," but accedes, "that's between you and him," reassuring Sarah, however, that Mike loves her. He just "can't bear to see the way you treat me." She goes on, saying, "You choose to see only the negative things because your heart is so full of hate." This is followed by an outburst of emotion (I can picture Nell shouting these words): "Jesus Christ is the answer Sarah! He will put LOVE in your heart and everything else will follow. Yes! I will try to cram it down your throat because it is the <u>way</u>."

Her closing paragraph is calmer, more reasoned, but still admonitory: "You have a lot of mixed up thoughts and feelings and a great many of them are way off base. It might help you to talk to someone (like a counselor) that can help you with your feelings. I wish it could be me but we don't have good communication. If where you need to be is with Joe then I will support you but just be careful and please please please get it through your head that all I've ever wanted for you is the <u>best</u>—nothing less." When I read the way she signs off, with "Love always!!!" I get chills. It is the way Sarah closes her letters to me, either with that or a symbol of a heart, followed by "always." There is a "P.S." as well where Nell says, "I <u>love</u> your poetry and I have told you before you just didn't <u>listen</u>. Yes it does bother me that some of it is so very sad."

Reading this letter makes me feel so very sad because in it I see catalogued so many of the problems Sarah had told me about already, but I see them from a different perspective, and I understand, intensely, that Nell seemed to be hurting every bit as much as her daughter.

■ ■ ■

On my last visit with Sarah Nickel, I finally told her that I no longer believed she had no involvement in "the plan," or that she simply complied with Ridgway's demand to bring her mother outside because she was afraid that he would kill her if she didn't. I remember preparing for the visit, sitting in my rental car, a red Toyota, outside the prison. The sun, so bright and intense for the past few days, had gone into hiding behind a scrim of gray cloud. I removed my jewelry—bracelets, ring, necklace, and earrings—divesting myself of its warmth, the comforting glint of silver against my bare skin. I was wearing a below-the-knee-length skirt and a blouse with sleeves, in keeping with visitor regulations. Still, I almost lost my sunglasses, having forgotten the rule against those—or maybe I had just forgotten that I had pushed them up onto my head on the drive to Columbia, when the sun retreated behind the clouds. For this the warden had to be called. He went through my visitation record to see if I had any other violations, or if I had visited recently enough that I should have known better than to slip up like this. Fortunately my visitation record lied, saying that I had never been before, or maybe the warden just felt sorry for me because I had come so far. Whatever the reason, he let me off with a warning.

There weren't many other visitors on this day at Camille Griffin Graham Correctional Institution. It was the Sunday before Mother's Day, so I figured a lot of friends and family were waiting for the big day, the next Sunday, when there might be a special treat like barbeque chicken for sale in the hallway outside the two visitation rooms, or maybe even a special performance, some praise dancing, perhaps. The visitation room had been cold and completely odorless, as usual, the asphalt tile floors sparkling in the way asphalt tile floors do only when they have been waxed and buffed.

This was one of Sarah's jobs at the time, and she was proud of the way the floors shined.

We'd been sitting at our table munching on salt-and-vinegar potato chips and Funyuns when I told Sarah that I no longer believed she had no involvement in "the plan," or that she simply complied with Ridgway's demand to bring her mother outside because she was afraid that he would kill her if she didn't.

Sarah's initial reaction was to tell me that *if* she had planned to run away, she changed her mind, "when I saw what they did to my mom." Then, about a week after I got home, I received in the mail an essay she had written, titled "Guilt." In the essay she states, "I not only ruined my life, but I ruined an entire family & b/c of me a woman lost her life. Not just any woman; my mother. A mother of 3. A woman beloved by many, but hated by only one solitary angry soul—me. I hated her for choosing her men over me. I hated her for trying to mold me into what she felt like I should be. She wanted me to be the perfect daughter & I couldn't be. So I tried to run away—not from her, but from myself. I hated myself for not being able to live up to her unreasonable expectations. She ruined my life & I have to live with the guilt and responsibility of ending hers. I did not kill her, nor did I want her to die. I only wanted to get away."

This, Sarah insisted, is the truth, the full extent of her involvement in her mother's murder. And I would have settled for this; indeed I did settle for this for a long time, because there simply wasn't enough evidence for me to know, *beyond a reasonable doubt,* that Sarah meant for her mother to die.

Now, however, I do know the truth.

33

When the Hurly-Burly's Done

My sister-in-law Vicki, who lives in Columbia, once had a job teaching at the same women's prison, Camille Griffin Graham, where Sarah is incarcerated. When I first started visiting Sarah, I would stop by and sometimes spend the night with Vicki during my stay. I remember debriefing with her immediately after my first visit, with her asking, "Well, does she say she didn't do it?" I had answered, "Yes . . . ," and Vicki proceeded to inform me that during the three years that she worked with the women in the South Carolina prison system, only one inmate who was accused of murder had ever admitted that she was guilty. That woman, Vicki said, had killed some children she had been babysitting. She was one of the saddest women that Vicki had ever met. I told Vicki that I thought that there was much about Sarah's story, and the way that she told it to me, that had the ring of truth. I was especially impressed that she had looked me in the eye and told me that she was innocent.

But that was a long time ago. Now I know that being able to look someone in the eye and convincingly deny that you did something means nothing, except that you could be a very good liar.

■ ■ ■

It is tempting just to quote Sarah's entire letters, because they are so condensed and contain so much material, stretching back to new information about her childhood, to more complete information about her relationship with John Ridgway, and finally up to her present decision to come, as she put it, "out of my fantasy world kicking & screaming."

As for the answer to the big question: did Sarah plan to kill her mother? It's a complicated yes, but a yes it is. She explains it thus, toward the end of her letter, after the part where she outlines all of Nell's many failures—as she saw them at the time—as a mother—how she wasn't affectionate, how she never showed Sarah how to do her hair or put on makeup, how she never explained about getting a period or being prepared for that when it came, and so on.

"Yes, I hated Nell & yes, in my mind I wanted her to die on numerous occasions. I was so delusional that, @ the time, I didn't realize my fantasy would have consequences. @ that time, consequences to any of my actions were irrelevant b/c I could always lie, cry, or manipulate my way out of anything I did. I didn't care about getting in trouble b/c I was not grounded in reality. I was in my own little bubble."

When she comes to the day of the murder, Sarah writes, "About Nell & what happened on Oct 20, 1999 was a huge mistake. It wasn't supposed to happen like that. Did John and I discuss it & plan it beforehand? Yes. Did either of us really think, in reality, that it would actually happen? No."

I should mention that elsewhere in the letter, when speaking of her relationship with John, she says that they had previously planned all kind of crazy things (she doesn't specify what), but none of them ever happened, except when they ran away and did drugs. But here she says, "I wanted it [the murder] to happen until it actually started happening but by then it was too late to stop it or do anything about it. Our 'plan' was a delusional fantasy based on drugs & mental illness & I truly believe neither John nor I expected the outcome as it occurred." After mentioning that, despite her failures as a mother, Nell did not deserve "to die in such a way," Sarah continues, "John & I were not evil, just lost & sick. While I am not as innocent as I have always made myself out to be, I am not the evil sociopath they portrayed me as. I was an immature, emotionally stunted kid & I made a bad situation worse & I hurt a lot of people. There is no amount of apology in the world to excuse what I did. I am so sorry if you feel like I lied to you—b/c I did. But I was lying to myself, too. I can't do that anymore."

In her second letter, Sarah writes about her decision to run away from John and Kevin after the crime had been committed. "U C, when all this happened, I immediately started thinking of a way 2 get myself out of it & I knew I couldn't stand by him [John] and do that. I knew most ppl would have a hard time seeing me as the villain in comparison to him and Kevin so I exploited that. I simply couldn't be 'the bad guy' so I made them out 2 be." Of John, with whom she is now trying to mend her relationship, she says she "probably broke his heart all because I wanted my way and he loved me enough to help me."

Why on earth did Sarah suddenly change her mind and decide to tell me the truth after all this time? I don't know for sure. In one letter she says it is primarily due to the influence of a new girlfriend, Pam who saw through Sarah's bullshit, saying, "At first I thought you had it all together in your perfect little life. You wear your mask well." Something about Pam inspired Sarah to trust her enough to finally tell her the truth, and the fact that Pam "learned the truth & didn't run screaming in the other direction" helped Sarah to be more at peace with herself and to accept her "true self." A later letter, written after she and Pam had broken up, is more convincing: "Once I threw up my hands & gave up my game, my life & my state of mind got a hell of a lot easier. When u have 2 truck around as many lies as I told then it gets 2 b pretty exhausting, ya know?" Then there is also Sarah's claim that she really wanted to mend her relationship with John, and she knew that telling the truth was the only way to do that: "I am so glad 2 b given the chance 2 mend things w/ John. I really, really missed him. Neither of us R the same ppl we were back then & we're both enjoying re-learning each other."

So Sarah finally told me the truth. Now it's time for me to tell her the truth about Nell, and what really happened the last time I saw her on that brisk but sunny afternoon in Georgia, just months before Sarah's birth.

■ ■ ■

The last time I saw Nell she was pregnant with Sarah, who would be the oldest of her three children. Even though Nell was still two months from her due date on that January afternoon, her belly was colossal, much too big, I felt, for her slight frame. Still, she was full of energy and optimism, happy with her husband, Joe Nickel, and her job as an x-ray technologist in Hilton Head, South Carolina.

That is how I began this story. With a lie. Here's the truth. The last time I saw Nell she was pregnant with Sarah, who would be the oldest of her three children. Even though Nell was still two months from her due date on that January afternoon, her belly was colossal, much too big, I felt, for her slight frame. She was full of energy, but it was a frenetic, electric charge. She bummed a cigarette from me, though she said she had quit smoking when she got pregnant, and just had one occasionally. She talked about how much she loved living in Hilton Head and bragged about her job at the medical center there. She also asked me if I knew where she could score some coke.

Sitting on the sofa across from Nell, I remember feeling as if I had stepped out of my everyday reality and entered some kind of fugue state, a waking dream, an Alice-in-Wonderland moment where what I was hearing and what I was seeing had no logical relationship. The Nell sitting in my grandmother's rocker on that sunny afternoon in January, I now realize, was someone who looked familiar, but whom I didn't know at all. She had continued to talk, telling me that she had a really good connection in Augusta, from whom she usually got "really good shit," but she hadn't been able to make contact this time, and she thought I might know somebody.

This was not an unreasonable assumption on her part. We had done various drugs together in the past, though our use of anything other than marijuana was highly sporadic. I got the definite impression, that day, that cocaine had become more than an occasional indulgence. But I simply could not believe Nell was using while she was pregnant, and I didn't want to ask, or question her judgment. All I wanted was to turn away, not get involved.

When Nell left, my mother said, "That was sure nice of Nell to stop by. I'm so glad you were home." I went to my room where I sat on the bed with my arms hugging my knees and persuaded myself that Nell was just gabbing, running off at the mouth, trying to impress or perhaps even shock me with this talk about cocaine.

Was Nell doing coke when she was pregnant? Or was she, like Amy Heath says of Sarah, all talk? I can't say. Nell may or may not have intended to do something terrible to her baby that day. I did do something terrible. I let Nell walk out of the house, and out of my life, forever, without doing a single thing to try to help her. That day I gave up on Nell. That is why I will not give up on her daughter, despite what, she now admits, she has done.

■ ■ ■

Over the course of our correspondence, Sarah has from time to time sent me essays she's written for a college-level English course she took through the University of South Carolina's extension service. One of the essays describes the Retired Racing Dog Adoption Program, in which she has participated. The essay talks at length about the special needs greyhounds have when they are adopted as adults. Because their experience has been limited to life at a dog track, where the surfaces they walk on are mainly dirt, clay, or sand, a retired racer is often terrified by a smooth tile or wood floor, on which they may scrabble to stay upright. She notes that windows are also a new experience for these dogs, who may run through the glass because they don't realize that it's solid. Some greyhounds have been known to crash through sliding glass doors because they want to chase something they see on the other side. Stairs can also pose a problem, again because of their novelty. And swimming pools are perhaps the most dangerous of all. With their deep barrel chests, greyhounds are notoriously bad swimmers. Some dogs, upon seeing a pool for the first time, perceive the surface as solid and then have to be fished out when they discover it's a liquid.

Reading Sarah's essay makes me wonder if the prison official who oversees the greyhound program understands the irony it poses, especially for women like Sarah. Incarcerated at the age of sixteen, before she had learned how to function successfully in the outside world, what will Sarah be like when, at the age of forty-two, she is released from prison? What surfaces will she scrabble on, metaphorically speaking, as she tries to maintain her emotional balance in a totally new environment? What windows will she attempt to walk through before she is cut by our society's prejudice toward former convicts? And if she is able to overcome that prejudice, will her mind still be nimble enough to climb the ladder of success; will she be able to succeed as a productive worker, able to support herself financially? And if she falls into a deep pool of despair, will someone be there to fish her out?

These are more questions for which I don't have any answers, at least not any definitive ones. But I can say this. In my heart I believe that Sarah did not really and truly want her mother to die. When she plotted her death, it was a fantasy borne of mental illness, abuse, and drug addiction. When the fantasy became real, she recoiled in horror. That is the other reason why I will not abandon Sarah. I can't replace her mother (or her Aunt Nini), but I will be there for her, to act as an advocate while she is in prison, and as a friend when she gets out. My friendship and support can never make up for the years, and the love, that she lost on the day her mother died, but I will do my best. And I believe that Nell, if she could, would give me her blessing.

Epilogue

In March 2012, more than twelve years after Nell Crowley Davis died, the Supreme Court of South Carolina delivered its final opinion in the case of *State of South Carolina vs. Sarah Nickel*. Dashing the hopes that had been raised by her successful PCR application, and her pursuit of the belated appeal that had been granted her by Judge Michael Nettles, the supreme court upheld the original ruling of the circuit court but did not bother to issue an opinion explaining their decision.

Acknowledgments

Thanks to Linda Fogle at the University of South Carolina Press, who helped guide the book to its final form, and to my family, and especially my husband, Paul Jobsis, who supported me throughout this process. I also owe a deal of thanks to Jessica Adams, who practically made me push through another revision by the force of her relentless cheerleading. I am grateful to the many people who assisted in my research: Debbie Szpanka, Detective James Bukoffsky, Detective Sam Roser, Detective JoJo Woodward, Sergeant Chris Sankowski, and various other personnel in the Beaufort County Sheriff's Office; to the Nelson family—Mary, James, and Heather, key witnesses in the case; and to Nell Davis's family, especially to Mike Davis and Joe Nickel. I also need to thank Gary Coggin and Brent Kiker, Sarah's lawyers. A very special thank you goes out to Gary for recommending that I send the manuscript of this book to University of South Carolina Press and for putting me up on one of my many visits to the Hilton Head area. I also appreciate the time that Gene Hood of the public defender's office and Solicitor Randy Murdaugh, who prosecuted the case, took to speak with me. Thanks to Judge Luke Brown, who gave me some of the most surprising information, and to Vic Bradshaw, for letting me stay at his apartment on my first visit to the area and for helping me navigate my way to all the sites I needed to visit.

Last but not least, I want to thank Sarah Nickel, John Ridgway, and Kevin Bergin. Without their openness and willingness to communicate with me, this book would have been a pale reflection of what it is today, and while I deplore their actions in bringing about the death of an innocent, beloved woman, I believe that each of them has much that is good within them, which I hope they will be able to hang on to once they are released from prison.